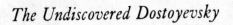

The Undiscovered Dostoyevsky

Photo: Society for Cultural Relations with the U.S.S.R.

FYODOR DOSTOYEVSKY

The

Undiscovered

Dostoyevsky

BY

RONALD HINGLEY

GREENWOOD PRESS, PUBLISHERS
WESTPORT, CONNECTICUT

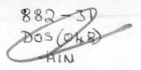

Library of Congress Cataloging in Publication Data

Hingley, Ronald.
    The undiscovered Dostoyevsky.

    Reprint of the ed. published by H. Hamilton, London.
    Bibliography: p.
    Includes index.
    1. Dostoevskiĭ, Fedor Mikhaĭlovich, 1821-1881--
Criticism and interpretation. I. Title.
PG3328.Z6H55 1975   891.7'3'3   74-5549
ISBN 0-8371-7506-2

Contents

Foreword

AMONG the reasons for attempting this study is a conviction that criticism of Dostoyevsky, voluminous and valuable as it is, still has gaps waiting to be filled. One significant aspect in particular has almost escaped attention—his humour. Dostoyevsky was many things besides a humorist, but humour certainly deserves to be more widely recognized than it is as an integral part of his work.

Failure to appreciate Dostoyevsky's humour has perhaps been due to the over-solemnity with which he has often been approached, and which, though intended as a tribute to his genius, seems rather to detract from it. Dostoyevsky's mature fiction represents a pyrotechnic display of creative talent. It is breathless, grotesque, exaggerated, outrageous—everything except solemn. In attempting to discourage an over-solemn approach it has again been my hope to do something to redress the balance.

Another feature of Dostoyevsky's work which has been insufficiently stressed in criticism (in this case criticism available in English, for Russian criticism is more forthcoming) is his skill as a craftsman. This has often been overlaid in English studies by a preoccupation with his ideas. These ideas are of course important, and an attempt is made to give due weight to them here. But it should not be forgotten that very few people would be much interested in Dostoyevsky's ideas if he had not been a master of the novelist's craft. An apparent lack of discipline in his work has sometimes blinded readers to the tough and controlled technique which lies beneath the surface. It has therefore seemed important to devote adequate space to discussing the devices which contribute to this technique.

Dostoyevskian criticism has not always gained from having been practised by admirers of his religious and philosophical teaching. It is natural that those who have been inspired to write about Dostoyevsky should include many who find themselves in harmony with his thought, but such critics err when they imply, as they often do, that Dostoyevsky can only be appreciated fully by those who have

vii

accepted at least some of his doctrines. This seems to me particularly mistaken because I am in no doubt about the vividness of my own appreciation of Dostoyevsky, while being if possible even less in doubt about the extent to which I reject his philosophical, political and religious ideas. This does not lessen my admiration for him as a man and as a novelist. The fact is that enjoying Dostoyevsky's work and sharing his ideas are two completely different things between which there is no correlation.

Despite these reservations there is, of course, a great deal to be learnt from both English and Russian criticism of Dostoyevsky. One work in particular, the long study by the émigré Russian critic Mochulsky (unfortunately not available in English) has helped more than any other to formulate my views. The influence has been one of attraction and repulsion. Like every reader of Mochulsky, I have been impressed by his erudition and eye for the significance of details which had escaped previous commentators, so that to read his work is to enjoy a series of revelations. On the other hand, Mochulsky was to a great extent a disciple of Dostoyevsky's ideas, and even seems concerned in his book to convert others to that strange body of doctrine. I have found the irritation caused by this approach just as valuable a mental stimulus as the many examples of Mochulsky's insight into Dostoyevsky's art.

*

Though this is a critical study, I have drawn on biographical material wherever this seems to illuminate criticism, relying on the sources to which reference is made in the footnotes and Bibliography. But the biographical material is subordinated to the critical, being introduced without reference to chronological sequence wherever it is needed to illustrate a literary point. Aspects of Dostoyevsky's life without important bearing on his writing have been ignored, and one result of this method is that more attention is given to early biographical material than to later.

The student of Dostoyevsky is in the privileged position of having access to the preliminary notes which he made when planning his later novels. This material has been taken into account, and is frequently referred to in the text. However, I have resisted the temptation to burrow too deeply into the creative origins of Dostoyevsky's novels because that would have distracted me from my main aim, to present a picture and interpretation of the finished product.

Students who read Russian can make use of the published Notebooks, while those who do not read Russian will find a condensed account of Dostoyevsky's creative processes, as revealed by the Notebooks, in Ernest J. Simmons's useful study. These works are listed in the Bibliography.

I hope that my book will be taken as an appreciation as well as an interpretation, because I feel bound to Dostoyevsky by a special tie of personal affection and gratitude. As a schoolboy I happened to pick up a dog-eared copy of Constance Garnett's translation of *The Brothers Karamazov*, which excited me so much that I immediately decided to learn Russian. This was many years ago, but I have never lost my enthusiasm for Dostoyevsky's great novels, which I have read more times than I can remember. I therefore hope that my admiration for Dostoyevsky will not be concealed by the many occasions when I describe his doings and beliefs as ridiculous, perverse and inconsistent.

The translations from Russian in my text are my own. The dates are 'old style' (twelve days behind our calendar in the nineteenth century). I am deeply grateful for the encouragement and advice of my colleagues, Mr. I. P. Foote, Mr. H. M. Hayward, Dr. George Katkov and Mr. John Simmons; and also of my wife.

Frilford, 1962   RONALD HINGLEY

A*

CHAPTER ONE

EARLY WORKS

WHEN Fyodor Dostoyevsky entered his twenty-fourth year in October, 1844, his future seemed unpromising. Five years' study at the Military Engineering School in St. Petersburg had earned him the rank of second lieutenant in the army. Now he had resigned his commission shortly after receiving it, abandoning the only career for which he had equipped himself because he had decided to become a writer or starve. His debts, poor health, neurotic temperament and spectacular inability to look after himself suggested that the second of these ambitions was the more likely to be realized.

However, as he laboured with his first novel, *Poor Folk*, in the winter of 1844–5, he had one potential advantage besides his unproven talent—that of writing in a climate of passionate concern for literature. For a century and more there had been Russian literary movements of one kind and another. But now in the eighteen-forties Russian intellectuals, who were entering their great period of national self-consciousness, had suddenly realized that in Pushkin and Gogol Russia had at last produced two writers who need not fear comparison with any foreigner. More were eagerly awaited. In this fevered atmosphere a young man could find himself promoted to genius overnight.

This could happen the more easily because the destinies of Russian literature were almost in the personal control of a single energetic figure, V. G. Belinsky, whose favour could rapidly put a new author on the map and who remains to this day the greatest name in Russian criticism. Dostoyevsky was lucky to find himself at only two stages removed from this powerful influence.

The first person to take a serious interest in his work was a young writer of his own age, D. V. Grigorovich, whom he had originally met as a fellow-cadet at the Engineering School and with whom he had shared a small flat in St. Petersburg. During the winter Dostoyevsky had been unwilling to talk about the manuscript on which he was known to be working, but on a May morning in 1845 Grigorovich

was permitted to read the finished novel. He was so impressed
that he insisted, against the author's protests, on taking *Poor Folk*
to a friend, N. A. Nekrasov, his immediate superior in the chain of
literary command. Nekrasov was of almost the same age as Dostoyevsky and Grigorovich, but had been publishing poetry since he was
sixteen and was already an established writer.

What followed was deliciously typical of the period and country.
Grigorovich, whose emotions were never far from the surface, found
that by the time he had reached the last page of Dostoyevsky's
novel, 'I could no longer control myself and began to sob.' Even
Nekrasov, a more hard-bitten customer, had tears on his face.[1] The
time was now four a.m., but as this was the period of the white
nights in St. Petersburg, it was light outside. So the two friends
decided to go straight to Dostoyevsky and offer congratulations
('We'll wake him up. This is loftier than sleep!').

Thirty-two years later Dostoyevsky recorded his own version of
the incident.[2] His account differs from that of Grigorovich, the
memory of both authors having obviously become blurred by the
passage of time, but the emotions aroused by the visit had remained.
Dostoyevsky recalls that he was not in bed when the two young
men arrived, having just returned from a party where, as was a
custom of the time, the company had spent the night reading Gogol
aloud. He was in exactly the state of excitement to do justice to
the embraces, tears and exclamations of Grigorovich and Nekrasov.

This is not how Grigorovich remembers the incident. According
to him Dostoyevsky showed embarrassment on seeing a stranger
(this was the first occasion on which he had met Nekrasov) at this
unreasonable hour of the morning, 'grew pale and for a long time
could not answer a word'. Grigorovich's version is the more plausible
for if there is one thing on which observers of the young Dostoyevsky are agreed it is his awkwardness with strangers. But this does
not greatly matter. What is interesting is that Dostoyevsky was left
with a lifelong memory, which he greatly prized, of a delightful
scene of youthful enthusiasm.

From Nekrasov the manuscript passed up the line to Belinsky,
with the recommendation 'a new Gogol has arisen'. Belinsky, who
liked to spot his own Gogols, retorted that Gogols grew like mush-
rooms in Nekrasov's imagination, but consented to read *Poor Folk*.
Such was the effect of his reading that when he next met Nekrasov

he was overwhelmed with emotion. 'Bring him here at once!' So Dostoyevsky was brought into Belinsky's presence, awed by the reputation of a critic from whom even praise must have been something of a nervous ordeal. 'Do you yourself understand what it is you have written?' Belinsky shouted, his eyes blazing. 'Have you comprehended the *whole of the* terrible truth which you have pointed out to us? It's impossible that you at the age of twenty should understand it.'[3]

However much Dostoyevsky did not understand, it was quite clear that he had arrived on the literary stage even more rapidly than he himself, with his extravagant ambitions, might have hoped.

*

The dust stirred up by *Poor Folk* has long settled, and modern readers may be puzzled by the ecstatic reception given to it in Russia of the eighteen-forties. How could such a mediocre novel create so great a sensation? How could it have been written by the author who later created *Crime and Punishment* and *The Brothers Karamazov*? The answers to these questions are important in helping to trace Dostoyevsky's early development.

Poor Folk is a short epistolary novel, a form never again attempted by Dostoyevsky except in a trivial work of 1847 called *A Novel in Nine Letters*. It consists of the correspondence, covering just under six months, between a middle-aged Government clerk, Makar Devushkin, and an attractive young girl, Varenka. The plot revolves round Varenka's virtue and the prospects of it surviving the assaults of various lechers, among whom the most formidable is the rich landowner Bykov, assisted by his agent, the procuress Anna Fyodorovna.

When the correspondence begins, Varenka is hiding from Bykov, who had previously seduced her. Or had he? It is characteristic of Dostoyevsky's approach that this is left vague.

It is clear that she was poor, but she was honest, and not so clear to what extent she had yet become victim of a rich man's crime. Perhaps Bykov had merely insulted the girl by importuning her with improper proposals. Be this as it may, a modern reader might easily be betrayed into dismissing *Poor Folk* as a Victorian melodrama with Russian trimmings. It is one of those novels in which all the characters are very good or very bad. Vice clashes with virtue, and in the end vice triumphs.

Much of Dostoyevsky's mature work also consists of a clash between good and evil, for this is a central theme in *Crime and Punishment*, *The Idiot*, *The Devils* and *The Brothers Karamazov*. But to mention this is to emphasize the gulf between these mature works and *Poor Folk*. In *Poor Folk* the conflict of good and evil, later to be developed in so tempestuous, original and complex a manner, is a simple black-and-white affair.

To be virtuous, within the moral framework of *Poor Folk*, is to be misfortune-prone. The misfortunes of Makar Devushkin, the mild and kind-hearted hero of the book, include poverty, unsavoury living-quarters (a screened-off section in a stinking slum kitchen), down-at-heel boots and a tattered civil servant's uniform. The object of general ridicule, he suffers among many mishaps the indignity of being brought back to his lodgings by the police after a four-day drinking bout and of being thrown downstairs by an officer—one of the many assailants of Varenka's virtue on whom he had called to protest.

This is the first in a series of similar incidents in Dostoyevsky's work where his downtrodden heroes are flung or escorted from various premises in humiliating circumstances. It is characteristic of these incidents that Devushkin's assailant was an *officer*, that he was thrown *downstairs* (staircases being a dominant theme throughout Dostoyevsky's work) and above all that such a feeble hero as Devushkin cannot even get himself thrown downstairs in hearty, full-blooded style. There is nothing more typical of Dostoyevsky in *Poor Folk* than Devushkin's own comment on this episode: 'They threw me downstairs. That is, they didn't exactly throw me but just sort of pushed me out.'

No less misfortune-prone is the young heroine Varenka, who is found on April the ninth suffering from fever and shivering. On the tenth of June she gets her feet wet and catches cold (a recurrent misfortune among the virtuous characters of the novel) and on the twenty-seventh of the same month reports a nasty cough, adding: 'I know that I shall soon die. Who will bury me? Who will feel pity for me?... My God, how sad life is, Makar Alekseyevich!' By August the thirteenth Varenka has recovered enough to have an accident with a flat-iron, on which she burns her left arm. By early September she is again well enough to be found once more brooding on her imminent death.

At the end of the novel both Varenka and Devushkin are in

desperate condition. She has been forced to accept an insulting offer of marriage from the infamous Bykov, who offhandedly explains that his main motive in seeking her hand is a wish to disinherit a nephew whom he dislikes. Devushkin is abandoned on the last page, bereft of Varenka, whom he dearly loves.

The novel also has minor figures whose lot is yet more desperate. These include the wretched Gorchkov, a fellow-lodger of Devushkin's, whose death and that of his small son are made much of. They also include the consumptive student Pokrovsky, another admirer of Varenka's, whose funeral is, of all the incidents in the book, the most tearfully pathetic.

These are characters and incidents of which it might be said that 'he must have a heart of stone who can think of them without laughing'. Yet it was such episodes which reduced Grigorovich, Nekrasov and many less eminent contemporaries to tears, an indication of the extent to which literary taste has changed since the mid-nineteenth century.

*

The vogue of *Poor Folk* owed much to the special circumstances of the country in which it was written. Not often in Russian history has it been possible for persons opposed to Government policy openly to advocate political and social reform. The latter part of Nicholas I's reign, during which *Poor Folk* was written, was certainly not such a time. But what could not be done openly in public meetings and articles, could be done indirectly and by implication in works of imaginative literature, admittedly only within narrow limits. Thus it came about that Russian authors were expected to do two things. Besides writing good poems and novels, they must contribute to the reform of society. To many readers and critics at the time when Dostoyevsky began writing the second of these objectives was beginning to seem more important than the first, and literature was coming to be regarded as a branch of social welfare or politics.

Though Belinsky himself did not go so far in this direction as some younger Russian critics, he was a founder of the trend. It is therefore not surprising that one of the elements which appealed to him in *Poor Folk* was that it could be made to carry a social message. He was attracted by the compassion which Dostoyevsky appeared to be expressing for the poor and downtrodden. 'Honour and glory',

Belinsky wrote, 'to the young poet [It was customary in this period to refer to all writers of *belles-lettres* as poets] whose Muse loves those who live in garrets and basements, and speaks of them to the inhabitants of giided halls, saying: "These also are men and your brothers!" '[4]

Belinsky's insistence on the compassion in Dostoyevsky's work has been followed by Russian critics down to the Soviet period. With the passage of time phrases like 'sympathy for the Little Man' in his 'suffering, spiritual purity and human dignity',[5] have acquired such an odour of priggishness that one can scarcely bring oneself to quote them, all the more so as these and similar clichés tend in present-day Soviet critical parlance to be applied without discrimination to most writers of note in the history of the human race. In the case of Dostoyevsky the more extreme practitioners of this approach almost suggest, for example, that the chief value of *Crime and Punishment* lies in its function as an exposé of scandalous housing conditions in nineteenth-century St. Petersburg.

Weary though one may become of such critical bromides as 'sympathy for the Little Man', *Poor Folk* does lend itself in some degree to this interpretation. It is true that it lays bare the sufferings of the poor and downtrodden and attempts to arouse the reader's sympathy for the Devushkins, Varenkas and Gorchkovs of mid-nineteenth-century Russia. It also conforms with another canon of philanthropic literature of the time by 'mercilessly lashing' (to adopt another ritual phrase of Russian criticism) the rich, heartless and privileged in the persons of Bykov and Anna Fyodorovna.

However, there are objections to this interpretation. Does not Dostoyevsky perhaps protest a little too much as he describes the sufferings of his *Poor Folk*? Does he not seem to be piling on the agony with some excess of gusto? This view was eloquently expressed in a well-known essay on Dostoyevsky, 'A Cruel Talent', published in 1882, by the populist writer N. K. Mikhaylovsky. According to Mikhaylovsky, Dostoyevsky, far from being any philanthropist, was a fictional sadist preoccupied with 'cruelty and torture and precisely from the point of view of their attractiveness'.

> Simply in order to torment some Sidorov or Petrov [that is, a Russian 'Smith' or 'Robinson'] created by himself, and to torment the reader at the same time, he will pile on him an incredible mountain of misfortune . . . drag him through a thousand calamities and insults of the most fantastic and improbable kind.[6]

Mikhaylovsky's criticism is a corrective to the excessively philanthropic interpretation of Dostoyevsky's approach, but goes too far in the opposite direction, and in a sense Mikhaylovsky commits the same error as the philanthropic interpreters with whom he joins issue. On both sides of the argument it is implied that the literary value of Dostoyevsky's work derives directly from its social usefulness. One side values a novel such as *Poor Folk* highly because it can be interpreted as preaching kindness, while the other puts a low value on the book precisely because it can be interpreted as preaching unkindness.

The arguments of both sides would have greater point if Dostoyevsky had been, not a great novelist whose work calls for careful appreciation, but an applicant for the post of treasurer to some charitable foundation of which the critics concerned happened to be trustees, Dostoyevsky having offered his literary work as evidence of suitability for the appointment. If this had been the situation Mikhaylovsky would have been right in casting his vote against the applicant. Such an appointment would have been disastrous.

The compassionate element in Dostoyevsky's work is not really a central problem at all. Excessive emphasis on it, which persists in Soviet and other criticism to this day, has distorted his image. It has led to undue prominence being given to minor 'philanthropic' works like *Poor Folk* and the later, equally mediocre *Insulted and Injured*. There was a long period in the Soviet Union under Stalin when the publication of Dostoyevsky's works was almost restricted to such trivia.

To dismiss the element of compassion in Dostoyevsky as a minor issue is not to suggest that it is not an issue at all. 'Poor Folk' of various kinds keep cropping up in his novels and there will be occasion to notice them again. They play a part, for example, in *The Brothers Karamazov* where the death of little Ilyusha, the Tiny Tim of the novel, is described in a manner reminiscent of *Poor Folk*. This is, therefore, an element which one cannot ignore, though it must be put in its proper place.

That its proper place is a modest one is due less to the fact that literature is not a branch of social welfare than to the fact that Dostoyevsky was not especially well equipped as a writer in this particular compartment. His endless descriptions of the sufferings of starving children, consumptive mothers and miserable, poverty-stricken fathers usually leave something to be desired from the artistic point of view. The main point here is that literary taste has changed, but also perhaps that at some subconscious level Dostoyevsky enjoyed contemplating the sufferings of others, though it is impossible to go all the way with Mikhaylovsky and brand him as an out-and-out sadist.

That Dostoyevsky's handling of the poor and downtrodden was among the weaker elements in his artistic equipment can be clinched by comparison with another writer who was superbly equipped in this department, Chekhov. In his story *In the Ravine* Chekhov describes the murder of a baby by scalding and the effect of this tragedy on the unfortunate young mother. This is again a story in which, as in *Poor Folk*, cruelty and vice clash with innocence and virtue. But Chekhov has handled his material with a skill beyond Dostoyevsky's reach in this particular field, even if the novels of his maturity are admitted for comparison alongside juvenilia such as *Poor Folk*.

One reason for Chekhov's superiority in this is that he was more interested in the poor and downtrodden than in the emotions which they aroused in his own breast. Chekhov was an observer of others, while Dostoyevsky, particularly at this stage in his life, was an observer of Dostoyevsky. There could be few more fascinating subjects for observation, so that this introspective approach was a strength as well as a weakness. But it did not fit him to write moving accounts of human misfortune, an exercise which, as Chekhov shows, can often be more effectively carried out by quiet understatement and emotional self-control than by piling on the agony.

This is not to say that Chekhov was a greater writer than Dostoyevsky, for there are many departments in which Dostoyevsky's talent was superior to Chekhov's. But it is important to clear out of the way the persistent myth of Dostoyevsky as a great literary philanthropist so that the reader may be free to hack his way through the difficult territory which was Dostoyevsky's own.

*

Dostoyevsky's second novel, *The Double*, was published hard on the heels of *Poor Folk*, which had been slightly delayed, so that both works appeared in early 1846. But at the time when Dostoyevsky was writing *The Double* the success of *Poor Folk* had already been assured by the interest of Belinsky and his circle. Dostoyevsky in his second novel might therefore have been tempted to repeat the successful formula of the first.

He did not attempt to do so, having already at this early stage the conscientiousness of an artist who continued to develop early themes and ideas, but is rarely found repeating himself from one work of fiction to the other—his writings as a journalist are another matter. This was conscious policy. 'I have thrown up the whole affair,' he remarked in a letter of late 1846 to his brother Mikhail with reference to a story which he was planning at the time, 'for it all adds up to nothing more than a repetition of old things which I have said long ago. . . . Monotony is ruin to one in my position.'[7]

The most obvious superficial difference between *The Double* and *Poor Folk* lies in the abandonment in the second novel of the humanitarian element which had aroused tears of sympathy in the first. Sentimental contemporaries, who had identified Dostoyevsky as a writer to whom one could go for a good cry, were having to think again, being now confronted with a story which contains not a single sympathetic character.

Belinsky himself was baffled by the contrast between the two works, admitting that it was hard to define wherein Dostoyevsky's special quality as a writer lay. 'Judging by *Poor Folk* we had almost concluded that a deeply humanitarian and pathetic element . . . constitutes the fundamental feature in the nature of his talent. But after reading *The Double* we saw that such a conclusion would be too hasty.'[8] Even a critic with Belinsky's flair could not have forecast the development of a writer as original as Dostoyevsky on the basis of a few early works, but it is interesting that his first instinct was to rate *The Double* above *Poor Folk*. 'To anyone to whom the secrets of art are accessible', he wrote in his usual grand manner, 'it is obvious at the first glance that *The Double* contains even more creative talent and depth of thought than *Poor Folk*.'[9]

This judgement shows how risky it may be to apply to Belinsky the stereotype of the 'civic' critic who always assesses a work of art by its social utility, for there are no edifying social messages to be extracted from *The Double*. Belinsky eventually retracted this favourable judgement and came closer to later criticism, which has tended to give the preference to *Poor Folk*. An extreme expression of this view is that of E. H. Carr, who calls *The Double* 'an almost complete failure . . . nobody would read it on its merits now'.[10]

Whatever may be said about the comparative merits of the novels, one thing becomes clear when one compares Dostoyevsky's early work with his mature achievement—he was making a deeper penetration into his own peculiar territory in *The Double* than he had made in *Poor Folk* or than he was to make in any of the other works which preceded his arrest in 1849. That this has not been more generally recognized was Dostoyevsky's own fault, for though the ideas of *The Double* are original and foreshadow much of his later work, the execution of those ideas is not impressive. The defects of the novel are repetitiveness and lack of clarity, combined with an irritating manner of writing modelled on the highly personal style of Gogol. Thus Belinsky, while conceding that *The Double* contained 'a vast amount of masterly artistry', also drew attention to Dostoyevsky's 'terrible incapacity for controlling and disposing economically of the superfluity of his own strength'.[11]

With *The Double* one is accordingly dealing with a botched masterpiece, whereas *Poor Folk* was a more skilfully executed, but relatively unexciting work. To put it differently, in *Poor Folk* Dostoyevsky achieved what he wanted to achieve, but what he wanted to achieve was not especially worth achieving. In *The Double* he may have fallen short of his target, but was aiming higher.

More than thirty years after the first publication of *The Double*, Dostoyevsky gave his own verdict on it.

> I completely failed to bring the story off, but the idea of it was rather bright and more serious than anything else which I have ever carried out in literature. But I utterly failed with the form of the story. . . . If I were to take up this idea now and to expound it anew, I should choose quite a different form. But in 1846 I had not discovered this form and did not master my story.[12]

It is difficult to dissent from this assessment, but Dostoyevsky went too far when, a few lines later, he remarked of *The Double*: 'Everyone's forgotten the story, and that's what it deserves.'

*

What exactly is the peculiar Dostoyevskian territory? The best short phrase which conveys it is 'humanity under strain'. It was this interest which led him to concentrate on the abnormal and to by-pass the ordinary, healthy *homme moyen sensuel* in order to consider the mentally and physically deranged person, the criminal, the suicide and the lunatic.

Humanity under strain had already been Dostoyevsky's concern in *Poor Folk*, but the strain there was a relatively straightforward affair, resolving itself purely into the question of poverty. There was little wrong with Devushkin, Varenka and their satellite underdogs which could not have been cured by a few hundred roubles. This is not the case with Yakov Petrovich Golyadkin, the hero of *The Double*, a point which Dostoyevsky stresses at the beginning of the novel where he informs the reader that Golyadkin has saved a fair sum of money, 750 roubles. But this cannot protect him from his developing insanity, the central theme of *The Double*.

As this choice of theme shows, Dostoyevsky is now reaching into the realm of the abnormal which he was to make so much his own. In fact he almost overreached himself, for actual insanity did not become a major theme in his mature work. There he is more concerned to show characters on the verge of madness. A few lunatics do occur on his later pages, but they are minor figures.

Golyadkin's insanity takes the form of imagining that he meets his own Double, a person who resembles him physically and also has the same name, being another Yakov Petrovich Golyadkin. The Double is at first a dimly apprehended figure, obviously a hallucination as he emerges from the mists of St. Petersburg, but as the novel progresses he begins to put on flesh and to acquire increasingly terrifying characteristics.

The Double obtains a post in the government office where the original Golyadkin (referred to as 'Golyadkin Senior') works as a clerk. By an effective literary device Dostoyevsky describes the Double ('Golyadkin Junior') as being visible to the other characters in the novel, who treat his appearance as a matter of course. For example, the other clerks in the office are not unduly put out when they suddenly find themselves working with two men of identical appearance who bear the same name. Golyadkin Senior is horrified, especially as the only response which he can evoke from his departmental head, when he tries to interest him in the matter, is the urbane remark, 'You're quite right. There really is a striking resemblance.'

This dead-pan treatment of the fantastic had become a peculiarly Russian recipe, and in this matter Dostoyevsky, as in so much else in his early writings, was copying Gogol. For example, Gogol, in his celebrated story *The Nose*, describes how another Government official wakes up one morning to find that his nose is missing, and at once sets about making inquiries with the police.

From mild beginnings Golyadkin Junior develops into the personification of *naglost* (brazen impudence), later to become a key concept in Dostoyevsky's writings. For instance, he manages to get credit with his boss for an important piece of work, in fact executed by Golyadkin Senior, by snatching the relevant documents off his namesake. He tyrannizes and humiliates his victim in increasingly absurd scenes. These include the episode where Golyadkin Senior, having consumed a single tart in a café, finds himself presented with a bill for eleven tarts, the extra ten having been eaten by 'Junior', who has escaped without paying.

As this incident shows, there is much humour in *The Double* and this is another feature of the novel which makes it a forerunner of the later Dostoyevsky. Of particular importance is one of the most painfully humorous scenes in *The Double*, where Golyadkin Senior intrudes uninvited into a reception given by a high official, with whose daughter he imagines himself in love. This episode is a landmark in Dostoyevsky's work, for it shows him tackling a Scandal scene for the first time.

A chain of improprieties committed at a public gathering or on a social occasion—this is something which can occur in any country, but there is something particularly Russian about the idea of a Scandal, deriving from the Russian tendency to impart to public occasions an extra air of bogus decorousness. Scandals are to this day the salt of Russian life, and are just as likely to erupt in the middle of a lecture by a Soviet academician or of an address by the Chairman of a Collective Farm as on the pages of Dostoyevsky.

As Dostoyevsky himself later remarked in the prelude to the greatest of all his Scandals (that which occurs at the ill-starred fête in *The Devils*): 'A Russian takes incredible delight in every kind of scandalous public upheaval.' His permanent interest in the Scandal is one of the features which make him so peculiarly and delightfully Russian in his writings, for there is something more authentically 'Russian' about a vintage Russian Scandal than there is about the 'Russian soul', a concept which now happily preoccupies the foreign reader of Russian literature less than was the case a few decades ago.

Compared with the grandiose Scandals which erupt in the later novels, Golyadkin Senior's experiences at the reception in *The Double* are a tame affair, but they already show the outlines of what was to come. An attempt is made to introduce suspense. Golyadkin has already once attempted to gain entrance to the house where the reception is being held, but has been turned away by a servant who has received specific instructions not to admit him. There can be no doubt that he will not be welcome when he turns up a second time later in the evening, and manages to intrude on the glittering company in the ballroom.

Typical also are the elements of slapstick which attend this second appearance.

> Moved by that same spring which had caused him to burst into a ball to which he had not been invited, he stepped forward. . . . In passing he bumped into a Counsellor and squashed his foot. He also trod on the dress of a highly respected old lady and slightly tore it, jogged a servant with a tray, jogged someone else as well. . . . At that moment it would have given him the greatest possible pleasure to be swallowed up into the earth.

It is such scenes which led Mikhaylovsky to accuse Dostoyevsky of tormenting his own creations, for seldom was any character so systematically tormented by his author as Golyadkin in this scene, which loses some of its force just because too much is made of it. Dostoyevsky was later to learn more exact balance in managing such episodes.

Amongst other humiliations in the ballroom Golyadkin clashes with an officer, an incident typical, as has been indicated above, of Dostoyevskian underdogs in search of humiliation. In order to draw attention away from his own isolation and from the fact that he has no friends in the ballroom, Golyadkin has decided to pretend that he is reserving chairs for the daughter of the house and for one of the guests.

> Nearest to him stood some sort of officer, a tall handsome fellow, before whom Mr. Golyadkin felt like a complete insect.
>
> 'These two chairs are taken, Lieutenant. One for Klara Olsufyevna and one for Princess Chevchekhanova, who is also dancing here. I am keeping them,' pronounced the panting Mr. Golyadkin, looking imploringly at the Lieutenant. The Lieutenant gave a murderous smile and turned away without speaking.

After a number of similar incidents the climax comes when the victim is taken out and thrown downstairs as a burst of music erupts from the orchestra.

*

Can the hero of *The Double* be considered a self-portrait? There seems little in common between a successful young author and a downtrodden, middle-aged clerk who disappears from the pages of the novel when he is removed by carriage to a lunatic asylum. However, this question illuminates an important aspect of *The Double*. It is posed by Dostoyevsky himself in a letter to his elder brother Mikhail, written while he was engaged on the novel. Dostoyevsky complains of his loneliness and says that he envies his brother, who had a wife and children. Of himself he remarks: 'I am now a real Golyadkin.'[13]

This problem links Golyadkin with the other underdogs who dominate Dostoyevsky's writing up to the publication of *Crime and Punishment* in 1866. The most notable specimen is the 'Underground Man', hero of *Notes from Underground*, which immediately precedes *Crime and Punishment* and represents Dostoyevsky's deepest reflections on the theme. Among other variants are the narrator of *Insulted and Injured*, the underdog-tyrant Foma Fomich Opiskin in *The Village of Stepanchikovo*, and several in the short stories of 1846-9.

These submerged figures are variations on a common theme, being Dostoyevsky as he saw himself in a series of distorting mirrors. In a sense the self-portraits are a hallmark of his literary immaturity, but this does not mean that they lack interest. Apart from their intrinsic fascination, the preoccupations which surround them did not end with the publication of *Crime and Punishment*. A study of these early variants is therefore helpful in understanding the mature Dostoyevsky.

Of the self-portraits of the eighteen-forties it is Golyadkin who most closely reflects Dostoyevsky's preoccupation with himself, as becomes evident when one compares what Dostoyevsky has to say about his hero with what friends and acquaintances had to say about Dostoyevsky as an adolescent and young man. The emphasis is everywhere on his loneliness, secretiveness, unsociability and awkwardness in company, all qualities which he shared with Golyadkin Senior, though there he had exaggerated them to the point of lunacy. For example, Grigorovich writes of Dostoyevsky's 'innate reserve of character', of a 'lack of youthful expansiveness and frankness. . . . He kept to himself, took no part in games, but would sit immersed in a book and would seek some solitary spot.'[14]

Seldom was anyone less adapted for an army career, and it is not surprising to learn from the memoirs of fellow-cadets that, though he was rarely idle on parade, he could never look like a soldier. Uniform did not suit him, nor after his retirement from the army did he cut much of a figure in civilian clothes. He dressed neatly, but 'bore himself clumsily, like a seminarist' (i.e. a student at a theological training college).[15] It must have been his inability to fit into army life which caused his obsession with handsome, well-dressed officers.

The link between *The Double* and Dostoyevsky's experiences as an army cadet is emphasized by evidence about the St. Petersburg Engineering School from Grigorovich and others. The worst feature of the school was the tormenting of new boys. This took ingenious forms—pouring water down the backs of their necks, spilling ink on their exercise books and making them lick it up. This is the sort of schoolboy trick which Golyadkin Junior is continually playing on Golyadkin Senior in *The Double*. Such was the Engineering School as seen by what may be called unofficial observers, but, as was inevitable in Russia, there was also a decorous official picture of the School, which knew nothing of such goings on. 'In this little world,' the instructor Savelyev wrote sententiously, 'young men prided themselves on their rank, honour, disinterestedness, respect for personality and on the other qualities of a man who understands his moral rights and duties.'[16]

Dostoyevsky himself was bullied at the School and this early experience must have inflamed his interest in humiliation as a theme. According to several observers Dostoyevsky never took part in bullying and would defend the victims from their tormentors, so that he was at least no thorough-paced Golyadkin. But though his occasional defence of the humiliated underdog cadet shows him in an agreeable and even noble light, he also had his share of weaknesses. As befitted so introspective a character, he was very largely aware of them, as he was also aware of the lack of self-control which might have held them in check. He was quick to take offence and in common with many of his fictional characters, often enjoyed the experience.

If this touchiness derived from pride, it was pride which quickly provoked a fall. Hardly had Dostoyevsky become established as the darling of the St. Petersburg literary vanguard before he had succeeded in transforming himself into a figure of fun. Whether through genuine conceit, or simply because he lacked the art of getting on with people, he contrived to turn everyone against him. He had a violent quarrel with Nekrasov, and Belinsky himself was soon saying that he had 'been taken in by this idea of Dostoyevsky

as a genius'. Where he had once been lionized, Dostoyevsky now
became the butt of witty epigrams and funny stories, being nick-
named the 'literary pustule'. The most persistent story concerned
Poor Folk, of which the literary memoirist P. V. Annenkov wrote
that Dostoyevsky had 'quite calmly, and as a condition belonging
to him by right, demanded that it should be distinguished from all
other items in the almanac [in which it was first published] by some
special typographical sign'.[17] (He is alleged to have wanted the novel
printed with an ornamental border.) The story was probably invented, but the fact that it gained currency is an indication of
the ease with which Dostoyevsky could cut a Golyadkin-like figure.

This was particularly evident in his relations with Turgenev,
who, with his aristocratic manner and imposing appearance, had
almost been designed by nature to put Dostoyevsky in his place.
At first Turgenev was cordial. Dostoyevsky wrote to his brother
that, 'The poet Turgenev has just got back from Paris and has
grown so attached to me that Belinsky explains it by the fact that
he's fallen in love with me.'[18] But when Dostoyevsky fell from
grace in the literary set, Turgenev soon became the most prominent
of his persecutors.

Dostoyevsky's character as a young man thus exhibits two
violently opposed trends. There was a consciousness of his own
inferiority and a tendency to abase himself before others. On the
other hand there was a fierce pride and self-importance, combined
with a wish to dominate others.

But were these two elements really as different as they might
seem? Were they not perhaps opposite sides of the same coin?
Dostoyevsky himself must have begun to realize this, at least subconsciously, when he created his two Golyadkins, the one a victim
of humiliation and the other its purveyor. He returned to this theme
in the works which follow his imprisonment in Siberia. Other 'self-
portrait' characters, such as the Underground Man in *Notes from
Underground*, oscillate like Dostoyevsky himself in real life, up and
down what may be thought of as a 'humiliation slot', now cringing
before more powerful characters, now themselves tyrannizing the
weak. But it is only in *The Double* that Dostoyevsky treats the
'humiliation slot' in precisely this way, creating two characters,
Golyadkin Senior and Golyadkin Junior, which are in effect the
same character with one pole fixed at each extreme.

*

The Double almost seems to bring Dostoyevsky to a full stop as a writer. Thirteen years pass before he makes an advance on the achievement of this remarkable second novel with the publication of *Uncle's Dream* and *The Village of Stepanchikovo* in 1859. The chief reason for the hiatus was his arrest in 1849, followed by nearly ten years' imprisonment and exile in Siberia, but it was not Siberia alone which hindered his advance, for three years of intensive literary activity intervene between *The Double* and his arrest. During these three years (1846–9) he came near to collapsing as a fiction-writer without the assistance of external catastrophe.

Not that he dried up, for the period saw the publication of eleven titles, all short stories except for the unfinished novel *Netochka Nezvanova*. None of these has made a mark in literary history, and in fact they include a lot of rubbish, but they do show Dostoyevsky as a determined experimenter never content to rest on his laurels and always eager to play with new themes and new techniques. Reading through these juvenilia in the light of his later achievement, one has the impression of an immense latent talent temporarily out of control. But the stories of 1846–9 are notable for the development of themes touched upon in *Poor Folk* and *The Double*, and because they contain the seeds of themes which ripened later on.

Among echoes of former achievements is Dostoyevsky's continued obsession with St. Petersburg, which seemed to many Russians the most fantastic city in the world with its mist, drizzle and sleet in winter, the 'white nights' of its short summer, its innumerable canals and bridges, and the contrast between its huddling slum tenements and spacious imperial palaces. Dostoyevsky was not the first important Russian author to write about St. Petersburg, having been preceded here by Pushkin and Gogol. But it was Dostoyevsky who, as it were, inaugurated a literary cult of the Russian capital, which forms the setting of almost all these early stories, as of his two first novels. It remained the chief setting of his work during most of his life, and even when he deserted it, as in *The Devils* and *The Brothers Karamazov*, he continued to prefer an urban background. Hence one big contrast between Dostoyevsky and his two leading contemporary rivals, Turgenev and Tolstoy, who were novelists of the countryside.

During these early years Dostoyevsky was already staking his claim to be regarded as the 'poet' of the city, but it is to be noted that one of the better early stories, *The Little Hero*, is set in the countryside in an atmosphere which critics have described as 'Turgenevesque'. However, this kind of background did not long attract him.

Against the St. Petersburg background Dostoyevsky continues to experiment with the isolated individual, adding further portraits to the gallery which had begun with Devushkin and Golyadkin. These include fantastic eccentrics such as Mr. Prokharchin, the miser-hero from the story of the same name, who, like so many Dostoyevskian heroes, lives out his lonely life in *a little corner* (*ugolok*; the word is used again and again to describe the living-quarters of Dostoyevsky's underdogs) behind a tattered screen.

These isolated figures also include some who correspond more closely to Dostoyevsky himself, being introspective young men described as 'dreamers' (*mechtateli*), another recurrent term in his writings of the period. Such is the hero of *White Nights*, one of his most remarkable early 'poems' of St. Petersburg. In this story a virtually new theme is broached, that of love. That these young heroes should be unsuccessful in love is axiomatic. This is true of Ordynov, hero of the grotesque story *The Landlady* (perhaps the least successful of all Dostoyevsky's works), who loses his beloved Katerina to the aged Murin, a fantastic character described as a kind of wizard. But the hero of *White Nights* goes further than this, in a manner prophetic of Dostoyevsky's own life and future writings. He makes no serious attempt to woo the girl with whom he has fallen in love one night on a St. Petersburg canal bank, but assists his rival.

The most forward-looking of these early works is also among the weakest, the unfinished novel *Netochka Nezvanova*. The idea of a 'big novel' (by Russian standards *Poor Folk* and *The Double*, with a mere hundred-and-fifty-odd pages apiece, are mere snippets) was among ambitious projects which attracted Dostoyevsky during these years. At one stage he planned, probably in imitation of Gogol, to spend eight months in Italy writing it, and even worked out that he would receive 1,200 roubles for the first part, enough to finance a two-month excursion to Paris.

Netochka Nezvanova did not live up to these expectations. It remained unfinished, being interrupted by Dostoyevsky's arrest, and is not of the stuff of which big novels are made, as the three completed sections show. These are three protracted short stories, united by the personality of the narrator, the young girl whose name appears in the title. Each section ends in a dramatic dénouement foreshadowing Dostoyevsky's mature method in which such explosive crises loom large, but the crises of *Netochka Nezvanova* are built up in a feeble way. They lack the dynamic urge which was to infuse the preparation for crisis later on.

Looking back on *Netochka Nezvanova* and some of the short stories of its period in search of a clue to their weakness, one is struck by the relatively small use made of direct speech, which occupies a much bigger place in the mature novels. It is this widespread use of dialogue which helps to make Dostoyevsky the most dramatic of the great Russian novelists, so that much of his work has lent itself to adaptation for stage or screen. If he had hit on this technique earlier, he might have freed himself from long passages of constipated narrative.

Netochka Nezvanova is the first work in which Dostoyevsky seriously concerns himself with children, an interest which would never desert him. It is shown in the portrait of the young girl Netochka, and also in *A Little Hero*, where the narrator is an eleven-year-old boy. Both works are concerned with the topic of love, portrayed, as in the later Dostoyevsky, as a source of suffering. This is the theme of the central and most interesting section of *Netochka Nezvanova*, where the heroine becomes infatuated with Princess Katya, a little girl of her own age.

Katya is beautiful, wayward and imperious, the ancestor of such 'infernal women' in Dostoyevsky's later work as Nastasya Filippovna in *The Idiot*. Like her successors, she oscillates between love and hate, emotions which, in Dostoyevsky's work, tend to be separated by a hair's breadth. Thus the 'love affair' between the two nymphets Netochka and Katya anticipates later Dostoyevskian love affairs between adults of opposite sexes.

> We embraced and eagerly clung to each other [Netochka relates of one of these anticipatory crises]. The Princess kissed me with abandon. 'Netochka,' Katya whispered between her tears, 'my angel, I have loved you for such a long time. . . . Listen, I used to want to love you very much, and then I'd suddenly take it into my head to hate you. . . . Then I would notice that you could not live without me and think "Now I'll torment her, the bad girl." I used to wonder whether I'd kiss her or pinch her to death.'

Much play has been made by critics with Dostoyevsky's abiding interest in children, an interest shown in real life as well as in repeated fictional studies. He was devoted to his own children and, as a journalist, showed on the pages of his *Diary of a Writer* as deep a concern for the welfare of actual Russian children as he did for the children in his novels. It has been pointed out that he anticipated the findings of Freudian psychology by detecting sexual elements in the emotional life of the young child.

For these and other reasons Dostoyevsky's studies of children have been rightly regarded as an important and original aspect of his work, but there is something unsatisfactory about Dostoyevsky's children as fictional characters. They may shed light on previously neglected aspects of human psychology, but do they really come over as children? By the side of Tolstoy's and Chekhov's children most of them do not.

The point is not so much whether Dostoyevsky's children are really children, as that so many of his characters, however old they may be, tend to be of the same emotional age. For example, Nastasya Filippovna in *The Idiot* is a more developed and interesting fictional character than Princess Katya, but is she emotionally more adult? What, indeed, is the emotional age of a typical character from Dostoyevsky? The parent of young children who is also a reader of his work might be inclined to put it at the two-year-old stage or even at that of the infant in arms, such are the gusts of uncontrolled emotion and oscillations from love to hate to which these characters are liable.

Perhaps Dostoyevsky has tended by a daring literary convention to attribute to many of his supposed adults the emotional colouring of infancy. If indeed the buried experiences of infancy have on adults the potent subconscious hold generally claimed for them, this may be one of the reasons for Dostoyevsky's grip on generation after generation of readers, who are able when reading his work to relive the emotions of the cradle, without perhaps realizing that they are doing so.

*

In the switch-back progress of Dostoyevsky's career there was no more disastrous swoop than that which occurred in 1849 when he was arrested as a member of the group of political conspirators whose leader was M. B. Petrashevsky. Outside a Russian context 'conspiracy' is too strong a term to describe many of the activities of a discussion group for the airing of socialist, liberal and atheistic ideas, to which the young Dostoyevsky had become an enthusiastic temporary convert. But in Russia the expression of unorthodox views has commonly been a crime punishable by death or imprisonment. Moreover, Petrashevsky's followers did include determined revolutionaries as well as social theorists, and Dostoyevsky's involvement was deep enough to put him in extreme danger. Arrest was followed by months of imprisonment in the Petropavlovsk Fortress in St. Petersburg, concluding in a trial at which Dostoyevsky amongst others was sentenced to death. As is well known, the sentence was countermanded at the last moment, after Dostoyevsky and his colleagues had actually been led out for execution, the most shattering event of his life and one too sharply seasoned even for a person with his craving for strong sensations.

Dostoyevsky did not lose his life, but lost something almost equally precious, nearly a decade of literary activity during the period when he was a convict in the prison at Omsk for four years and thereafter a conscript soldier and officer in a Siberian infantry regiment. But what might have been disaster to a more ordinary man was not disastrous for Dostoyevsky, and may even have been a blessing. To judge from his letters, written from the Petropavlovsk Fortress to his brother Mikhail, his arrest brought him something which five years of feverish activity as a free man in St. Petersburg had been unable to give him—peace of mind.

Despite his sombre surroundings and uncertain future combined with ill health (he was suffering from insomnia, scrofula and piles) it seems that his morale had never been so high in his life as during this pre-trial period. 'I expected something much worse, and I now see that I have such a store of vitality that it can't be exhausted.'[19] The emphasis on vitality recurs: 'Never have such abundant and healthy stores of spiritual vitality seethed within me as now.'[20]

Literature remained a major interest. 'Shall I really never take up the pen again?' he wrote only an hour or two after his mock execution. 'I think there will be a possibility in four years' time.... I shall perish if I can't write. Better fifteen years' imprisonment and a pen in my hands.'[21] In prison he had already worked out the ideas for three stories and two novels. Only one of these came to fruition (*The Little Hero*) and it is significant that this short story, the least sombre of his early works, should have been written at a time when his future seemed so black.

There were reasons for this paradoxical state of affairs. The previous five years had been so hectic and disorderly that almost any change would have provided relief. Dostoyevsky's financial troubles alone had been almost enough to drive anyone to seek refuge in prison. No topic occurs more persistently and tediously throughout his large correspondence than money, for seldom can any man have possessed more talent for involving himself in a financial mess. His entanglements involved the acceptance of advances from publishers for projected work. To one publisher in particular, Krayevsky, he felt that he had sold himself into slavery. Then there had been endless arguments with his brother-in-law, Kurepin, who was executor of his father's small estate. Dostoyevsky strongly disliked Kurepin, whom he once described as 'a son of a bitch and blackguard of the first grade', and it has been suggested that Kurepin served him as model for the occasional pompous bourgeois, such as Luzhin in *Crime and Punishment*. However this may be, anyone who had to deal with Dostoyevsky in money matters deserves some sympathy. Apart from these troubles there were also the ramifications of Dostoyevsky's borrowings from friends. No attempt will be made here to do something which was beyond his own powers—to keep track of these matters. But it is important to remember that financial complications pursued him throughout most of his life to an extent which it is impossible to exaggerate. Later on such complications began to play a larger part in his fictional plots than in his early period.

Though Dostoyevsky was always complaining about money worries, it is doubtful if these cut very deep. More genuine distress probably arose from the relative failure of his literary career. This, combined with the frenzied introspection of the 'St. Petersburg dreamer', as described in so many works of fiction, meant that the vehicle of his imagination was rattling itself to pieces without progressing anywhere. Thus, although one cannot guess what would have happened to Dostoyevsky without his decade of prison and exile, it is likely that he received a reprieve from more serious mental breakdown.

A commentary on this topic is supplied by a short story of 1848, *A Weak Heart*. It describes how a young man goes mad for a reason unlikely to occur outside the pages of Dostoyevsky—he was too happy. This hero, another 'St. Petersburg dreamer', is unlucky enough to be engaged to a young girl with whom he is deeply in love, and also to enjoy the goodwill of his official superior, who as a sign of favour gives him extra copying work to be done after office hours. This combination of good fortune is too much for him and drives him out of his mind. Perhaps Dostoyevsky felt that something of the sort had threatened him after the spectacular success of his first work. His letters of the period show considerable unbalance, as in his repeated threats to commit suicide if his literary plans should fail, either by hanging or by throwing himself into the Neva. He later refers to a 'mental illness' from which he suffered during the period, 'before my trip to Siberia where I got cured'.[22] Whatever the correct interpretation of *A Weak Heart*, it becomes less surprising that Dostoyevsky should have welcomed ill-fortune in the shape of imprisonment when one remembers that he had recently conceived a character who broke down entirely through excess of good fortune.

To these considerations must be added the special role assigned to punishment and suffering in so much of his later writing. He often thought of these as desirable—witness the attitude of many of his characters, such as Raskolnikov in *Crime and Punishment* and Dmitry Karamazov. Was Dostoyevsky less distressed than he might have been by his arrest because he wanted to be punished?

An explanation has been offered which is perhaps less facile than it may sound, and which relates Dostoyevsky's attitude to suffering and guilt to an event which occurred when he was eighteen. At that time his father was murdered by his own serfs in the village of Chermashnya, which he had bought a few years previously. No one was brought to justice for the crime, partly perhaps because of the connivance of surviving relatives, who in any case benefited from the results of letting the case drop, for so many serfs had been implicated that the value of the estate would have decreased if all the culprits had been sent to Siberia.

Had Dostoyevsky, accordingly, 'murdered his own father' in the Freudian sense? And even profited from the crime? One can only say that if this was the case his attitude to guilt and punishment, which otherwise defies explanation, falls easily into place. There is no direct evidence that Dostoyevsky hated his father, who appears, particularly in his later years after he had become widowed and taken to drink, to have been a hateful man, although the evidence here is conflicting. In any case such hatred would presumably only have been truly guilt-provoking if it had been subconscious, in which case one would not expect to find direct evidence of it.

B

What one does find in Dostoyevsky's letters to his father, written from the Engineering School, is a lack of intimacy and candour. Dostoyevsky addresses his father with oleaginous deference and in an old-fashioned prose style modelled on authors such as Karamzin whom they had read aloud to each other in the family circle. How far these letters, which combine flowery professions of devotion with urgent requests for money, were actually hypocritical and how far they derive their quality from stylistic convention, it is hard to decide. It is perhaps significant that Dostoyevsky, so prone to muse about events of his past life—he returned again and again, for example, to the episode of his near-execution in St. Petersburg —never made reference to his father's murder. But this may have been merely the result of agreement amongst the family, in which case it is less significant than it might seem.

More interesting is the fact that one of his strongest plots, that of *The Brothers Karamazov*, hinges on the murder of a father. This theme from youth took forty years to mature.

CHAPTER TWO

THE SIBERIAN NOVELS

OF Dostoyevsky's ten years' enforced absence from St. Petersburg, only the first four, the period of his imprisonment, excluded all literary activity. After his release from prison in February, 1854, he was able to take up the threads, but only to a limited extent. As a private soldier in the Seventh Siberian Battalion of the Line, stationed in the Siberian town of Semipalatinsk, he was not ideally placed to launch himself anew.

His first need was for reading matter. In answer to urgent requests his brother Mikhail sent books on which Dostoyevsky flung himself like a starving man. It was Mikhail who acted as his literary agent during the six years of exile which remained and who began placing Dostoyevsky's work in the magazines. *The Little Hero*, written in prison in 1849, appeared in 1857 and was the first work to break the long silence.

Meanwhile Dostoyevsky had been working out new ideas, and there are references in letters of 1856 to a comic novel which he was then planning. This may have been the prototype of *Uncle's Dream* or *The Village of Stepanchikovo*, the two humorous novels which mark his reappearance on the literary scene in 1859.

These Siberian novels are similar to each other in tone, and in many ways stand apart from the rest of Dostoyevsky's work. The rural setting is among the points of difference. Here only *The Village of Stepanchikovo* goes the whole way, being staged, like so much of Tolstoy's and Turgenev's fiction, on a Russian country estate. To mention this is to be struck at once by the contrast between the stately sweep and elegiac atmosphere of the rural scenes in Tolstoy or Turgenev and the indecorous upheavals which take place at Colonel Rostanev's country seat at Stepanchikovo. *Uncle's Dream* is not quite so rural, being set in an imaginary country town called by the comic name Mordasov, but the atmosphere of this ridiculous provincial centre of gossip and intrigue is hardly metropolitan. Dostoyevsky had temporarily abandoned his vocation as an urban novelist.

Another peculiarity of the two novels is the element of farce which pervades them. This had appeared in earlier writings, notably *The Double*, and had dominated one trivial early story, *Another Man's Wife and the Husband under the Bed* (1848), of which the less said the better. This comic element eventually became an ingredient in Dostoyevsky's mature novels, where it is mixed, in a manner which lends these gigantic works much of their strange piquancy, into his preoccupation with broad philosophical problems, with the existence of God, with sin, crime, madness and disease, and with the nature of man in his political, social and religious life.

It is interesting that Dostoyevsky now chose to concentrate on the comic ingredient. Because of the importance of humour in his later work, the two novels of his Siberian period occupy a crucial place among the elaborate experiments which he conducted before eventually finding himself as a writer. The Siberian novels helped him towards this destiny by bringing something new to his narrative technique, the element of pace.

Of the works written before Dostoyevsky's arrest, only *The Double* conveys the sense of proceeding from one place to another, and even here he often loses momentum because of the frequent repetitions. As for the inferior early works, he often appears to be wandering about without knowing where he is going. In *Uncle's Dream* he first gives the impression of driving his furious narrative along the road chosen for it. The road is not a very interesting one, the novel being too farcical to command serious respect, but the impetus of Dostoyevsky's attack does something to remedy this. When in *The Village of Stepanchikovo* he succeeded in whirling the reader through more notable scenery—for he now had a worthwhile and serious comic theme—he produced his most impressive work to date.

The two novels occupy an important place in the development of the Dostoyevskian Scandal, each being built on an eruption of riotous improprieties. As these scenes show, Dostoyevsky had come a long way as the practitioner of the fictional Scandal since the occasion when Golyadkin Senior was thrown out of the ballroom in *The Double*, thus inaugurating this memorable series.

The two novels caused disappointment in St. Petersburg, where Dostoyevsky seemed cut off from reality. It must be remembered that at this period the Russian countryside was in ferment. Emancipation of the serfs was the topic of the moment, and would be realized in 1861. Yet here was Dostoyevsky on the eve of this event writing about the countryside as if the peasant problem did not exist, for the occasional rustics who lumber across his pages are the idealized bumpkins of an eclogue—enough to infuriate the radical critics and publishers who set the literary pace.

It was probably for this reason that Nekrasov in effect turned down *The Village of Stepanchikovo*, by offering too low a fee, when it was submitted to his review, the *Sovremennik*. Soon Mikhail Dostoyevsky was damning both novels by implication when he wrote to Fyodor: 'You've absolutely got to write something effective for the New Year. . . . Above all you must remind the public of yourself with something grandiose and passionate, and do it quickly.'[1]

Dostoyevsky's own comments on the Siberian novels show no illusions about their importance. Writing about *Uncle's Dream* in 1873, he said: 'I find it bad. I wrote it in Siberia, my first thing after imprisonment, with the sole aim of beginning my literary career again and in terrific fear of the censorship'—which, as he went on to explain, might be especially severe on a former convict.[2] About *The Village of Stepanchikovo* he spoke differently, saying that, despite certain defects, it was the best of his works so far. 'I've put into it the whole of my soul, flesh and blood. I don't want to say that I've expressed everything which I have to say there. That would be rubbish! There will be plenty of other things to express yet.'[3]

*

The central figure of *Uncle's Dream*, the 'uncle' of the title, is Prince K., an even more farcical caricature than any of the other figures. He is described as so aged and decrepit that anyone looking at him 'couldn't help thinking that he might immediately fall to pieces'. Everything about this 'idiot prince' is artificial. He wears a wig and also sidewhiskers, moustache and espagnole beard—all false. He uses powder and rouge. 'It was also maintained that he wore a corset, having somewhere lost a rib when jumping awkwardly out of a window during one of his amorous escapades in Italy.' The Prince wears a monocle—over a glass eye—and resembles 'a corpse on springs'. Yet this is the character whom Dostoyevsky himself describes as the only serious figure in the story.[4]

Prince K. does have one thing about him which makes the designing mammas in the town of Mordasov take him seriously—he is a rich landowner, being the possessor of four thousand serfs. It might even be possible to marry one's daughter to a man so out of rapport with the outside world without him really being aware of what was happening. This is the plan of Marya Aleksandrovna Moskalyova, the leading gossip of the town, whose greed for power has caused her to be compared with Napoleon. Moskalyova has a beautiful twenty-three-year-old daughter called Zina, whom she plans to marry to the Prince.

Moskalyova is the first in the series of masterful middle-aged women in Dostoyevsky's work. Such predators must always be provided with a foil—a weak and passive character who can be bullied and ordered about—and in *Uncle's Dream* this victim's role goes to Moskalyova's husband, Afanasy Matveich. He is described as a man of imposing appearance, 'but all this dignity and impressiveness disappeared the moment he opened his mouth'. Moskalyova regularly refers to her husband as 'my fathead'. She will not allow him to live in the town with her, but keeps him in a village three versts away. Afanasy Matveich plays only a small part, but is the most amusing figure in the novel.

The daughter, Zina, is a caricature too, but differs from the other characters—all monsters of frivolity and self-seeking—in being a caricature of nobility and the only virtuous figure. She does eventually fall in with her mother's unscrupulous plan to marry her to Prince K., but only because this would provide her with funds to help the man with whom she is in love. He is a young tutor who is dying of consumption and seems to have staggered into *Uncle's Dream* from the pages of *Poor Folk*. An exotic detail is that his illness is described as self-induced—after a quarrel with Zina he had tried to commit suicide by drinking a decoction of tobacco. He had also further shown the perversity of a Dostoyevskian character in love by circulating a letter, written to him by Zina, among the town gossips, thus compromising the girl's reputation. A writer of verses and a 'dreamer', the young man is a hang-over from Dostoyevsky's pre-arrest period, being one of the most distorted in the series of self-portraits.

The Scandal in which these stresses reach breaking point is the funniest scene which Dostoyevsky had yet written. Just before it erupts Prince K. has proposed to Zina, only to be persuaded immediately afterwards by one of her unsuccessful suitors that his proposal had not taken place at all, but had presented itself to him in a dream. This challenge puts Moskalyova's intrigues in such danger that she summons her idiot husband Afanasy Matveich from the country to lend her support, on the strict understanding that he will not open his mouth except to say 'h'm!' Unfortunately he departs from this brief, and incidentally gets the funniest line in the whole of this scene, which has hitherto hinged on whether Prince K. proposed to Zina in actual fact or merely in a dream. Afanasy Matveich suggests a third alternative—perhaps it was his wife herself who had dreamed the whole thing. 'At this point a burst of uncontrollable laughter filled the whole room.'

There is no point in dwelling longer on *Uncle's Dream*—except to point out that it was to some extent a preliminary sketch for the greatest of Dostoyevsky's novels, *The Devils*. This aspect of *Uncle's Dream* is developed and slightly exaggerated in K. Mochulsky's study of Dostoyevsky.[5] Mochulsky finds in Prince K. a forerunner of one of Dostoyevsky's most memorable creations, Stepan Trofimovich Verkhovensky in *The Devils*. He points out that both are Europe-orientated Russians, a type which Dostoyevsky came to despise. But in fact this link between the two characters does not go much further than the possession of a common affectation, the habit of interspersing their sentences with French phrases. More notable is the parallel of intrigue. Stavrogina (the Moskalyova of *The Devils*) tries to marry her ward Dasha to Stepan Trofimovich, just as Moskalyova tries to marry Zina to Prince K. In each case the projected marriage is blown up by a Scandal.

The provincial town of Mordasov in *Uncle's Dream*, with its futility and emptiness, is an adumbration of the fuller study of 'our town', the background of *The Devils*. There are also many sentences in the early novel which seem to belong in spirit to the later, not least:

> Through the whole town suddenly spread a strange and almost incredible rumour, welcomed by one and all with a transport of malicious and violent delight, as we usually do welcome every unusual scandal when it involves one of our neighbours.

*

In one of his letters Dostoyevsky explains why he considered *The Village of Stepanchikovo* his most successful work to date: 'It contains two vast and typical characters, the result of five years of *creation* and *note-taking*, characters which have been given a flawless finish (in my opinion), which are completely Russian and which have so far been indicated poorly in Russian literature.'[6] These two characters once more present the confrontation of predator and victim, but the predator-victim duel, which forms the theme of the novel, shows points of contrast with previous duels.

This is partly due to the greater subtlety of the character-drawing. The two protagonists are extravagant figures, but are not pure caricatures like the Golyadkins and the Moskalyov husband and wife. They also have a new characteristic—mobility within the humiliation slot. Whereas Golyadkin Junior and Moskalyova remain fixed at the extreme pole of predatoriness, while their victims, Golyadkin Senior and Afanasy Matveich, remain fixed at the opposite pole as butts and victims, it turns out that the protagonists of *The Village of Stepanchikovo* can change roles.

Foma Fomich Opiskin, the prime predator of the novel, had once been at the receiving end of Dostoyevskian humiliation. During the period before the action begins he has fulfilled the part (familiar from other works of Dostoyevsky) of the 'hanger-on' or parasite—in the house of a wealthy general, where, in return for his keep, he was expected to perform the role of buffoon. During this period the General, who happens to be the stepfather of the prime victim of the novel, Colonel Rostanev, has tyrannized and humiliated Foma Fomich.

When the General dies, Foma Fomich manages to attach himself as a hanger-on in Colonel Rostanev's house, at the same time switching his role from victim to predator. On this transformation the important comment is made: 'A mean spirit, emerging from oppression, itself becomes an oppressor.'

To the parasite Foma Fomich, his victim Colonel Rostanev proves an ideal host. Despite his gigantic build, his career as an officer of Hussars and his position in society as a country squire, the Colonel has the spirit of a mouse. 'It was hard to imagine a man meeker or more ready to agree to everything. If anyone had taken it into his head to ask him to carry someone a couple of versts on his shoulders, he would perhaps have done it.' Yet the Colonel too can switch roles, and the climax of the novel comes when he rounds on his tormentor and hurls him through a french window.

Each protagonist has a train of sympathizers. Foma Fomich's camp includes the Colonel's mother, who combines the acceptance of subsidies from her son with denunciations of his ingratitude.

Surrounded by a nimbus of female hangers-on, lap-dogs, poms and Chinese cats, she is devoted to Foma Fomich, being always ready to produce hysterics or give ear-splitting screeches in furtherance of his intrigues. Prominent among her entourage is her confidante, the spinster Perepelitsyna, 'an overripe and ubiquitously hissing creature in a wig, without eyebrows and with small carnivorous eyes'. Such is the camp of Evil. As for the camp of Good (and this is another novel in which virtue and vice are dispensed on the all-or-nothing principle), its main representative after the Colonel himself is the Narrator of the novel, a young man of twenty-two called Seryozha, who is the Colonel's nephew.

When the action begins, Seryozha has just been summoned to Stepanchikovo by his uncle in order to help out in a crisis which has suddenly arisen. Foma Fomich has decided to marry Colonel Rostanev to a Tatyana Ivanovna, 'a highly peculiar female, over-ripe and almost entirely half-witted'. The Colonel, who is used to taking orders, might have minded this less if he had not already been in love with someone else, a girl called Nastasya, the governess of his two children by a former marriage. He is too timid to aspire to marry Nastasya himself, but fears that his mother and Foma Fomich are going to use the occasion of his marriage to throw her out of the house. Nastasya is another representative of the Good camp, and her family relationships bring with them a whiff of *Poor Folk*. She is the sole support, through her earnings as governess, of her aged father (a subsidiary buffoon in the novel and a forerunner of Marmeladov in *Crime and Punishment*) and also of seven brothers and sisters. The Colonel wishes to help her by marrying her to Seryozha.

One of the reasons for the success of Foma Fomich and Colonel Rostanev as character-studies is that Dostoyevsky has managed to avoid self-portraiture as well as the extremes of caricature. It has been suggested above that his successful rise to maturity went hand in hand with a tendency to rid himself of an excessively introspective approach in the creation of character. It is noteworthy that the one character in *The Village of Stepanchikovo* who does obviously spring from introspective origins (Seryozha) is a less odious sample of self-portraiture than his predecessors.

Seryozha, who is subtly observed, is perhaps the nearest of all the portraits so far drawn of the Dostoyevsky who made a fool of himself in St. Petersburg literary circles in the late eighteen-forties.

He exhibits the same shyness combined with self-assertion, for Seryozha is another oscillator up and down the humiliation slot.

It is Seryozha the Victim who stumbles into the tea-party at Stepanchikovo at the beginning of the novel, the first in a chain of increasingly outrageous Scandals. 'Seeing the whole gathering at the tea-table, I suddenly tripped over the carpet, staggered, and while trying to save my balance, unexpectedly flew into the centre of the room. Embarrassed . . . I stood motionless, blushing like a crayfish and gazing stupidly at the assembly.'

The gathering soon forgets Seryozha's unsuccessful entrance as the representatives of Evil revert to their favourite party game of mocking Colonel Rostanev. After one of these sallies 'Obnoskin [a minor evil satellite] gave a loud guffaw, throwing himself back in his arm-chair. His mamma gave a smile, while the spinster Perepelitsyna emitted an especially foul snigger.' Seryozha too joins in the fun of mocking his uncle, thus appearing in the role of predator. He is checked by a reproachful glance from Nastasya. 'I understood her glance and guessed that, by my mean-spirited and odious wish to make Uncle ridiculous in order to divert some of the ridicule from myself, I had not gained greatly in the girl's favour.'

The novel again raises the question of Dostoyevsky's children, but not because of what it has to say of the two actual children who figure among the dramatis personae. These are the Colonel's eight-year-old son Ilyusha and fifteen-year-old daughter Sasha, who are simple representatives of the camp of the Good and lack the usual perversities of Dostoyevsky's children. Sasha and Ilyusha seem like adult characters when they are compared with some of their seniors.

'He was really a forty-year-old child'—this comment by the Narrator on his uncle Colonel Rostanev provides a clue to much which might be mysterious about the novel. No such comment is made about Foma Fomich, but a survey of his antics suggests that he too is an odious child rather than the man of fifty as whom he is presented. Examples of his childish capriciousness are the occasion when he decreed that it was a Wednesday when it was in fact a Thursday and his tendency to claim that his birthday is a movable feast which may be deemed to occur on any day when he thinks he is not getting his full share of attention.

There are accordingly aspects of *The Village of Stepanchikovo* which confirm that Dostoyevsky, when purporting to describe adults, was often in a sense describing infants or adolescents, a literary device of which he was probably not conscious, but which may be one of the springs of his originality.

One important feature in the handling of Foma Fomich is the use made by Dostoyevsky of a 'build-up', such as he later gave to other villains like Svidrigaylov in *Crime and Punishment* and Stavrogin in *The Devils*. It was Dostoyevsky's practice to keep these Bogeymen waiting in the wings until he had worked up a great feeling of suspense. A characteristic Dostoyevskian fog is spread over Foma Fomich's antecedents, as in the following sentence: '*It was said* . . . that he had *at some time* been *somewhere* in Government service, that he had *somewhere* met with misfortune . . . *it was also said* that he had *at one time* devoted himself to literature in Moscow.'[7]

Thus, long before Foma Fomich appears—about a third of the way through the novel—the reader has already been furnished with much tantalizing and ambiguous information about him. It is also typical that Foma Fomich should finally erupt on to the stage at the end of a chapter and with a verbal formula which Dostoyevsky often uses at points of crisis: 'The door opened, and . . .' Thus, at the end of Chapter Five of *The Village of Stepanchikovo* the reader is at last told: 'The door opened, and Foma Fomich in his own person appeared before the astonished audience.'

The skilful use of suspense is a reminder of the advance registered in this novel towards the methods of the mature Dostoyevsky. Suspense, which plays no great part in his preceding fiction, and which is often handled ineptly where it does appear, is a vital element in his mature technique. Now for the first time he is to be seen dispensing it with an exact sense of measurement.

Once Foma Fomich is on the stage, suspense is increased by relatively innocent scenes in which, assisted by his evil entourage, he baits the Colonel. One of the Colonel's weaknesses is his interest in learning, but since he is an ignorant man, he can easily be put in his place even by the equally ignorant Foma Fomich. When the Colonel dares to interrupt one of Foma Fomich's discourses on literature, he is told 'Leave literature alone. It will not be the loser if you do, I can assure you.' Then the Colonel tells a long and pointless story about how he once made a fool of himself, and ends by laughing heartily at his own joke. 'But in vain did poor Uncle laugh. In vain did he look around him with his kind and happy glance. A dead silence was the answer to this funny story.' At last Foma

Fomich speaks: 'Have you quite finished? Are you quite satisfied now that you have interrupted a pleasant literary conversation between friends and thereby satisfied your petty conceit?'

Foma Fomich's persecution of the Colonel encroaches on more dangerous territory when he involves Nastasya, with whom the Colonel is in love. One night he finds the Colonel kissing Nastasya in the garden, and thus compromising her reputation. The Colonel accordingly writes a letter to Foma Fomich in which he implores him to keep the incident secret. So he does for a time. At the beginning of the grandiose Scandal which forms the main crisis of the novel the reader meets a chastened Foma Fomich, who at first says little except to reveal that he has been praying. Then it turns out that he is leaving the household for good and has had his luggage put on a hired cart. 'A few favourite books, two changes of underwear—and nothing more.' At this news the Colonel's mother utters one of her shrieks. 'Her confidantes grew petrified. At that moment distant rumbles of thunder were heard. A storm had begun.'

Now the real struggle is joined. Foma Fomich begins to lecture the Colonel. 'Understand, Colonel . . . in your house even I, an elderly and contemplative man, am already beginning to have serious fears for the purity of my morals. . . . Restrain your passions! And if the corrupting poison has not yet seized on the entire building, then, so far as possible, put out the fire! . . . Moderate your passions.'

The Colonel tries to calm him down, but soon Foma Fomich has produced the fateful letter in which he was implored not to compromise Nastasya, and has torn it up demonstratively. 'I spit on this letter. I trample it underfoot.' Now the Colonel reveals that he has proposed marriage to Nastasya, and Foma at last over-reaches himself. 'You have seduced this girl and are trying to deceive me by offering her your hand. For I saw you both last night in the garden under the bushes! . . . Out of one who was hitherto the most innocent of maidens you have succeeded in making the most corrupt of women.'

A characteristic moment has now been reached, the pay-off. The Colonel seizes Foma Fomich by the shoulders, turns him round like a piece of straw and hurls him at the french windows. They fly open and Foma Fomich hurtles down seven stone steps to collapse in the yard. Then the Colonel tells a servant to dump him in a cart and get him away from Stepanchikovo. A 'soul-searing wail' comes from his mother, the spinster Perepelitsyna is robbed of her faculties, while the chorus of female hangers-on give vent to sighs and groans. The thunderclaps grow louder and a downpour of rain raps the windows. Of this storm the comment has been made: 'The storm, its approach, development and explosion—these are the symbols of the construction of Dostoyevsky's novels.'[8] It would be hard to improve on this image, which illuminates the whole of his mature work, but it can be reinforced with other images. To read Dostoyevsky's mature work is like watching someone blowing up a balloon. The tension grows greater and greater, but still the balloon does not burst. Dostoyevsky pauses for breath at artistically calculated moments—and finally there comes the big bang, usually an explosion of violence, as someone has his face slapped, is thrown out of the house or is murdered.

This aspect of *The Village of Stepanchikovo* makes it an important forerunner of the future. The characteristic fact must also be noted that the whole operation covers only two days, though over two hundred pages are required to describe that brief period. This reminds one, for example, of *The Idiot* and *The Brothers Karamazov* where there is a similar pelting onrush of narrative which seems to carry the reader forward over a great stretch of time. Yet, when he pauses to calculate, he may find that time actually covered by this onrush is to be measured only in hours or days.

In the handling of the central plot *The Village of Stepanchikovo* is a worthy though much inferior forerunner of the mature novels. But it does suffer from artistic defects because of certain peripheral intrigues. These include the elopement of Tatyana Ivanovna, a scene which has no connection with the central plot and was clearly inspired by the elopement scene in Dickens's *Pickwick Papers*.

*

The failure of the elopement scene in *The Village of Stepanchikovo* draws attention to the question of literary influences on Dostoyevsky. His interest in literature goes back to childhood when it was customary for such early nineteenth-century Russian writers as Karamzin, Derzhavin and Zhukovsky to be read aloud in the family circle. This was before Pushkin, who died in 1837, had yet found a footing in Russian education, so it is likely that Dostoyevsky and his elder brother Mikhail discovered Pushkin for themselves. They at once became passionate admirers.

The news of Pushkin's death reached the two brothers shortly after the death of their own mother. If he had not already been in mourning, Fyodor (as is noted in the reminiscences of his younger brother Andrey) 'several times repeated that he would have asked his father's permission to wear mourning for Pushkin'.[9]

Dostoyevsky set Pushkin aside from other writers, whether Russian or foreign, as a figure whom he almost worshipped. This passion ran through his whole life, reaching its supreme point in June, 1880, when (as will be described below) he pronounced his famous 'Pushkin speech' in Moscow, the greatest public triumph of his career. In this speech, as elsewhere in Dostoyevsky's many pronouncements on Pushkin, one misses any serious criticism, for these are the dithyrambs of a worshipper addressing his god. But the extremes of emotion which ran through Dostoyevsky when he thought of Pushkin, and to a lesser extent when he thought of other great writers, are important in understanding his attitude to literature, in which his emotions were so deeply involved that he rarely wrote of it without passion.

This passion led Dostoyevsky to lay the foundations of his immense reading in childhood and adolescence. The exhausting drills and manœuvres of the Engineering School could not seriously hinder his addiction, and if he was unable to read during daytime, he would do so at night. A vivid picture of this is drawn by one of his instructors at the School.

> In the middle of the night one would notice F. M. Dostoyevsky sitting at work by a little table. Throwing a blanket over his underclothes, he seemed not to notice that there was a strong draught from the window by which he was sitting. . . . When I used to point out that it would be more healthy to get up earlier and work in his clothes, he would politely agree with me.[10]

But though Dostoyevsky would obediently put away his work and make signs of going to bed, he would be back again at his table with the blanket over his shoulders a few minutes later.

Thus Dostoyevsky acquired early in life a knowledge of world literature in which few other great Russian writers could rival him. D. V. Grigorovich reports that, 'The extent of his reading astounded me. What he told me about the work of writers whose names I had never heard of, was a revelation to me.'[11]

Much evidence of this early interest and of the passion with which it was pursued is to be found in letters written by Dostoyevsky in the late eighteen-thirties to his brother Mikhail, with whom he seemed to consider himself to be in competition.

> You boast that you've been doing a lot of reading [he wrote just before his seventeenth birthday], but please don't imagine that I envy you. I myself have been reading . . . no less than you. The whole of Hoffmann in Russian and German . . . almost all Balzac (Balzac is immense! His characters are products of the mind of the universe. Not the spirit of the times but whole millennia have prepared by their struggle such a dénouement in the soul of man). Goethe's *Faust* and his short poems . . . also Victor Hugo except for *Cromwell* and *Hernani*.[12]

Similarly, a few months later, he protested:

> You wrote to me, brother, that I had not read Schiller. You're wrong, brother! I have learned Schiller by heart, talked his language and raved about him. Fate has never made any happier incursion into my life than when it allowed me to get to know the great poet at this epoch of my life.[13]

To survey Dostoyevsky's reading at this time is almost to give a catalogue of all the great names in world literature . . . Homer, Shakespeare, Victor Hugo, Voltaire, Racine, Corneille are a few among the many whom he devoured. When he went to prison and was scarcely able to get hold of any books, this deprivation apparently weighed on him more than mere physical hardships, and he came out of prison in a state of ravening hunger.

> If you can, do send me this year's magazines . . . [he wrote to Mikhail, breaking the four-year gap in their correspondence which had occurred during his imprisonment at Omsk]. But this is what is essential. I must have (it is a case of extreme need) the ancient historians (in French translation) and the modern, the economists and the fathers of the Church. . . . Send me the Koran, Kant's *Critique of Pure Reason* . . . send me Hegel without fail, in particular his *History of Philosophy*. My whole future is bound up with this![14]

A little later he was asking for the works of Herodotus, Thucydides, Tacitus, Pliny, Flavius, Plutarch and Diodorus.

These interests show Dostoyevsky temporarily diverted from his great love, imaginative literature. But this was not neglected. 'I remember', he wrote more than twenty years later, 'that when I came out of prison in Siberia in 1854 I began to read through the whole of the literature written during my five years' absence.'[15]

Amongst contemporary Russian authors whom he read at this time was Turgenev, whose 'great talent', according to Dostoyevsky—and it is amusing to read this criticism from him at this period—went with 'a great deal of lack of restraint'. He liked Tolstoy, who was just beginning his literary career, but (surely one of the most inaccurate prophecies on record) 'in my opinion he won't write much'.[16]

Dostoyevsky's first printed work had been a translation of Balzac's *Eugénie Grandet*, and Balzac remained an influence on his writing. The same is true of other writers of world stature mentioned above. The influence of Dickens, detectable in a minor episode of *The Village of Stepanchikovo* has already been mentioned. Other aspects of the same novel can be traced to Molière's *Tartuffe* and to Gogol.[17]

The last-named writer was the most important influence of all, and the most obtrusive. To trace the influence of many other writers on Dostoyevsky one has to dig and delve. Much research has been devoted to the topic, which has an enormous literature of its own. But these influences, apart from that of Gogol, cannot play any great part in the kind of general study attempted here. The influence of Gogol, Dostoyevsky's greatest and most original predecessor as a master of Russian fiction, is another matter. It sticks out as other influences do not. Dostoyevsky had to come to terms with it, and almost deliberately to expel it from his work, as he did in *The Village of Stepanchikovo*, before he could reach his full stature as a writer. It was Gogol who had given him his original boost, but by now Gogol was holding up progress.

It was no accident that Nekrasov had originally brought the manuscript of *Poor Folk* to Belinsky with the exclamation 'A new Gogol has arisen.' For the work derives from Gogol to an extent which no one in Belinsky's Gogol-obsessed circle could miss. This is not merely a matter of stylistic echoes, such as one finds in *Poor Folk*, and even more abundantly in *The Double*. In addition to these, *Poor Folk* derives from and is to a large extent a commentary on a single work of Gogol, *The Greatcoat*. This remains the most famous short story in Russian. It describes the misfortunes of a petty official, who decides at great sacrifice to provide himself with a new greatcoat to protect him from the rigours of the St. Petersburg winter. The greatcoat turns into the obsession of his life, and the tragedy of the story comes when he loses it in the streets one night to thieves.

Like Gogol's official (Akaky Akakiyevich), Dostoyevsky's hero in

Poor Folk (Makar Devushkin) is a man obsessed with one idea, the welfare of his young friend Varenka. Just as Akaky Akakiyevich loses his coat to robbers, so Devushkin is robbed of his treasure by the infamous Bykov. The important point is that Dostoyevsky sought to emphasize, not the resemblances between the two works, but the differences, by conducting a literary dialogue with Gogol through the mouth of Devushkin.

In one letter to Varenka, Devushkin discusses his reading, which has included *The Greatcoat*. But he objects to the story because Gogol seems concerned to ridicule the poor official who is his hero. Recognizing Akaky Akakiyevich as an attempted portrait of someone like himself, Devushkin protests and to drive home his point draws another parallel—with Simeon Vyrin from Pushkin's *Station Inspector*. Devushkin finds Pushkin's portrait of an underdog kind and sympathetic, whereas Gogol's is cruel.

Another contrast with *The Greatcoat* is that the centre of the dehumanized Akaky Akakiyevich's obsession is an inanimate object, whereas Devushkin's is a human being. This contrast is further emphasized by Dostoyevsky's choice of a surname for his hero. 'Devushkin' derives from *devushka*, 'a girl', whilst Akaky Akakiyevich Bashmachkin's surname derives from an object: *bashmak*, 'a shoe'.

Dostoyevsky is thus to be found struggling against Gogol's influence from the beginning. Yet in his second work, *The Double*, it is equally in evidence. To some extent *The Double* is the same kind of commentary on another story of Gogol's, *Notes of a Madman*. The stylistic influence is even more obtrusive. Here it is a retarding influence, without which the possibilities of *The Double* might have been realized more effectively. But it is an idle speculation to imagine *The Double* shorn of Gogol's influence, for without Gogol it could not have been written at all.

The minor works of 1846-9 show a slight slackening of Gogol's influence, and an attachment to other influences such as that of Hoffmann, who helped to feed Dostoyevsky's interest in the fantastic. But Gogol emerges again in full strength in *Uncle's Dream*. Here the stylistic echoes are as thick as ever. The atmosphere of the trivial, gossip-mongering town of Mordasov echoes (admittedly feebly) the atmosphere of the preposterous provincial town which had been the centre of the first part of *Dead Souls*, Gogol's supreme masterpiece.

It is in *The Village of Stepanchikovo* that Dostoyevsky finally rounds on his teacher, for the villain of the story is in part a hostile caricature of Gogol himself. Here Dostoyevsky satirizes the Gogol who abandoned literature in the later years of his life in order to preach directly to his fellow-Russians. It is the Gogol of the moralizing work *Select Passages from Correspondence with Friends* who is parodied in Foma Fomich's long moralizing tirades. These even include direct quotations from Gogol. Dostoyevsky, as he often showed later, could be savage when he decided to set upon a fellow-writer.

Dostoyevsky's whole life and career were in a sense intertwined with Gogol's. The main charge against him when he was put on trial in 1849 was that of having read aloud Belinsky's celebrated Letter, a notorious document of the political opposition in which Gogol is attacked for the publication of *Select Passages*. Dostoyevsky followed Gogol by gravitating to a position of extreme political reaction and by adopting Gogol's view that the only hope for society lay in the moral transformation of individuals through religion, not in the reform of social and political institutions. Dostoyevsky too eventually emerged as a preacher, particularly in his *Diary of a Writer*, a work only a little less absurd than Gogol's *Select Passages*. Fortunately he did not follow Gogol by becoming mentally deranged.

Thus if there is any single writer without whose influence Dostoyevsky's whole career is unimaginable, it is Gogol. But there were few more important turning-points than the moment when he decided to reject Gogol as a direct literary influence in *The Village of Stepanchikovo*. If Dostoyevsky once more murdered his father when he set upon Gogol in *The Village of Stepanchikovo*, it was a crime from which he was to draw profit.

CHAPTER THREE

'INSULTED AND INJURED' AND
'THE HOUSE OF THE DEAD'

WHEN Dostoyevsky was released from prison in 1854 he began a difficult and lengthy process of self-rehabilitation. It was not until early in 1859 that he at last obtained permission to return to European Russia, where he had to spend several dreary months in the provincial town of Tver before being allowed to reside in either of the 'two capitals', Moscow and St. Petersburg.

To move the Russian bureaucratic machine has never been easy for an isolated individual, and it is embarrassing to contemplate the humiliating postures which Dostoyevsky adopted in attempting to re-establish himself. Sycophantic letters were dispatched from Siberia and Tver to influential individuals from the Tsar Alexander II downwards. To show that he was no longer a 'political criminal', Dostoyevsky even wrote patriotic doggerel verses, the spirit of which is conveyed in the following translated extract, attacking Russia's enemies in the Crimean War:

> Shame on you, apostates from the Cross,
> Extinguishers of God's light.
> But God is with us! Hurrah! Our cause is holy.
> And who will not be glad to give his life for Christ!

An ode in similar style was written to celebrate the coronation of Alexander II in 1856.

Dostoyevsky's difficulties in this period remind one of the shabby treatment which great Russian writers, from before Pushkin to Pasternak, have often received from official Russia. None of the hurdles which he had to jump was more important than obtaining permission to print his writings, denied to him for some years after his release from gaol in 1854. Apart from his burning ambition to succeed, this was vital to him financially. In spite of all difficulties he did manage to produce the two Siberian novels discussed in the previous chapter, but these did not match his ambitions. He looked

on them as works of light entertainment sufficiently innocent not
to jeopardize his return to literature. Such light-weight stuff could
not satisfy him, and he began to brood increasingly on something
which could, a 'big novel'. 'I am in a completely feverish condition',
he wrote in 1860. 'The reason is my novel . . . I know that the
whole of my literary career depends on its success.'¹

He was now determined to profit from errors of the past when,
by accepting advances from publishers, he had found himself forced
to produce hurried work. He decided to publish a collection of
previous writings which, according to his calculations, would bring
in enough money to keep him for at least two years, 'so that perhaps
for the first time in my life I might have the chance . . . of writing
not to order, not for money, not to a time limit, but conscientiously,
honestly, deliberately, not selling my pen in return for a bite of
daily bread'.²

Here Dostoyevsky was returning to an old dream. From his
earliest days as a writer he had seen himself as a literary business
man destined to make his fortune by publishing his own works.
This idea persisted. 'Look at other people', he wrote to his brother
Mikhail from Tver in November, 1859. 'No talent, no ability. But
such a man makes his mark and builds up capital. Yet you and I
struggle and struggle. . . . I am convinced for example that you and
I have much more adroitness, ability and knowledge of the business
. . . than the Krayevskys and Nekrasovs. [Krayevsky and Nekrasov
were among Dostoyevsky's own publishers.] Why, they're just a
lot of yokels in literature.'³

Not all Dostoyevsky's publishing ventures were disastrous, and
they occasionally earned enough to tide him over. They never made
his fortune, for the business acumen which he attributed to himself
was imaginary. One publishing enterprise, the journal *Vremya*,
enjoyed fair success until it was closed down by Government order.
The journal was founded in 1861 by Dostoyevsky and his brother
Mikhail, who acted as business manager and nominal editor. In the
same year it printed *Insulted and Injured*, the 'big novel' to which
Dostoyevsky attached so many hopes.

In spite of his resolve to work slowly and carefully on the new
novel, it turned out another rush job.

It has often happened during my literary career [he wrote in 1864]
that the beginning of a chapter . . . was already at the printer's and
being set up, while the end was still sitting in my head, but had to be

written by the following day *without fail*. . . . This was exactly what I did with *Insulted and Injured*. . . . The result was a barbarous piece of writing, but there are about fifty pages in it of which I am proud.[4]

The new novel was popular with the public, but unworthy of Dostoyevsky. It falls short of his mature stature and is inferior to the best work which had preceded it. The achievements of *The Village of Stepanchikovo*—the strong central plot, humour and surging impetus—seemed to have been thrown away.

The novel's weakness derives from a feeble plot. As his later work shows, Dostoyevsky needed a strong central situation involving violent crime. When such a situation was present the complexities of his plots fell into position. In *Insulted and Injured* the complexities are found without the inner core. The absence of humour in *Insulted and Injured* is also striking, and perhaps derives from the over-solemnity with which Dostoyevsky approached his first 'big novel'. If so he was making a mistake which is not repeated in the long novels from *Crime and Punishment* onwards.

Another reason for the failure of *Insulted and Injured* may be its excessively introspective origins. Dostoyevsky plunges back again into St. Petersburg after his recent excursions into the countryside and also reintroduces in a major role a 'St. Petersburg dreamer' such as had figured prominently in the early stories. The introspective and autobiographical inspiration is here increased, for Ivan Petrovich, the Narrator of the novel, is a fairly direct self-portrait of Dostoyevsky himself during the period before his arrest. It is true that he is given a different name, but certain features of the novel show that Dostoyevsky was thinking of himself and did not mind the description being recognized. Ivan Petrovich is presented as a young novelist who had scored a great success with his first novel. This novel is not named, but from the description given of it it corresponds with *Poor Folk*. References to the 'critic B.', who 'was as delighted as a child' by the novel, point to Belinsky, while the literary *'entrepreneur K.'*, to whom some passing sarcasms are devoted, was Krayevsky.

Ivan Petrovich presents himself as a dying man, writing down the events of *Insulted and Injured* to pass the time in hospital. He comments that after his death the pages of his manuscript will be useful for pasting over cracks in the hospital window. As this detail shows, he is a weak-spirited creature who represents Dostoyevsky in self-pitying moments, such as had been frequent in the late eighteen-forties.

The resilience and courage which enabled Dostoyevsky to triumph again and again over ill health and misfortune were not attributed to Ivan Petrovich.

Insulted and Injured also draws heavily on an episode which engrossed Dostoyevsky during part of his Siberian period, his courtship of his first wife. This is, accordingly, by far the most autobiographical of all Dostoyevsky's novels if one excludes *Notes from the House of the Dead*, which is in fact a book of memoirs and only nominally a novel.

The most striking feature of *Insulted and Injured* is the love interest. In no other novel of Dostoyevsky is it so prominent. Love had played only a minor role in his earlier fiction—for example, one can scarcely regard the relations of Devushkin and Varenka in *Poor Folk* as a love affair. In the later novels love does play an important part, but never dominates the plot as in *Insulted and Injured*. Here perhaps is another reason for the novel's failure. Although Dostoyevsky had new and surprising things to say about love, his full strength as a novelist was only revealed when he handled other topics. Love always remained a relatively weak point in his armoury.

The plot of *Insulted and Injured* hinges on two separate intrigues which are linked by the participation in both of the two main characters, the Narrator (Ivan Petrovich) and Prince Valkovsky.

The less prominent intrigue centres round a thirteen-year-old girl called Nelly, who will be considered first because she provides clues to the novel as a whole. Nelly revives previous themes in Dostoyevsky's fiction. She belongs to the 'Poor Folk' strand, for her predicament at the beginning of the narrative reproduces that of Varenka in Dostoyevsky's first work. The evil Madame Bubnova, her landlady, here plays a role similar to that of Anna Fyodorovna in *Poor Folk* by trying to turn the girl into a prostitute. Nelly fulfils another 'Poor Folk' requirement by being seriously ill—she eventually expires piteously. She also revives the 'nymphet' theme treated in *Netochka Nezvanova*. It eventually becomes clear that this nineteenth-century Lolita is in love with Dostoyevsky's Narrator, who rescues her from Madame Bubnova and gives her shelter for a time. This itself established a precedent, for it was beginning to seem axiomatic that self-portrait characters such as the Narrator in *Insulted and Injured* could only love other people. There had been no question previously of anyone loving them.

Dostoyevsky's interest in little girls as the object of sexual exploitation is notorious, and receives its most brutal expression in the 'banned chapter' from *The Devils* where Stavrogin confesses to having raped a small girl who afterwards committed suicide. The theme also occurs on the many occasions when a young and innocent girl is confronted by that minor but persistent Dostoyevskian type, the Dirty Old Man, as in a minor story of 1848, *The Christmas Tree and the Wedding.*

Dostoyevsky's obsession with the sexual involvements of little girls is not one of the most important aspects of his fiction. It is no doubt evidence of a morbid streak in his own make-up, but should also be considered in a wider context. One of his claims to originality arises from his readiness to make reconnaissances into unexplored areas of human behaviour. The topic under discussion was only one of these, and one in which his forays were not particularly fruitful.

When Dostoyevsky described Nelly he may, as has been suggested, have been providing an acute psychological study of the emotional life of an adolescent girl on the threshold of womanhood. But it is not easy to take this suggestion entirely seriously when one begins to notice the close parallels between Nelly's behaviour and the behaviour of other characters in the novel who are not on the threshold of womanhood—for example Ikhmenev, the elderly father of the chief heroine (Natasha). Except for Prince Valkovsky, the Bogeyman of the novel, all the other characters are of the same emotional age as Nelly, indulging like her in swift unpredictable changes and perverse tantrums.

Nelly is the most perverse in the gallery of perverse portraits in *Insulted and Injured.* It happens that one of her outbursts provides a short paragraph which forms a useful commentary on the novel as a whole. This occurs when she is visited by a kindly doctor who gives her medicine. She refuses to take it and deliberately splashes it over his clothes, to which he replies by mildly offering to prepare a second dose. In quoting this paragraph the phrases most important to the understanding of the novel are italicized.

She was expecting us to be angry and thought that we would start scolding and reproaching her. And perhaps *subconsciously* that was all she was after at the time—*so as to have an excuse to burst out crying and sobbing*, as if in hysterics, to throw the medicine about again as she had just done, and even to break something out of pique, and by means of all this to satisfy the urges of her capricious, aching little heart. It is not only ill people and not only Nelly who have such whims. How many times in the old days I used to walk up and down my room with an *unconscious wish for someone to do me an injury or to say a word which could be taken as an insult*, so that I could then vent my anger on something.

This paragraph helps to explain the love affairs in Dostoyevsky's fiction, where love almost always appears as a source of unhappiness. It also illuminates the early love affairs in Dostoyevsky's own life. He has already been described as a seeker of suffering and punishment, as was certainly the case repeatedly in his life, whether or not support is given to the explanation linking this drive with a supposed feeling of guilt for his father's murder. To suggest that he subconsciously engineered his own arrest and imprisonment in order to involve himself in suffering and punishment might be going too far. But when one considers his first two love affairs—the courtship of his first wife, Mariya Isayeva, and (a few years after the publication of *Insulted and Injured*) of his mistress Apollinariya Suslova—one may be less diffident. It seems clear that at this stage of his life Dostoyevsky could not be bothered with a love affair at all unless it offered a prospect of misery. Isayeva and Suslova were picked as purveyors of anguish. They could provide Dostoyevsky with constant 'excuses to burst out crying and sobbing'.

Dostoyevsky first met Isayeva shortly after his release from prison, at the beginning of his long period of exile in the army at Semipalatinsk. She was already involved in a 'Poor-Folkish' situation of her own, since her first husband was unemployable and was drinking himself to death, while she had a small son to look after. Her situation thus made her a promising target for a Dostoyevskian love affair. Her character, perverse, neurotic and with a streak of sadism, made her doubly desirable.

The husband soon died and Dostoyevsky wished to marry Isayeva, but having no money realized that the marriage might have to be postponed until he could print his writings. Meanwhile she was stranded in the town of Kuznetsk, five hundred versts away, a distance which did not prevent her from tormenting her suitor. She once wrote that local matchmakers were trying to marry her to an elderly man of means. What was Dostoyevsky's advice? Should she accept the proposal? Her letter had the desired effect on him. 'It was as if I had been struck by lightning', he told his friend A. E. Vrangel, in whom he confided details of the courtship. 'I staggered, fainted and spent the whole night crying.'[5]

Dostoyevsky now saw himself in the position of Devushkin in *Poor Folk*, with Isayeva in the role of Varenka and the unknown suitor playing the part of Bykov. 'She's in the position of my heroine . . . who marries Bykov. (So I'd prophesied my own doom!)'[6]

Later Isayeva admitted that she had invented this story in order to test her lover's devotion. Other trials were in store when, in the summer of 1856, Dostoyevsky managed to pay a visit to Kuznetsk despite the difficulty of transporting himself through the Siberian wastes, his lack of funds and the need to obtain leave from the army. In Kuznetsk he discovered that he had been supplanted by a rival. 'She wept and kissed my hands, but she loves another.'[7] The young man was a schoolteacher called Vergunov, described as handsome, but four years younger than Isayeva (who was twenty-nine) and just as penniless as Dostoyevsky.

Dostoyevsky now found himself taken out of the world of *Poor Folk* and plunged into that of his other early story, *White Nights*, where the young 'dreamer' hero had fallen in love with a girl who was herself in love with someone else, and instead of urging his own suit had tried to help his rival. This was how Dostoyevsky now behaved, seeking to enable Vergunov to take an examination in Tomsk which would enable him to get a job at a thousand roubles a year, enough to marry on. 'Now', he reported in December, 1856, 'he is dearer to me than my own brother.'[8]

By cultivating his rival in love Dostoyevsky revealed a trait which would persist into middle age, a wish to extract maximum emotional vibration out of his experiences. Early in 1857 he reported that his relations with Isayeva had engrossed him 'during the whole of the last *two years*. At least I have been *living*! I may have suffered, but I lived!'[9]

His wooing came to an unsatisfactory conclusion—it was successful, and he married Isayeva in February, 1857. Now the transports of enthusiasm about Isayeva in Dostoyevsky's letters, about her beauty, intelligence and skill as a housewife, abruptly disappear. The marriage began inauspiciously when Dostoyevsky had a severe epileptic fit on his wedding night. (He had first suffered from epilepsy in Siberia, or possibly earlier, and from now on fits occurred at irregular intervals. The most severe attacks left him prostrated for days on end, thus adding to the catalogue of obstacles which he so heroically surmounted in pursuing his literary career.) His wife became more seriously ill, with tuberculosis, being true to the canons of Dostoyevskian fiction down to this detail. The marriage was an unhappy one. Dostoyevsky was virtually separated from her during the last years of their marriage, but did his best to care for her when her illness reached its critical stage.

In the main love intrigue of *Insulted and Injured* Dostoyevsky reproduces the triangular situation as it had existed between himself, Isayeva and Vergunov before his marriage. The Narrator (=Dostoyevsky) is in love with Natasha Ikhmeneva (= Isayeva) who deserts him to live with Alyosha (= Vergunov), handsome son of Prince Valkovsky. The Narrator helps his rival by running errands and carrying letters. Like his predecessor, the hero of *White Nights*, and like Dostoyevsky himself, he lacks the element of male aggressiveness in love.

Natasha also shows herself a true Dostoyevskian character in love. She too has chosen unhappily, for her lover Alyosha himself falls in love with a beautiful young girl called Katya, who has a dowry of two million roubles and has been picked for him by his unscrupulous father. Natasha has the true Dostoyevskian attachment to suffering, so this arrangement no doubt suits her very well. 'We must somehow suffer our way anew to our future happiness', she tells the Narrator at one point. 'We must purchase it by some new torments. All is purified by suffering. . . . Oh, Vanya, how much pain there is in life.'

The novel thus contains a typical Dostoyevskian chain of unsuccessful love attachments: Nelly loves the Narrator; the Narrator loves Natasha; Natasha loves Alyosha. The chain breaks down at the end, for the love of Alyosha and Katya seems to be reciprocal. But the others have as many 'excuses to burst out crying and sobbing' as they could wish.

Dostoyevsky was breaking new ground by drawing so much attention to love's perversities, to the way in which it can oscillate with hatred and to the streaks of sadism and masochism which may lurk within it. There can be few adults so 'normal' as to find these things incomprehensible. But the defect of love as described by Dostoyevsky is that it so often consists solely of the perversities, without any admixture of the normal. Dostoyevsky does not usually convey any feeling for the sensual element in love such as a skilful novelist can suggest without necessarily being frank about the physical details of sex. Tolstoy shows this in *Anna Karenina*, but in this respect Dostoyevsky never managed to rival him. Even in the novels of his maturity the love intrigues tend, depressingly, to follow the scheme laid down for them in *Insulted and Injured*. The chief exceptions to this are the love affairs of Dunya Raskolnikova and Razumikhin in *Crime and Punishment* and of Gruskenka and Dmitry in *The Brothers Karamazov*. Elsewhere Dostoyevsky continues, as in *Insulted and Injured*, to present his readers with love without sex, an omission for which new contributions to the study of human psychology cannot quite compensate.

A foretaste of the mature Dostoyevsky is provided by Prince Valkovsky, the first in the series of Dostoyevskian Bogeymen. This character-type was to become much more important than an earlier Dostoyevskian type with which it has some affinities, the Dirty Old Man. Valkovsky forms a strong contrast with the other characters in *Insulted and Injured*, all weak, downtrodden, miserable or ineffectual. While Dostoyevsky's Narrator in *Insulted and Injured* is a portrait of Dostoyevsky himself in the eighteen-forties, Valkovsky is an inverted self-portrait. At every point—his wealth, influential connections, social ease and success with women—he offers so marked a contrast to the poverty-stricken, isolated, and socially awkward 'dreamer' as to suggest that he too is just as introspective in origin.

It is Valkovsky's distinction to participate in the first great philosophical debate in Dostoyevsky's fiction. This occurs in the scene where he argues with the Narrator in a restaurant, attacking the romantic, self-sacrificing philosophy of the Narrator, which he calls 'Schillerism'. Here Valkovsky executes a typical Dostoyevskian *volte face*, by swinging from initial politeness to *naglost* (brazen impudence) which has already been noted as a key concept. There is also a characteristic harping on the theme of power. Valkovsky (as the Narrator reflects while describing the scene) 'was one of those who, seeing a man to be to some slight extent in their power, at once make him feel it. . . . His tone suddenly changed, becoming increasingly impudent, familiar and mocking.'

Valkovsky sneers at the Narrator's poverty and ineffectualness. 'You live on nothing but tea and shiver in your attic. . . . Here's Alyosha taking your girl friend off you . . . and you, like some Schiller, crucify yourself on their behalf, assist them and have almost made yourself their errand-boy.' Valkovsky offers the Narrator money if he will agree to marry Natasha (it must be remembered that Valkovsky wishes to detach Natasha from his son Alyosha so that Alyosha can marry the heiress Katya). When the Narrator says that Valkovsky must be mad, he retorts, 'Ha! ha! ha!' (an exclamation frequent in Dostoyevsky, but nearly always used to convey contempt rather than amusement). 'Why, you're almost on the point of hitting me.'

> He played with me [the Narrator comments] like a cat with a mouse, supposing me to be entirely in his power. It seemed to me . . . that he found some sort of pleasure, perhaps even some sort of sensual delight [*sladostrastiye*] in his own baseness, in the insolence and cynicism with which he was at last tearing off his mask in front of me.

Valkovsky defines the pleasure which he derives from this kind of conversation.

> There is a trait in my character which you have not yet got to know— hatred for all these vulgar, worthless naïveties and pastorals. One of my most piquant pleasures has always been to begin by affecting to take on this line myself, to get into this current—to encourage and treat with kindness some eternally young Schiller. And then suddenly to disconcert him by raising my mask in front of him, changing my solemn expression for a grimace and putting out my tongue at him at the very moment when he least expects such a surprise.

This scene reproduces the confrontation of a predator with a victim such as has been noticed earlier in Dostoyevsky's work, the new feature being that the conflict here takes a philosophical form. The confrontation yields in interest to later philosophical debates in Dostoyevsky, notably to the argument about God between Ivan and Alyosha Karamazov. But it is interesting to notice here a similar kind of inner dialogue, with Dostoyevsky using fictional characters to express contrary points of view which fought for dominance in his own mind. The moral defeat sustained by the Narrator in *Insulted and Injured* suggests that Dostoyevsky had now turned his back on the naïve and romantically philanthropic approach of *Poor Folk*, but had so far found nothing to replace it with except the cynicism of a Valkovsky. Later he would try to make religion take its place.

*

Dostoyevsky's next work was published in 1860–2. This is *Notes from the House of the Dead*, which describes his experiences as a convict in the prison at Omsk during 1850-4. He puts the book forward as a novel, presenting it as the reminiscences of an imaginary landowner called Goryanchikov who had served ten years for murdering his wife. But these reminiscences, as most readers must realize, are Dostoyevsky's own.

The House of the Dead represents the greatest achievement before Crime and Punishment. Here at last is a fully authoritative work from the pen of a great writer. The fact that it was published at the same time as Insulted and Injured shows Dostoyevsky failing with an imaginative work (for such Insulted and Injured is despite its partly autobiographical inspiration), while succeeding with a book which scarcely derives from his creative imagination at all. A literary diagnostician might now reasonably have advised Dostoyevsky to abandon the novel and to become a chronicler of Russian life. However, Dostoyevsky remained unpredictable and soon reversed the roles of fiction and description of Russian life. The descriptions of what he sought to pass off as Russian life in his Diary of a Writer were to be as absurd and unconvincing as anything in Insulted and Injured, while his great works of fiction are the most impressive achievement of any Russian imagination.

In answer to complaints that Picasso's figures sometimes possess the wrong number of eyes or legs, the painter's defenders can point to other pictures which show him with the technique of representational art at his command. Similarly readers who feel that Dostoyevsky could only portray humanity in a distorted way will obtain a more complete impression of his range if they remember the skill with which he depicts humanity with a relative lack of distortion in The House of the Dead. The absence of distortion in his literary method should not be obscured by the fact that he was on the whole describing distorted humanity, mainly murderers, in this book.

Another paradox about The House of the Dead is that it consists of the author's own reminiscences, yet is the least introspective work which he had so far written. 'My personality will disappear', he had correctly predicted when writing about the book to Mikhail Dostoyevsky in October, 1859.[10] The House of the Dead shows lively curiosity about the nature of Dostoyevsky's fellow-men and less curiosity about Dostoyevsky himself than had hitherto been found in his writings. If it is true that the excessively introspective nature of his early inspiration was now proving a handicap, this could be one explanation for the success of his prison memoirs.

The most surprising feature about *The House of the Dead*, at least to those who know Dostoyevsky's later journalism and the system of ideas propagated in it, is the empirical approach. It is Dostoyevsky the painstaking accumulator of evidence whom one meets in *The House of the Dead*, not Dostoyevsky the leaper to conclusions. On this one short passage from the book is especially significant. It occurs where Dostoyevsky, fearing that he is becoming too abstract and schematic in discussing his fellow-convicts, calls himself to order. 'Incidentally I am now endeavouring to put our entire prison into categories. But is that possible? Reality is infinitely varied when we compare it with even the most cunning deductions of abstract thought, and it does not tolerate sharp and harsh divisions.' As this passage indicates, it was in the spirit of an observer that Dostoyevsky approached human nature in *The House of the Dead*. The time had not yet come when, in *The Diary of a Writer*, he would seek to dispense revealed truths. He was still a seeker, not yet a finder.

The difference between Dostoyevsky the investigator in *The House of the Dead* and Dostoyevsky the later pedlar of revealed truths is most strikingly illustrated in his attitude to the *narod* (the Russian common people). In the later Dostoyevsky the word *narod* developed into a pure nonsense-concept, as it has in the mouths of many other Russian political thinkers of both the left and the right. It was then that Dostoyevsky began to attribute to the Russian people such surprising qualities as deep, instinctive wisdom and an unrivalled capacity for promoting the universal brotherhood of mankind. He would whirl the word *narod*, loaded with portentous overtones, round his head like a bludgeon, and what he then had to say about the Russian people had nothing to do with actual Russian persons.

In the eighteen-fifties the word had not yet acquired such fuzzy outlines in his head. It is instructive, for example, to study what he has to say about the *narod* in a letter written to his brother Mikhail in February, 1854. This long letter, written while his prison experiences were still fresh in his mind, is in effect a preliminary sketch for *The House of the Dead*, which reproduces, in some cases literally, ideas contained in the letter. One passage from the letter is noticeably harsh in what Dostoyevsky has to say about the *narod*, among which he had lived as a convict.

It is a crude, irritated and embittered *narod*. Its hatred for the gentry [*dvoryane*] passes all bounds, for which reason it met us representatives of the gentry with hostility and malicious pleasure at our misfortune.

They would have eaten us if they could. . . . 'You gents with your iron noses always pecking us! Once you were a gentleman and tormented the *narod*, but now you're the lowest of the low. You've become one of us. . . .' Such was the theme which was played for four years. There were a hundred and fifty enemies who never wearied of persecution. It was an amusing occupation for them. If there was one thing which saved us from misfortune it was our indifference, our *moral superiority* which they could not fail to understand. . . . *They always recognized that we were their superiors*.[11]

One trembles to think what brainstorm would have been provoked if Dostoyevsky had chanced to read this letter, and especially the phrases italicized here, during the period when *The Diary of a Writer* was being written. A few pages later in the same letter he is found judging the *narod* less harshly.

How many types and characters of the common people I have brought out of prison! . . . How many stories of tramps and robbers! . . . Enough to fill whole volumes! What a wonderful *narod* it is! In general I didn't waste my time. If I didn't get to know Russia, then at least I did get to know the Russian *narod* well, better perhaps than many other people know it.[12]

The House of the Dead maintains this attitude towards the *narod* as a subject for study rather than rhapsodizing. Only in a few passages of the book is a foretaste of Dostoyevsky's future idealization of the Russian common people to be found—for example: 'The loftiest and most distinctive trait of our common people is a feeling for justice and a longing for it. . . . Our pundits haven't got much to teach the common people. They themselves ought to learn from the people.' Here Dostoyevsky is seen expressing a view diametrically opposite to that contained in his letter of 1854, quoted above, to the effect that people of his own class were superior to the common man. By the time he finished *The House of the Dead*, he had come round to the opinion, expressed on almost the last page of the book, that the convicts were really the élite of Russia: 'How much great strength has perished here in vain! Why, these are perhaps the most talented and strong of all our people.'

Among the influences which shaped this view were figures of towering moral strength among the convicts, whom Dostoyevsky terms 'powerful personalities'. They include a soldier called Petrov, sentenced for stabbing his commanding officer on parade. Petrov, the 'most decisive character in the prison', felt sorry for Dostoyevsky because he seemed so helpless. (The 'I' of *The House of the Dead* will be referred to here as 'Dostoyevsky' despite the fiction that the book presents the memoirs of an imaginary character called Goryanchikov.)

> He considered me a sort of child, almost a baby, and thought that I did not understand the simplest things in the world.... It seemed to me that he had decided, without troubling his head much about the matter, that I was the sort of person who couldn't be spoken to like other people, that I couldn't understand a single thing except a conversation about books.

It was Petrov who shepherded Dostoyevsky through the steam bath, which the convicts occasionally took *en masse*, helping him to take off his underclothes over the fetters on his feet—a tricky art—and even washed him. The bath scene is the *pièce de résistance* of the book, and one of the episodes which led contemporaries to compare it with Dante's *Inferno*.

Another powerful personality was called Orlov. 'I can state positively that I have never in my life met a stronger man, or one of more iron character than he. . . . There wasn't a creature in the world who could have exercised influence on him by authority.' Dostoyevsky questioned him about his crimes.

> But when he understood that I was trying to touch his conscience and to extract at least something in the way of repentance from him, he looked at me with contempt and arrogance as if I had suddenly become in his eyes some silly stupid little boy with whom one could not discuss things as with an adult.

Another powerful personality was an enormous Tartar called Gazin, one of the main dealers in contraband spirits among the prisoners (such smugglers eluded the warders by going about wreathed with the entrails of oxen, which had been cleaned and filled with vodka). Gazin, renowned as a torturer and murderer of small children, used to get raging drunk once or twice a year and attack his fellow-convicts with a knife, whereupon it was the custom for a gang to set upon him and beat him senseless. In one horrific scene he came near to murdering Dostoyevsky and another prison intellectual with a heavy tray, and was only deflected from this when someone had the happy idea of telling him that his store of hooch had been raided.

Contrasting with the strong personalities are sympathetic and kind-hearted characters, such as the Caucasian youth Aley, sentenced for brigandage, whom Dostoyevsky taught to read and write. There was an elderly Old Believer, whom everyone trusted with money and who seemed to bear his captivity serenely, except when he could be heard weeping bitterly in the middle of the night. Perhaps Dostoyevsky's memory had succeeded in polarizing the convicts along the lines of the figures in his fiction, where the contrast of strong and active characters with humble and passive characters is so often met.

Another feature of Dostoyevsky's fiction, preserved in several anecdotes about his fellow-convicts, is the sudden change of roles, from passive to active. A truly Dostoyevskian *volte face* is executed in one particularly 'Russian' anecdote from *The House of the Dead*. This concerns an unnamed convict of meek behaviour, who for several years had done nothing more violent than read the Bible. One day he went and told his N.C.O. that he did not intend to report for work. The matter was taken to the Major, who rushed along to investigate such outrageous behaviour, whereupon the convict tried to hit him with a brick with which he had equipped himself for the purpose. But he missed (a characteristic Dostoyevskian touch), and after being punished by flogging, died three days later, saying that he wished no one any harm. *He only wanted to suffer.*

Perhaps it was in considering such episodes that Dostoyevsky first stumbled on a theme which would become the pivot of many an incident in his later novels: the outrageously absurd act, committed by a man in defiance of his own interests and as an assertion of his freedom as a human being. The connection of the concept of freedom with the outrageous act is already made in *The House of the Dead*.

The entire meaning of the word convict is that of a man without freedom. . . . [Dostoyevsky uses the word *volya*, which combines the idea of freedom with that of 'will'.] The authorities are sometimes surprised when a convict, having lived . . . quietly for several years suddenly, *à propos* of nothing, as if a devil had got into him, misbehaves, goes on the binge, starts a brawl, and sometimes even takes the risk of committing a criminal offence—showing gross disrespect for senior authority, killing or raping someone and so on. They see this and are astonished. Meanwhile perhaps the sole reason for this sudden explosion from a man from whom one might least of all expect it, is an anguished, feverish expression of his own individuality . . . a wish to assert himself and his humiliated personality.

C

The motive of self-assertion is a unifying theme in many of the Scandals which were continually breaking out and which no doubt helped to reconcile Dostoyevsky to prison life. Among these was the ritual of the solitary drinking bout, a phenomenon on which Russians have always looked with something like religious awe. The celebrant on these occasions

> would get as drunk as an owl and make a point of staggering and blundering round the barracks, trying to show everyone that he was drunk, that he was 'on the binge'—and thereby to earn general respect. A drunk man everywhere enjoys a certain sympathy among the Russian common people, but in prison people even became respectful towards a man on the spree. About prison carousals there was a kind of aristocratic element.

Throughout Russian history official harshness has generally been tempered with an equal degree of inefficiency, which explains how the convicts could get hold of liquor, play cards and introduce prostitutes into the gaol. The prisoners had their own bankers, financiers and moneylenders. The wealthier ones could even bribe the warders to let them out into the town to enjoy some sensational debauch.

They were united by a fierce pride which produced a rigid code of behaviour. It was a point of honour never to betray surprise, a principle which must have been strained by the constant eruptions of Scandals. With few exceptions they were dry, reserved and formal in their manner to each other. They were acutely conscious of status.

> About ranks and senior officials, who was senior to whom, which of them could put another in his place or would find himself put in his place, the convicts dearly love to converse, even arguing and quarrelling about generals almost to the point of fighting. One might wonder what advantage this brought them. But an exact knowledge of generals and of higher authority . . . is an index of the extent of a man's knowledge and understanding, and of his status in society before he became a prisoner.

Since the Omsk prison was a military establishment, the prison officers held army rank and it is these officers who receive the severest comment from Dostoyevsky. They include the drunken Major with purple face and bloodshot eyes who, at the first sign of disorder, would rush out like a spider to seize a fly caught in his web. Though un-

named in *The House of the Dead*, he is obviously to be equated with
the Major Krivtsov of whom Dostoyevsky wrote to his brother
Mikhail in the first letter after his release as 'an almost unique swine,
a petty barbarian and trouble-maker, a drunkard, the most revolting
person imaginable'. His first act when Dostoyevsky entered the
gaol had been to threaten him with corporal punishment if he should
put a foot wrong.[13]

Dostoyevsky was particularly harsh about officers who had risen
from the ranks and combined a tyrannical attitude to their subordinates with sycophancy towards their superiors, thus reminding
one of the axiom from *The Village of Stepanchikovo*: 'A mean spirit,
escaping from oppression, itself becomes an oppressor.'

The most loathsome figure among the prison officers was a fat,
sadistic lieutenant with a jolly laugh, called Zherebyatnikov. His
favourite pastime was to preside over the punishment known as
'going through the ranks' (running the gauntlet), when the victim
stumbled through files of soldiers who beat him as he passed. On
such occasions Zherebyatnikov would 'invent various refinements
and unnatural acts in order to titivate and pleasantly tickle his fat-
encased soul'. Sometimes before a beating an offender would appeal
to be let off lightly, and it was the Lieutenant's pleasure to agree if the
offender promised to behave better. But as soon as his victim began
to pass through the ranks the fat Lieutenant would execute a typical
Dostoyevskian *volte face*. 'Let him have it! Have his skin off! Roast
him!' The victim would begin to yell, while Zherebyatnikov ran
after him along the ranks, so helpless with laughter that he could
not stand up straight 'and in the end you even felt sorry for
him'.

Savage floggings, from which the victim sometimes expired, were
the vilest feature of prison life, but fascinated Dostoyevsky with his
permanent interest in humanity under strain. Among the most
interesting pages of *The House of the Dead* are those which he devotes
to the psychology of the *palach*—the 'executioner', as the word is
usually translated—who flogged offenders lucky enough to miss the
even more severe punishment of passing through the ranks. Once
again the common Dostoyevskian theme of self-assertion is encountered. 'The skill of the blow, the knowledge of his science, a
wish to show his worth to himself and the audience—these incite
his self-esteem.' Any self-respecting executioner would feel insulted
if the victim did not scream with pain. Sometimes, as the result of

long negotiations and a large bribe, he would agree to let the victim off lightly, but the first blow, which he regarded as 'his own', would always be given with maximum force. Before the beating every executioner undergoes an emotional crisis as he 'senses his power and feels himself a master'.

Dostoyevsky lets fall one especially significant comment in his discussion of this topic: 'The qualities of a *palach* in embryo are to be found in almost every modern man.' It is difficult to exaggerate the importance of this key sentiment in Dostoyevsky's later thought. It was in the early eighteen-sixties that he seems to have first become convinced of the essential evil of human nature. In this he ran against the current of contemporary thought, inclined to build political theories on the supposed perfectibility of man and on his essential reasonableness. To Dostoyevsky man was a dangerous, unpredictable, cruel creature whom he feared so much that it later became necessary for him to believe in God.

One amusing sidelight on *The House of the Dead* concerns the reaction of the censor, who at first showed signs of objecting to the book, but not, as Dostoyevsky may originally have feared, because it gave too harsh a picture of prison life. The objection was that it made prison sound too attractive. Perhaps the idea was that the common people might be lured into seeking imprisonment by the thought of drinking bouts, card games and prostitutes as described by Dostoyevsky. But Dostoyevsky leaves the reader in no doubt about the extent of his own suffering as a prisoner, suffering which (as he repeatedly points out) bore more heavily on an intellectual like himself than on the *narod*. The most painful feature, worse than the fights, the noise, the smells, the lice and fleas, was lack of privacy. One was never alone, yet always felt lonely. Then there was the almost complete absence of reading matter, a particularly cruel deprivation to him.

As time passed these discomforts tended to recede to the back of Dostoyevsky's mind, and he was inclined more to stress the value of the experience, which, as he felt, had given him a knowledge of the Russian *narod* such as few other writers could claim. What is extraordinary, therefore, is the limited use made of this material in his fiction. In his mature novels there is not a single successful major figure from the *narod*, an omission which *The House of the Dead*, with its rich gallery of sketches of the common people, makes one regret. But unfortunately, as has already been indicated, the concept of the *narod* in Dostoyevsky's mind was soon to lose all connection with reality.

Perhaps the most important effect of *The House of the Dead* and of the experiences which it describes, was that it eventually put Dostoyevsky on to the subject of crime as a fictional theme. Dostoyevsky's fiction was waiting for crime as the parched land waits for rain. When, in *Crime and Punishment*, he eventually adopted the theme, it gave his work a new vigour and sense of direction. The whole of his fiction from the middle forties to the middle sixties had been waiting for one thing. Murder.

CHAPTER FOUR

THE THRESHOLD OF MATURITY

THE early eighteen-sixties mark another turning-point in Dostoyev-sky's development. So far he had been writing as a student—of himself in the early works of introspective inspiration and of other human beings in *The House of the Dead*. These writings had been full of original ideas, many of which would continue to haunt him, but he had so far been content to investigate these ideas without wishing to influence his readers. Even the philosophical debate between the Narrator and Prince Valkovsky in *Insulted and Injured* lacks any apparent didactic impulse. Although the cynicism of Valkovsky is allowed to defeat the naïve sentimentalism of the Narrator, one detects no wish on Dostoyevsky's part to rally the reader behind Valkovsky.

This situation changed in the early eighteen-sixties, when Dostoyevsky, who had so far been content to play with ideas, began to use them as a weapon. No longer a student, he now became a teacher.

The change coincided with the foundation of the monthly maga-zine *Vremya*, which he and his brother Mikhail began to publish in January, 1861. *Vremya* was closed down in May, 1863, because of an article on the Polish riots of that year, misinterpreted by officials as an attack on Government policy. Shortly after this the brothers were permitted to continue publishing a journal, but under a differ-ent name, *Epokha*. *Epokha* was less successful than *Vremya*, and was discontinued early in 1865, having struggled on for six months after the sudden death of its nominal editor, Mikhail Dostoyevsky. The death of his brother, who had always been closer to him than anyone else, was a great shock to Dostoyevsky. It closely coincided with another loss, the death of his wife. This brought release from an unhappy marriage and a protracted illness, but was naturally a severe emotional shock.

During the early eighteen-sixties Dostoyevsky's main energies were switched from imaginative literature to journalism, a foretaste of the years in the following decade when he became similarly engrossed with his *Diary of a Writer*. In a series of unsigned articles in *Vremya*, beginning in 1861, he begins to formulate a system of ideas important for the understanding of his future as a novelist. Since reference will be made repeatedly to this system of ideas, it is necessary to have a term by which to describe them, and they will be called 'Dostoyevskyism', with regret that no less cumbrous word suggests itself.

Dostoyevskyism did not spring in full panoply from its author's head in early 1861, but much of the armour was already in position. Certainly the central concept of the creed, an obsession with Russia and her role in world history, was already established. Dostoyevsky was not alone in this, for rarely has national self-consciousness been carried to such a pitch of inflammation as by nineteenth-century Russian intellectuals. But even among these, few ran so high an emotional temperature as Dostoyevsky when he spoke and wrote of his native land.

Basic among the axioms of Dostoyevskyism was the claim that Russia possessed, to a degree unique among the nations of the world, an attribute termed 'universal humanity'. It is perhaps futile for a non-Russian to attempt an explanation of this concept, especially since Dostoyevsky repeatedly asserted that it was incomprehensible to Europeans (when using the term 'Europeans' he generally excluded Russians and other Slavs). 'No, Messrs. Europeans!' he exclaimed in the first of the articles in *Vremya*. 'Don't ask us for the time being to give proofs of our opinion about ourselves.' Proofs of Russia's universal humanity, as of the other axioms of Dostoyevskyism, never would be forthcoming, for these were revealed truths outside the realm of argument or evidence.

Dostoyevsky conceived Russia, in contrast to the effete West, as a young and vigorous nation, which (according to a formula frequently invoked) was continually on the point of 'saying a new word'. The idea that Russia stood on the threshold of a new epoch was particularly natural in 1861, the year of the Emancipation of the Serfs. This event, according to Dostoyevsky's hopes at the time, was destined to end the rift between the privileged classes of Russia and the common people. He later became less optimistic about closing this rift, while remaining equally eloquent about the importance of closing it.

He was already making the claim, bewildering to any modern

student of nineteenth-century Russia, that Russian society lacked class distinctions as found in the West. Yet his first imaginative work of the period, the short story *A Nasty Anecdote*, contains a vicious satire on precisely those class distinctions which, in his journalism, he was simultaneously claiming to be non-existent. This kind of self-contradiction is typical and many examples of it can be found in his theoretical writings.

It is characteristic for example that, in one article in *Vremya*, he should deviate from a tirade about the virtues of Russia and her superiority to all other countries, in order to emphasize the Russian's 'sober view of himself and absence of any sort of self-elevation'. Such examples of self-contradiction combined with unconscious irony are of importance to the understanding of Dostoyevsky as a creative artist. Rarely has any human brain succeeded in simultaneously holding so many mutually self-cancelling ideas, a capacity which was of advantage to him as a novelist and contributed to his originality, but hardly conduced to clear thinking.

Though his conception of Russia had already matured in the early eighteen-sixties, many other features of Dostoyevskyism were added later. One was his lurch into the extreme political right wing. Already ecstatic references to the Tsar and sneers at contemporary 'progressives' indicated the future direction. But at the beginning of his career as a prophet Dostoyevsky took a point of view which is perhaps the most delightful paradox about this extreme and passionate reasoner: he believed that he could be a restraining influence. One of the initial aims of *Vremya* was to act as a bridge between Russian Westernizers, who wished to copy the West, and Slavophiles, who wished to develop Russia's native traditions. Before long he moved away from the Westernizers to a point where he was willing to admit himself, with some reservations, as a Slavophile.

*

The most notable excursion into journalism during this period is a series of articles published in *Vremya* in early 1863, *Winter Notes on Summer Impressions*. This contains Dostoyevsky's reflections on an event of importance in his emotional biography, his first visit to Western Europe. The visit had lasted two and a half months between June and September, 1862, and had taken him to Germany, Switzerland and Italy as well as to the two countries with which he is mainly concerned in his *Winter Notes*, France and England.

Love of humanity in the abstract had by now become an axiom of Dostoyevskyism, and it followed as a corollary of this (which will surpise no one attuned to the contradictory quality of his mind) that he on the whole disliked actual human beings. Of such love-hatred directed towards Western Europe, *Winter Notes* provide rich evidence. Thus, on the one hand, he pays enthusiastic tribute to Europe's influence on Russia: 'Everything, absolutely everything which we have in the way of progress, learning, art, civic virtue, humanity, everything, everything comes from there [Europe], from that land of holy miracles.' On the other hand he writes with withering contempt, individually and collectively, of the Englishmen and Frenchmen whom he met. He expresses similar contempt elsewhere for Germans, Swiss, Turks, Jews and other peoples, by no means always excluding the Slavs, among whom the Poles were always his least-favoured nation.

He sometimes spoke of himself as an ordinary tourist, but he was of course nothing of the sort. Sightseeing bored him. It was in the spirit of Jonah setting out for the city of Nineveh, not of Baedeker, that he descended on Western Europe.

The most striking pages in the articles are devoted to London, where he spent eight days which left him with a lurid vision of brightly decorated gin palaces, of hordes of prostitutes swarming under the flaring gas jets of the Haymarket, of the 'poisoned Thames' and of the 'air saturated with coal'. He had discovered that English husbands regularly beat their wives with pokers. One ray of sunshine illumines the gloom: 'there are no women in the world so beautiful as the English'. The building which most impressed him in London was the newly erected Crystal Palace, later used by him as a symbol in which the three concepts of orderly organization, Socialism and ultimate evil are so strangely united.

The French receive even severer treatment than the English. 'Honestly, the French are a people who make one sick', he had written in a letter from Paris.[1] It is the French, not the English, whom he describes as a nation of shopkeepers and hypocrites. The French air of superiority especially irritated him. 'The meanest little Frenchman, who's ready to sell his own father for twenty-five copecks . . . at the very same moment when he's engaged in selling his father, will adopt such an air of imposing dignity that one is overcome with bewilderment.'

He had met in London the most eminent of Russian political
c*

émigrés, Alexander Herzen. It seems likely that discussion with Herzen, whose ideas on some points were not far from Dostoyevsky's own, reinforced his impression that the materialist West was doomed, while the future lay with the spiritual and brotherly Russian.

＊

To the period 1862–5 belong three imaginative works: two short stories (*A Nasty Anecdote*, *The Crocodile*) and a short novel (*Notes from Underground*). These three works are remarkable for the reintroduction of humour, abandoned in *Insulted and Injured*, and also for a new element: the polemics of Dostoyevskyism now enter his fiction.

Dostoyevsky's humour was usually aggressive. It demanded a victim, such as Golyadkin Senior in *The Double* or Colonel Rostanev in *The Village of Stepanchikovo*. Now, in *A Nasty Anecdote* (1862), Dostoyevsky is found for the first time aiming this aggressive humour at an ideological target, attacking what was to become his supreme *bête noire*, the Russian 'progressive'. The story is therefore a landmark in his slide towards the extreme political right wing.

Curiously enough, the victim of the attack was a 'general'. It is perhaps necessary to explain that this figure, General Pralinsky, was not a military officer but a highly placed civil servant, for each of the fourteen grades in the 'table of ranks' of the Tsarist civil service was equated with a military rank. Many of Dostoyevsky's later 'generals'—Pralinsky was only one of a series—were also civilians. Pralinsky is a modern General, recently appointed, and sees himself in the vanguard of the 'new ideas' which were sweeping Russia during the decade inaugurated by the Emancipation of the Serfs. He prides himself on his humane attitude to his subordinates, and it must here be noted that the words *gumanny* (humane) and *gumannost* (humanity) were already becoming terms of abuse to Dostoyevsky.

Pralinsky, as the reader learns at the beginning of the story, was flattered by his reputation as a 'desperate liberal', and he is first encountered in argument with another General, a reactionary of the old school. Pralinsky tells him, over a bottle of champagne, that 'humanity is the most important thing, humanity with one's subordinates, remembering that they too are men. . . .' 'Tee-he-he!' is the reactionary General's only comment, and he must have been still sniggering at the end of the story, a moral tale intended to show the falsity of *gumannost*.

Flushed with champagne, Pralinsky stumbles out of the house with a single idea in his mind: he will perform a humane act. It happens that one of his subordinates, who lives in the neighbourhood, is celebrating his wedding. Pralinsky decides to intrude uninvited into the celebrations, and prove by his kindness and condescension in lending distinction to the proceedings what a humane person he is. He thus adds another episode to the line of gatecrashing scenes in Dostoyevsky, this one having the peculiarity that the gatecrasher is intruding on a lower social milieu. Skilled in providing premonitions of disaster, Dostoyevsky loads the situation with foreboding before his General has even crossed the threshold of the wedding reception.

The bridegroom, Pseldonimov, is a petty official who earns only ten roubles a month, he and his entourage belonging to the 'Poor Folk' strain in Dostoyevsky's fiction. He is terrified by the General's appearance and behaves like a recruit on parade. Pralinsky, already tipsy and embarrassed by the devastating effect caused by his arrival, continues to drink, while, realizing that the distinguished visitor is drunk, some of the guests make the characteristic Dostoyevskian *volte face* from sycophancy to *naglost* (brazen impudence). A chain of scandalous episodes follows, such as the trick played on Pralinsky by an unnamed student, who 'turned abruptly towards him with a sort of grimace, and moving his face towards his Excellency to a distance approaching impropriety, crowed like a cock at the top of his voice'.

Pralinsky tries to halt the developing Scandal by making a speech about *gumannost*, but is too drunk to be coherent and finds himself denounced to the company by a young man who is described as a correspondent of an imaginary paper called *The Firebrand*—the title is intended to be understood as a reference to *The Spark* (*Iskra*), a satirical journal of the period which attacked political reactionaries.

'Yes, you've come to boast about your humaneness! You've spoiled everyone's enjoyment. You've drunk champagne without realizing that it's too dear for an official with a salary of ten roubles a month, and I suspect you're one of those high officials who have a weakness for the young wives of their subordinates.'

Soon after this Pralinsky falls face foremost into a plate of blancmange, and then has to be put to bed in the only available place, the nuptial couch.

The most wicked touch comes several days later, when Pralinsky returns to his office and learns from an assistant that Pseldonimov has meanwhile put in for a transfer to another department. Giving his consent to this arrangement, he makes the outrageous comment: 'Tell Pseldonimov I don't wish him any harm. . . . On the contrary, I'm even prepared to forget what has happened.' The bankruptcy of *gumannost* has been demonstrated.

A Anecdote Story calls to mind remarks made by one of those gifted amateurs of Russian literature who did much to popularize the subject in England in the nineteen-twenties, but whose comments are sometimes more amateurish than gifted—Virginia Woolf.[2] She claims that Dostoyevsky has 'little sense of humour', and explains that a typical scene from his novels is one where 'we open the door and find ourselves in a room full of Russian Generals'. This, she claims, bewilders the English reader, because in an English novel 'we should find it very difficult not to laugh at a General'.

The suggestion that Dostoyevsky's generals were intended to be taken seriously is astonishing, for it is difficult to name a single Dostoyevskian General who is not a comic figure, whether one thinks of Pralinsky himself, of the preposterous General in *The Gambler*, the henpecked General Yepanchin from *The Idiot* or, most comic of all Dostoyevskian brass-hats, General Ivolgin from the same novel. Of course in Virginia Woolf's day many English translations of Dostoyevsky were so bad that they spread a film of equal incongruity over all his writing, whether humorously intended or not. Small wonder that some interpreters went wildly astray.

But Virginia Woolf is not the only English critic to deny Dostoyevsky a sense of humour. For example, E. H. Carr—who presumably read his works in the original—also writes that he 'has the smallest possible capacity for sustained humour'.[3] This point of view is not easy to challenge, since there is no department of criticism which lends itself less readily to demonstration than humour. It is also understandable for a number of reasons. Dostoyevsky's humour was sometimes heavy-handed, and is curiously compartmented. As has been noted, some long works such as *Insulted and Injured* entirely lack it. Furthermore, Dostoyevsky's letters are without humour, except for an occasional rasping sarcasm—a strong contrast, for example, to the letters of Chekhov. Then again, as has also been remarked, Dostoyevsky's humour was apt to be linked with cruelty, which has led some critics to describe him as a sadist. It is understandable that humour of this kind should not be to everyone's taste. And there is also the curious point that when one believes oneself to be laughing with Dostoyevsky, one may occasionally be laughing at him.

In spite of objections, it remains a firm contention in the present study that humour is one of the most important ingredients in Dostoyevsky's work, an ingredient to which increasing attention must be paid as the period of his maturity is approached. An attempt will be made to do full justice to this neglected element, but the suggestion will not of course be made that Dostoyevsky was no more than a humorist.

Nothing is more surprising when considering Dostoyevsky's writings on the one hand, and the vast amount of critical literature devoted to them on the other, than this wholesale failure of critics to react to his humour. The only treatment of this aspect of his work to have been traced during the preparation of the present study is Professor I. I. Lapshin's essay, 'The Comic in Dostoyevsky's Work'.[4] This contains some interesting ideas, but is itself so humourless as to be out of sympathy with the subject.

Dostoyevsky's own comments on the humorous side of his work are sometimes surprising because he is apt to attribute comic qualities to characters who do not really seem to possess them. These include Pyotr Verkhovensky in *The Devils*.[5] They even include the saintly Father Zosima in *The Brothers Karamazov*, of whom Dostoyevsky wrote:

> It was necessary to present a modest and majestic figure. Meanwhile life is full of the comic and is majestic only in its internal sense, so that I was compelled against my will and out of artistic considerations to touch even on the most trivial aspects in the biography of my monk [Zosima] so as not to injure artistic realism.[6]

This quotation is worth dwelling upon because it provides such a splendid commentary on Dostoyevsky himself, outwardly so often an undignified and even farcical figure, to whom it is impossible to deny a truly 'majestic' quality when one penetrates beneath the surface.

*

Evidence of the strange crannies into which Dostoyevsky's humour could penetrate is provided by another story of the period,

The Crocodile (1865). This is one of those pieces of dead-pan fantasy of which *The Double* and Gogol's *The Nose* had provided previous examples.

A man goes to see a crocodile on show in St. Petersburg. While teasing it with a glove he is seized by the beast and swallowed, an event which does nothing to inhibit his flow of conversation. He declares that he is fairly comfortable inside the crocodile, except for a slight smell of rubber, and resists attempts to extricate him. For it is his ambition to make his mark as a pundit. Hitherto little attention has been paid to his philosophizings, but now the situation has been changed by a lucky accident. How can humanity possibly ignore words of wisdom coming from so strange a source as the inside of a crocodile? He has found what a later age would call a 'gimmick', and intends to use it to propound a new social system.

This is an amusing *jeu d'esprit*, but its chief interest lies elsewhere. Contemporaries found in *The Crocodile* a vicious attack on the man who had become Dostoyevsky's main ideological enemy, the radical thinker N. G. Chernyshevsky. Chernyshevsky had been arrested in 1862, and had written in prison the didactic novel *What is to be done?*—the bible of the Russian progressive movement and of the 'nihilists' associated with it. To Dostoyevsky, Chernyshevsky was the premier heretic of the age, for it was to Chernyshevsky more than to anyone else that he attributed the supreme sin of advocating a society organized on rational lines.

Was Dostoyevsky's man pontificating from inside a crocodile intended as an attack on Chernyshevsky pontificating from inside the Petropavlovsk Fortress as he faced a long period as a political prisoner in Siberia? Could this be an example of Dostoyevsky kicking a man when he was down? Many contemporaries thought so, and Dostoyevsky later took the trouble to deny the charge at length in *The Diary of a Writer* for 1873. But this denial does not necessarily mean much. Dostoyevsky could be malicious when he wanted—witness his attack on Gogol in *The Village of Stepanchikovo* and his parody of Turgenev in *The Devils*. His denial was probably sincere, and it is even possible that the idea of Chernyshevsky's plight had not crossed his conscious mind when he was writing *The Crocodile*. But Dostoyevsky's right hand did not always know what his left hand was doing. He was a strange compound of genius and petty malice, and it would have been out of character if malice had not been present at some level of his consciousness when he wrote *The Crocodile*.

*

The most memorable production of the period now under consideration is *Notes from Underground* (1864), a short novel, the only short work which has exercised on Dostoyevsky's critics a fascination comparable with that of his later long novels. It has been spoken of as the 'prelude' to the five-act tragedy of the great novels from *Crime and Punishment* to *The Brothers Karamazov*. There are arguments in favour of this view, for the links with Dostoyevsky's future to be found in *Notes from Underground* are indeed numerous and important. In particular it is his first attempt at a philosophical novel, an enterprise into which he plunged with enthusiasm. This short work contains a greater proportion of theorizing than any of the fiction which followed it, not excluding *The Brothers Karamazov*.

The theoretical sections of the novel, like the narrative which follows, are put into the mouth of Dostoyevsky's unnamed Narrator, who will be referred to as the 'Underground Man'. As his title suggests, this is a figure from the past. The Underground Man is another in the series of 'St. Petersburg dreamers', being the most developed and interesting member of the group, but possessing the familiar stigmata. He is an isolated, lonely figure who lurks in poverty and introspective misery in his 'corner', and like other members of the group is a distorted portrait of Dostoyevsky himself during the eighteen-forties. There is reference to his 'touchiness', 'irritability' and 'pride,' all words which Dostoyevsky applied to himself on many occasions in his letters.

Dostoyevsky also attributes to his Underground Man his own passion for reading, together with the romantic dreams in which he had indulged in the eighteen-forties, those dreams termed 'Schilleresque' about everything 'noble and beautiful' which had incurred the sneers of Prince Valkovsky in *Insulted and Injured*. These romantic imaginings of the Underground Man are described as alternating with bouts of *razvrat* (debauchery), a word which occurs repeatedly in Dostoyevsky's writings. Dostoyevskian debauches usually take place off-stage, as it were, being hinted at in oracular language, and form part of the regular build-up of his Bogeymen. Here they are attributed to one of the self-portrait characters.

Sometimes I used to get terribly bored. . . . I used to feel the need of movement, and would suddenly plunge into dark subterranean, loathsome . . . petty debauchery. Because of my perpetual pathological irritability my passions were sharp and burning. . . . I used to feel a hysterical thirst for contradictions and contrasts—hence my plunges into debauchery.

Is the 'debauch' also autobiographical, and if so what kind of debauchery does Dostoyevsky have in mind?

Alcoholic debauchery can be ruled out. Though drunkenness figures in his fiction (Marmeladov in *Crime and Punishment* being his most notable alcoholic) this was not among Dostoyevsky's many human weaknesses. But it does seem almost certain that in the dark days of the eighteen-forties he was at least an occasional visitor to the brothels of St. Petersburg. The point is almost clinched in a letter of November, 1845, in which he remarks to his brother Mikhail: 'The Minnas, Klaras and Mariannas [these were intended to be understood as the names of prostitutes] have become excessively pretty, but are damned expensive.'[7] Unless Dostoyevsky was romancing here—always a possibility—this was his own brand of *razvrat*. If so this is another autobiographical trait in his Underground Man, whose visit to a brothel brings on the climax of the novel.

To the alternation between high thinking and low living must be added another more familiar contradiction which the Underground Man shares with his creator. This is his ambivalent attitude to humiliation. The Underground Man is yet another oscillator up and down the 'humiliation slot'. He is a predator and victim by turns, alternating between situations in which he courts humiliation and situations in which he himself humiliates and tyrannizes others. 'I'd been humiliated,' he remarks at one point, 'and so I wanted to humiliate. I'd been treated like a dishcloth, and so I too wanted to show my power.'

The Underground Man resembles previous self-portrait characters, such as the Narrator from *Insulted and Injured*, in being the product of introspective inspiration. But he differs from these characters, and even more strikingly from previous humiliation-oscillators (of whom Foma Fomich in *The Village of Stepanchikovo* was the most important forerunner) in the amount of introspective theorizing put into his mouth. This is his special characteristic. He outdoes all other characters in Dostoyevsky in the profundity of his self-analysis.

He is also one of the most sensitive, 'as if [he remarks of himself at one stage] I'd had my skin flayed off me and the mere touch of air hurt me'. This sensitivity, which he terms *soznaniye* (consciousness) is one of his main introspective preoccupations. He wishes, for example, that he had been equipped with only the ordinary human allocation of consciousness, 'that is a half or a quarter of the portion allotted to a highly developed man in our unhappy nineteenth century, especially to one who has the added misfortune of living in St. Petersburg, the most abstract and contrived city on the face of the globe'. All consciousness, he claims, is a disease.

Notes from Underground is curiously constructed, the first part of the book (about one-third of its total length) being devoted entirely to theory, while the second part contains the narrative. Part One is again subdivided into two sections, of which the first is devoted to this theme of 'consciousness' (Dostoyevsky's term will be kept here, although it may be helpful in attempting to understand his somewhat involved arguments to remember that 'hyper-sensitivity' perhaps conveys better what he had in mind).

The Underground Man's reflections on 'consciousness' are particularly revealing, the most significant pointers here being his pleasures. One of these is to commit some vile and irretrievable deed.

> I used to experience a sort of secret, abnormal, base little pleasure in returning on some excessively foul St. Petersburg night to my corner and in being *violently conscious* of the fact that here I was today having again committed a vile deed and that what I had done was again irretrievable. Secretly and internally I would gnaw, rasp and suck myself on account of it to the point when my grief at last turned into a kind of base and accursed sweetness, and finally into a positive and serious pleasure.

One comic feature is the imaginary dialogue which the Underground Man conducts with his reader, as when he goes on to discuss another and even more strange source of enjoyment—having toothache.

> 'Ha! ha! ha!' you will shout with a laugh. 'After this you'll even be finding pleasure in toothache!'
> 'So what? There *is* pleasure even in toothache,' I shall answer. 'I've had toothache for a whole month. I know what it is. This is of course something that people don't put up with in an angry silence. They groan. But these are not frank groans, they are groans with a dose of malevolence. And the malevolence is the whole point. It is precisely

in these groans that the sufferer expresses his pleasure. . . . I ask you, gentlemen, to have a good listen some time to the groans of an educated man of the nineteenth century who is suffering from toothache, say on the second or third day, when he is already beginning to groan differently from the first day, that is, not simply because he has toothache. He doesn't groan like some crude *muzhik*, but as a man touched by progress and European civilization. . . . He knows that even the audience for whom he's putting on the performance, and all his family have already begun to listen to him with loathing, don't believe him for an instant, and realize perfectly well that he could groan differently, more simply and without all these trills and twists.'

To this exotic pleasure may be added the satisfaction which the Underground Man claims that he would receive if someone were to slap his face, and the pleasure which he derives in the narrative section of the book from the many occasions on which he takes and gives offence.

These perversities of the Underground Man provide a key to an important quality in Dostoyevsky's own make-up—an addiction to violent sensation, with the important qualification that it was violent mental sensation which attracted him. To physical sensation he remained relatively indifferent, in spite of the attractions of toothache described in *Notes from Underground*. And it was precisely the violence of the sensation and not its quality which interested him. One might phrase it differently by saying that he would rather be violently unhappy than mildly happy, though his attitude to this changed in the last few years of his life. The same point is put in different words by the Underground Man, when he asks the rhetorical question: 'Which is better? Cheap happiness or lofty sufferings?'

Dostoyevsky himself was the same kind of emotional self-flagellant as his Underground Man, although it is necessary not to lose a sense of proportion here, for it was Dostoyevsky's habit in his fiction to take a human trait, whether observed in himself or others, and to carry it to the most extreme possible degree. It is doubtful whether Dostoyevsky was quite such an extreme example of 'consciousness', even in the difficult period of the eighteen-forties, as his Underground Man. But he was fairly far along the road. Reference has been made above to his courtship of Isayeva, in which he seems to have sought, not satisfaction in love, but extreme mental vibration. A love affair of the mid-sixties, in which this tendency was carried even further, must shortly be considered. To this will be added a new addiction exactly suited to maintain the shuddering vibrations in which he delighted—gambling.

More trivial matters also were exploited as a source of emotional vibration. An illustration of this is found in a letter written to his brother Mikhail when Dostoyevsky was eighteen.

You will not believe what a sweet trembling of the heart I experience when I am brought one of your letters. And I have discovered a new form of pleasure, a strange one—tormenting myself. I take your letter, turn it over for several minutes in my hands, feel it to see if it is of adequate weight, and, having looked my fill and taken my fill of delight over the sealed envelope, put it in my pocket. . . . You will not believe what a sensual [*sladostrastnoye*] condition of soul, feelings and heart this brings! And in this way I sometimes wait for about a quarter of an hour. In the end I fall greedily on the packet, tear the seal, and devour your lines.[8]

Dostoyevsky's craving for strong mental sensations perhaps explains his indifference to alcohol, a drug for those who wish to dull that 'consciousness' in which he found so much perverse pleasure. This craving for sensation is part of the secret of his art, since it is his ability to squeeze the last drop of emotional stimulation out of a scene which often contributes to his strongest effects.

The characterization of the 'conscious' man is completed by an analysis of his diametrical opposite, the 'man of action'. This term illustrates one of the points made about the conscious man, who is inhibited from action by his excess of consciousness. The man of action, also termed the 'normal', 'straightforward' and 'real' man, is saved by his stupidity. He can do things like taking revenge on someone who has insulted him, an activity denied to the 'violently conscious mouse', as the Underground Man describes himself.

So much for the beginning of the philosophical First Part of *Notes from Underground*. The passage continues with an apparent change of subject as Dostoyevsky settles in the saddle of what was to become his favourite hobby-horse and mounts his first full-scale fictional attack on the fashionable theory which he would from now on regard as the major heresy of his time: the idea that human society should or could be reorganized on the basis of enlightened self-interest. From now on Dostoyevsky's hatred of this idea remained the ruling passion of his life, but he rarely exceeded the eloquence with which he denounced it in *Notes from Underground*.

Tell me, who was it who first announced, who first proclaimed that the only reason why man commits evil deeds is that he does not know his own true interests? And that man, if he were enlightened and had his eyes opened to his true and normal interests, would at once cease to do evil, and would at once become kind and noble, because, being enlightened, and understanding his own real advantages, he would see his own advantage precisely in goodness, it being well known that no single man can knowingly act against his own interests? And that he would consequently start doing good compulsorily, as it were? Oh, babe! Oh, pure, innocent child! But when on earth, in the first place, has it ever happened in all the millennia that man has acted exclusively on the basis of his own interests? What on earth are we to do with the millions of facts which show that people have *knowingly*, that is, fully understanding their real interests, left them in the background and have rushed along another road, one of risks and hazards, not having been compelled to do this by any person or thing, but apparently because they have specifically not wanted the obvious road, but have obstinately and wilfully opened up a new road, a difficult nonsensical road which they seek out almost in darkness?

It is shortly after this point that the Underground Man introduces the image of the Crystal Palace to denote the ideal society which Dostoyevsky's opponents believe can be constructed in the future on the basis of the enlightened self-interest of men. What if the thing is actually built?

Why, I, for example [the Underground Man continues], won't be in the least surprised if suddenly, without any warning, there pops up in the middle of the general future harmony some gentleman with an ignoble, or let us rather say with a reactionary and sneering countenance, who will stick his hands on his hips and say to us all: 'Well, gentlemen, how about sending all this harmony to blazes with a single kick just so that we can consign all these logarithms to the devil and start living again by our own stupid whim?'

Thus Dostoyevsky began to settle accounts with the kind of social theory of which he himself had been an adherent in his twenties, and which he now attacked with that special venom reserved by a person of his strong intellectual passions for his own fallen idol. Although the main target of his outbursts were Socialist thinkers, with the prime offender Chernyshevsky as the villain of the piece, Dostoyevsky was a persistent heresy-hunter. Later on other ideologies, Catholic and liberal, were transfixed with the same arrows. All these schools of thought, however much their followers might imagine them to differ from each other, were guilty of the same crime. They wanted to build a paradise on earth by organizing man for his own good. Thank heavens this would never be possible while there were a few 'violently conscious mice' like the Underground Man around. Freedom, however extreme the perversities to which it might lead, was to be prized above happiness in Dostoyevsky's scheme of things.

Later on the charge-sheet against Dostoyevskian heretics would include an important new item: in attempting to reorganize the world exclusively on the basis of human reason they left out God. This idea had originally formed part of the argument of *Notes from Underground*, but the relevant section was cut by the censors. 'Those swine of censors', Dostoyevsky wrote, 'have passed the places where I mocked everything and sometimes blasphemed *for appearance's sake*, and banned the part where I deduced the need for a belief in Christ.'[9] Dostoyevsky did not attempt to restore the cut, and the passage to which he refers has been lost.

Having established a theoretical base in Part One of *Notes from Underground*, Dostoyevsky's Narrator proceeds to show himself in action in Part Two, which consists of narrative. Here he relates three episodes from his life as a young man. The first two describe him receiving humiliation from figures who correspond to the 'man of action', as defined in Part One. In the third he emerges as the purveyor of humiliation.

The first two episodes follow the traditions of Dostoyevskian humour by including an ejection scene and a gatecrashing scene. Traditional also is the fact that the chief purveyors of insults in both episodes are army officers, here equated with the 'man of action'.

The first episode begins when the Underground Man happens to look through the window of a tavern and sees some people fighting with billiard cues. One of them is thrown out of the window. 'I felt a stab of envy for the ejected gentleman, so much so that I even went inside the tavern into the billiard-room. With a bit of luck I too . . . might be thrown out of the window.' The passage continues, 'I was not drunk', of which it may be remarked that this formula is invoked so often in Dostoyevsky's fiction as to give the impression that all his characters are to be presumed drunk until proved sober.

The delicious thing about the billiard-room scene in *Notes from Underground* is that it does not even become an ejection scene. It is an ejection scene *manqué*, as befits the ineffectual character of the hero, whose incapacity for action is so total that he cannot even succeed in getting himself thrown out of a window.

> I was put in my place right away by a certain officer.
> I was standing by the billiard-table and barring his way without realizing it. Wanting to pass by, he took me by the shoulders and silently—without warning or explanation—transferred me from the place where I was standing to another, and then walked past as if without noticing anything.

The Underground Man retires quietly from the billiard-room, but this is only the beginning of the adventure. For years he is obsessed by the idea of revenge. He discovers the officer's name and address, writes a story denouncing him (which remains unpublished) and composes a letter challenging him to a duel (which is not dispatched). Then he discovers that his enemy is in the habit of walking on the Nevsky Prospekt each day between three and four o'clock. During these walks he gives way to Generals and other important personages, 'but people of my sort . . . he simply squashed, walking straight at them as if there was an empty space in front of him, and in no case did he give way'. It is, of course, the Underground Man who always gives way. But the thought suddenly strikes him: 'What if I don't give way on purpose, even if it means bumping into him?' At this point it is necessary to record the incidence of another common formula ('What if . . .?') which often precedes that typical Dostoyevskian event, the sudden, unpredictable outrageous act.

The Underground Man makes careful preparation for his revenge in a passage which Dostoyevsky uses skilfully to heighten the suspense surrounding the proposed collision. As is common in scenes where a Victim is courting humiliation, careful sartorial preparations are made in advance. New black gloves are bought, the colour yellow being rejected after some thought as too frivolous for the occasion. The Underground Man then borrows money in order to have a beaver collar attached to his overcoat, as his existing raccoon collar is too 'lackey-like'.

It is still some time before the Underground Man can bring off his coup, because he continually takes fright at the last moment. Finally, after a delirious night during which he runs a high temperature, he decides to abandon the project. However, next day on the Nevsky:

Suddenly, three paces from my enemy, I unexpectedly made up my mind, closed my eyes and—we banged hard into each other, shoulder to shoulder. I did not yield an inch and passed by on a completely equal footing! He didn't even look round, and pretended not to have noticed. But he was only pretending. I am convinced of that. I am still convinced of that! Of course I came off worse—he was the stronger. But that is not the point. The point is that I had attained my goal, had maintained my dignity, had not yielded a step and had publicly placed myself on an equal social footing with him.

The second adventure of the Underground Man occurs when he intrudes on a farewell dinner given by three of his former school-friends to a fourth, a young officer called Zverkov, who has just been posted to the Caucasus. Zverkov, the main 'man of action' in the narrative, is a happy, healthy, good-looking youth with a modest fortune. He has everything which the Underground Man lacks.

The dinner is a chapter of accidents. The Underground Man arrives at the hotel an hour early because the others, irritated by the fact that he has invited himself to the celebration against their wishes, have deliberately failed to inform him of a change of time. Zverkov, when he eventually arrives, is odiously patronizing and asks him how much he earns at the Government office where he works (the Underground Man is another in the series of poor clerks). The Underground Man flares up and demands what right Zverkov has to interrogate him. 'Actually I at once told him how much my salary was. I blushed terribly. "It's not much," Zverkov pompously observed.'

Further incidents include an insulting toast to Zverkov pronounced by the Underground Man, and a challenge to a duel, which makes the other four 'fall flat on their backs with laughter'. The isolation of the Underground Man is finally brought home after the dinner is over and the other four recline on a sofa drinking and talking, while the Underground Man spends three hours walking up and down the room in total silence, except for a single 'odious snort' which he emits when, at one point, Zverkov is heard to speak of Shakespeare.

These two adventures provide typical samples of Dostoyevsky's strange and original humour, revolving, as it so frequently does, round the Scandal. As in his second novel, *The Double*, the comic is here bound up with the tragic, but these two powerful scenes are written with a command of the material which had not been present in *The Double*. What had been experimental in *The Double* is here found in fulfilment. A comparison of the two works shows how far Dostoyevsky had travelled as a writer in the first two decades of his development.

The Underground Man's third and final adventure lacks the comic element of the first two, and is one of the most painful scenes to have come from Dostoyevsky's pen so far. Here the Underground Man, abandoned by his four enemies, pursues them to a brothel with the aim of slapping Zverkov's face. But he does not find them, and instead meets a young prostitute called Liza. Like her successor, Sonya Marmeladova in *Crime and Punishment*, Liza is a 'pure prostitute', and she has only been in the business for a fortnight. The Underground Man at once sums her up as a simple and trusting girl who offers him almost unlimited scope for mental self-flagellation. Zverkov and the other humiliators are forgotten as he makes the characteristic switch in the 'humiliation slot' from Victim to Predator. He sets himself to torment the girl, drawing an appalling picture of the future which awaits her in the stews of St. Petersburg —beatings, illness and a premature death. He dwells on her funeral, when, according to his predictions, she will be thrown in a cheap coffin into a waterlogged grave, and he torments her with the future which might have been hers as a happy wife and mother.

Out of all this rubbish Liza succeeds in grasping only one thing —the man who is trying to make her unhappy is himself desperately unhappy. She feels sorry for him and comes to love him. This, of course, is the ultimate provocation to the Underground Man, for whom love must inevitably become tyranny, and in the supremely painful climax of the novel he viciously insults her by pressing on her, in return for her love, a five-rouble note.

At the end of the novel the Underground Man addresses the imaginary audience with which he had conducted a dialogue in Part One. 'So far as I am concerned, I have only carried to the extreme in my life that which you did not even dare to carry even halfway.' The paradoxical 'anti-hero', as he describes himself, leaves the pages of *Notes from Underground* as its hero. At least this was what Dostoyevsky intended to infer. He had proved that man was too ingloriously perverse to be regimented for his own good by the schemes of social theorists. Freedom, even if man makes no better use of it than Dostoyevsky's 'violently conscious mouse', is always to be preferred to regimented happiness.

This is one of the most difficult of all Dostoyevsky's works. As already indicated, nowhere else in his fiction is he found juggling with so many ideas in so short a space, so much so that it has only been possible to indicate a few of them here. It is principally for this reason that the novel is the most important work (together with *The Brothers Karamazov*) for readers who are more fascinated by Dostoyevsky's thought than by his art. The power of *Notes from Underground* evokes sympathy for this point of view, even though the contrary emphasis is aimed at here.

The novel is also a notable example of Dostoyevsky's mastery of narrative. For here the sense of pace, the use of suspense, and the technique of the 'gathering storm' are applied with greater force and economy than before.

These are among the many elements in the novel which foreshadow the future. But the character of the hero does also, in a sense, herald the end of an era, since he is the fullest and most powerful of the Dostoyevskian 'self-portraits', of which he may be described as the *reductio ad absurdum*. From now on Dostoyevsky did not entirely abandon the introspective inspiration which led to the self-portraits. For example, the hero of *The Gambler*, which will be discussed next, is a specimen of the type. But Dostoyevsky's most important later character-studies, such as Raskolnikov, Prince Myshkin, Stepan Trofimovich Verkhovensky and the members of the Karamazov family, show him more orientated towards the outside world. In exploiting introspection so exhaustively with his Underground Man he had cleared the road for what was to follow.

*

The next work to be examined is another short novel, *The Gambler*. It is arguable that this involves a break in chronological sequence, since at the time when *The Gambler* was written, in October, 1866, *Crime and Punishment* had almost been completed. However, *The Gambler* had been maturing for over three years, and belongs in spirit to the works discussed in the present chapter. It draws heavily on Dostoyevsky's own experiences in the years 1862–3, notably on his two visits to Western Europe and on the two dramas there enacted: the beginning of his phase as a gambler and his love affair with Apollinariya Suslova.

The Gambler is an adventure story in which Dostoyevsky retreats from philosophical profundities, but without abandoning his favourite theme of humanity under strain. This is the only one of his novels which is not set in Russia, and its closest affinities of thought, among works of the early eighteen-sixties, are with *Winter Notes on Summer Impressions*. There Dostoyevsky had fulminated about the West European character. Now, in *The Gambler*, he takes the opportunity to create some West European characters, and thus to illustrate his fulminations with concrete examples.

From this ordeal by withering contempt the English emerge with least discredit in the person of the shy, reserved and honourable Mr. Astley, whose title 'Mr.' is never omitted, as befits so formal and withdrawn a personage. The French, always more potent provokers of Dostoyevskian bile than the English, are represented by two plausible rogues: a high-class tart called Mlle Blanche de Cominges and a handsome, urbane swindler called the Marquis De Grie, whose operations and antecedents are shrouded in a typical Dostoyevskian fog, hints being dropped that this is not his real name and that he is not really a marquis.

A few passing blows are aimed at the Poles and the Germans. By this time a miserable little foreigner of some kind, whether a 'wretched little Pole' (*polyachishka, polyachok*) or 'wretched little German' (*nemchik*), was becoming an indispensable seasoning to a Dostoyevskian Scandal. The main Scandal of *The Gambler*, which takes place when the eccentric 'Grandma' gambles away her fortune at the tables in Roulettenburg (the imaginary German town which is the scene of the novel), develops among a swarm of disreputable *polyachishki*.

As for the Germans, they are here put in their place in a theoretical tirade, along the lines of *Winter Notes on Summer Impressions*, put into the mouth of Dostoyevsky's Narrator, the 'gambler' of the title. This is a young Russian, Aleksey, who is the main mouthpiece of Dostoyevskyism in the novel. 'Into the catalogue of virtues and merits of civilized Western man,' he orates, echoing one of Dostoyevsky's favourite ideas, 'the ability to acquire capital has entered . . . as just about the most important item.' The Germans are the worst offenders here. 'I don't know which is more loathsome: Russian disorderliness or the German method of amassing money by honest toil.' But he himself would rather spend his whole life wandering around with a Kirghiz tent than bow down before the 'German idol 'I prefer to be a debauchee, Russian style, or to make my fortune at roulette'.

As well as xenophobia, Aleksey shares the addiction to strong sensation which was also so marked a characteristic of his creator. This is revealed in his relations with Polina, the heroine of the story, which reproduce the hectic atmosphere of Dostoyevsky's own second major love affair, with Apollinariya Suslova. She was an attractive girl, twenty years younger than he, whom he met in 1862 when she began to contribute stories to *Vremya*. What may have started as a casual affair soon developed into a great drama, as it became clear that Suslova was a kind of female Dostoyevsky. Like him, she preferred her love with a lacing of hatred. And she enjoyed endless 'scenes' in which she would do everything possible to torment her lover. As a purveyor of anguish she was even better equipped than his first wife.

When Dostoyevsky first met Suslova she was attending lectures at the University. In addition to her beauty and intelligence she brought extra spice to her affair with Dostoyevsky by being tainted with the 'progressive' ideas of the period to which he so strongly objected. She became his mistress in St. Petersburg in late 1862 or early 1863. Then they arranged to travel in Europe together, but Dostoyevsky had to send her on ahead owing to the chaos caused by the sudden banning of *Vremya*.

Meanwhile Suslova had not been marking time, and when in August Dostoyevsky at last managed to reach her in Paris, he found himself in a situation already familiar in his life and fiction. She was in love with someone else, Dostoyevsky having been supplanted by a good-looking young Spanish medical student called Salvador. This happy event proved a less potent source of anguish to Dostoyevsky than might have been hoped, for the Spaniard turned out too much of a weakling to sustain a thorough-paced love affair *à la Russe*. Scarcely had he seduced the girl before she found herself abandoned. It was particularly galling for her to see him one day on the streets, apparently in the best of health, shortly after he had sent word that he could not meet her because he had contracted typhus.

From now on Suslova and Dostoyevsky had to do their best without him. It was agreed that they should tour Europe 'as brother and sister', an arrangement which proved a rich source of anguish to Dostoyevsky. Suslova's idea of fraternization was to invite him into her bedroom at night, when she would appear in various stages of undress, but without permitting him to make love to her. Since she was an exceptionally attractive girl, and since Dostoyevsky's physical (as opposed to emotional) attitude to love was fairly normal, anguish must have been purveyed and received on these occasions in impressive quantities.

In the relationship between Aleksey and Polina *The Gambler* closely reproduces the atmosphere of the love affair with Suslova. Though Aleksey loves Polina to the point of anguish, and has many times offered to throw himself off a cliff to prove it, he also finds her hateful. 'There were times . . . when I would have sacrificed half my life in order to strangle her! I swear that if it had been possible to plunge a sharp knife slowly into her breast, I would, I think, have seized it with pleasure.' Polina holds him in a condition of 'humiliation and slavery', which is exactly what he wants. 'I tell you there is pleasure in the last degree of humiliation and insignificance. . . . The devil knows, perhaps there is pleasure in the *knout* as it falls on the back and tears the flesh to ribbons.' Again, as in real life, a handsome rival is supplied, for it transpires that Polina had been the mistress of the French intriguer De Grie, the Salvador of the novel.

Though Aleksey has often claimed that he would jump off a cliff if Polina should say the word, this ultimate sacrifice is not demanded of him. Instead of this she displays her perversity by requiring only that he should create a Scandal. He is to insult a fat Prussian Baroness, whom they know by sight and who happens at the appropriate moment to be taking the air of Roulettenburg with her pompous Prussian husband. Aleksey discharges the task with skill and enthusiasm, though the Baron is too taken aback at first to attack him with his stick, as Polina had hoped.

This absurd scene, managed with all the finesse which Dostoyevsky was now bringing to his Scandals, has even more amusing repercussions which involve most of the main characters. The Baron lodges a complaint with the preposterous General Zagoryansky, Polina's stepfather, in whose household Aleksey is employed as a tutor. The General now tells Aleksey that he has promised to dismiss him from his household on account of his misbehaviour to the Baron.

Dostoyevsky's Generals only exist in order to be taken down a peg, and Aleksey's reply is a masterpiece of insolence.

> General, the matter cannot end like this. I am very sorry that you have been subjected to unpleasantness from the Baron, but—you must excuse me—you have only yourself to blame. How did you come to take it upon yourself to answer for me to the Baron? What is the

meaning of the expression that I 'belong to your household'? I am
simply a tutor in your house and nothing more. I am not your son, nor
am I under your tutelage, and you are not in a position to answer for
my acts. I am myself a juridically competent person. I am twenty-five
years old, a post-graduate student of the University, a gentleman
[dvoryanin] and am completely unrelated to you. Only my unbounded
admiration for your virtues prevents me from immediately demanding
satisfaction from you.

Aleksey makes similar pompous and deliberately impertinent
threats to challenge the Baron to a duel, which complicates matters
from the General's point of view owing to the tightly woven intrigue
of love and money in which all the main characters are involved. The
General, who has mortgaged his estates to De Grie, is in love with
De Grie's accomplice Blanche, over whom the Baron has some sort
of hold. And Blanche will not agree to marry the General in his
present impecunious state. She is holding off until he gains an
expected inheritance from his aunt, the 'Grandma' of the novel,
whose death is believed to be so imminent that the General has been
sending telegram after telegram to Russia in the hope that the happy
event may already have taken place.

It is the sudden arrival of this supposedly dying Grandma which
leads to the big scene of the novel. The imperious old lady erupts
into the main hotel of the town with a retinue of servants and is
dumped in front of the horrified General, who has been imagining
her in her coffin. She may be in her second childhood and have lost
the use of her legs, but this does not prevent her having herself
carried straight off to the gambling tables, where she proceeds
ostentatiously to hazard the vast fortune on which the whole of
General Zagoryansky's future depends, brushing aside his desperate attempts to distract her with more innocent pleasures such as
the view from a famous local beauty spot. The General's attempts to
restrain her include some delicious touches. 'You are bringing shame
on the name of Russia, Madam', he shouts. 'The police must deal
with this.' But Grandma only has him chased off with a stick. She
has lost a hundred thousand roubles and become the talk of Roulettenburg before she finally takes the train back to Russia.

Hardly has Grandma disappeared from the scene when Aleksey
himself, who has so far only staked money for other people, makes
a move which he has long been planning and takes over the role of
major gambler in the novel. At his first attempt he is outstandingly

successful and leaves the casino with a small fortune, after breaking the bank at two of the tables. Already he is beginning to discover that it is not money, but sensation, which he craves. 'Perhaps the soul does not grow sated after passing through so many sensations, but is only irritated by them and demands more sensations, ever stronger and stronger until the point of final exhaustion.'

One of Aleksey's motives in gambling had been to enable Polina to pay a large sum which she owed to her former lover, the scoundrel De Grie. She appears to reject the offer. 'The mistress of De Grie is not worth fifty thousand francs!' However, her next remark ('I hate you!') forms the natural prelude to a night of love together, after which she hurls the money in his face and rushes from the room. She now seeks refuge with Mr. Astley, another of her admirers, although it is made clear later that she really loves Aleksey. But Aleksey is now in the grip of a stronger passion. 'From the moment when I touched the gambling table yesterday and began to rake in packets of money, my love seemed to retreat into the background.' Aleksey spends his winnings with true Russian abandon on a wild orgy in Paris with the complaisant Mlle Blanche, but news at last comes of Grandma's death and Blanche marries the General after all. As for Aleksey, he returns to the tables, doomed to spend the rest of his life in the grip of his obsession.

The study of gambling as an obsession is the most autobiographical feature of the novel. Dostoyevsky himself was already so much of an addict that even his eagerness to meet Suslova in Paris in summer 1863 had not stopped him from breaking his journey for four days in Wiesbaden. Here he won five thousand francs at the tables, and also discovered a system: 'one must be continually restraining oneself . . . and not get excited'.[10] But this was not a programme which Dostoyevsky was equipped to follow, and the system broke down almost as soon as it was enunciated. Many times in the coming years he would be in the same position as his Aleksey in the last lines of *The Gambler*, where he stakes his last florin. 'There really is something special about the sensation when one is alone in a foreign country, far from one's homeland and friends, and stakes one's very last florin without knowing what one is going to eat that day.'

The Gambler is a relatively light-weight work, but one which shows Dostoyevsky with a tighter grip on his own brand of fictional craft than any which have so far been discussed. In addition to the ferocious humour, riotous action and full-blooded Scandal scenes, such as had appeared earlier in his work, an important new development is to be noted: the successful description of characters who were not just so many distorted Dostoyevskys. The General, Grandma and Mlle Blanche do not stand with the great characters of his fiction, but they are alive and amusing, and do not bring the whiff of introspection which many of the important early characters carried. Even Aleksey, the self-portrait of the novel, is more independent of his author than the self-portrait characters in the early fiction. *The Gambler*'s closest links among the great novels of Dostoyevsky's maturity are with *The Idiot*, where Nastasya Filippovna emerges as a more developed Polina and is caught in a similar web of love-and-money intrigues.

CHAPTER FIVE

'CRIME AND PUNISHMENT'

DOSTOYEVSKY had flowered early as a writer of the second rank, but at the age of forty-four showed little promise of developing into one of the world's great creative artists. Now this position changes with the publication in 1866 of *Crime and Punishment*, the novel with which he attains maturity and makes the biggest stride in his career. The experimental period is over, and cogwheels which had revolved frantically without connecting are now set to drive the machine.

The transformation coincides with the choice of murder as a pivot of the plot. Murder had an importance to Dostoyevsky which can hardly be exaggerated, as the briefest consideration of the five long novels of his maturity emphasizes. One can almost call the first and last in the series detective stories—of a contrasting type. In *Crime and Punishment* the criminal's identity is revealed before the murder, the suspense hinging on his prospects of being caught, while *The Brothers Karamazov* is more of a 'whodunit', in which suspense hinges on the murderer's identity. In each novel the murder takes place at an early stage. *The Idiot* and *The Devils* less resemble a detective story or thriller, but·in each of them a murder, occurring towards the end of the narrative, forms its main climax. Finally, the remaining novel in the series (*A Raw Youth*) dispenses with murder, a significant omission, because it is surely no coincidence that *A Raw Youth* is also the weakest novel of the five. Dostoyevsky was lost without murder.

One feature of *Crime and Punishment*, surprising in the context of Dostoyevsky's previous development, is its effectiveness as a piece of construction. Hitherto he had shown little skill as a fictional architect. His best-constructed novel had been *The Village of Stepanchikovo*, but even there rambling discursions had unbalanced the main plot. His most skilful building had gone into *The House of the Dead*, where the loose form of the memoir will not blind the thoughtful reader to the careful disposition of the material. As for his only previous long novel, *Insulted and Injured*, that had shown complete incompetence in its construction. But *Crime and Punishment* suddenly confronts the reader with a masterpiece of construction, although Dostoyevsky (as was his invariable custom) was still completing the novel when large parts of it were already in print.[1] Like his other major novels it first appeared in serial form, for he could never afford to hold on to early instalments until a whole book was completed. It was, however, his habit not to venture into print until he was satisfied with the detailed plan of a novel.

Crime and Punishment owes its structural perfection to the simplicity of a plot which can be expressed in one sentence: the student Raskolnikov murders an old pawnbroker and her sister, a crime which he eventually confesses, being condemned to imprisonment in Siberia. To make a similar summary of *Insulted and Injured* or *A Raw Youth* would be impossible, a symptom of their structural inferiority.

The simplicity of the murder plot in *Crime and Punishment* goes with much complexity in the analysis of the murderer's mind, and with that persistent probing of his motives and reactions which is one of the novel's chief merits.

To the murder plot are appended two sub-plots which revolve round the misfortunes of the Marmeladov family and the love life of Raskolnikov's sister. These are as complex in their details as the central plot is simple, but their complexities are held by the pull of the central plot. The sub-plots are also free from the weight of analysis attached to the central plot. As an additional element of symmetry, each sub-plot furnishes a character of outstanding ideological importance. These are Sonya Marmeladova, personifying Dostoyevskian Good, and Svidrigaylov, the embodiment of Dostoyevskian Evil. Between them the soul of Raskolnikov swings like that of Everyman.

The novel is also a landmark as the first long work in which Dostoyevsky operates as a teacher, and because it contains for the first time a character (Sonya) who is offered as a model to the reader. The four long novels after *Crime and Punishment* all contain a figure similarly designed to serve as a model of the Dostoyevskian Good, though this is less true of *The Devils* than of the other three. Just as Sonya is followed by Dostoyevskian saints, so Svidrigaylov is followed by Dostoyevskian Satans. Central figures, oscillating between Good and Evil, offer variants of Raskolnikov's predicament,

D

and reproduce the *pas de trois* first introduced in *Crime and Punishment*.

Crime and Punishment also marks a big advance in characterization, now a powerful weapon in Dostoyevsky's armoury. The preceding works include few really effective character-studies except for the Underground Man. But in *Crime and Punishment* Dostoyevsky suddenly creates a series of unforgettable figures including both major and minor characters.

The most important portrait is that of Rodion Romanovich Raskolnikov, who so dominates the novel that he only departs from the stage on a score or so pages out of about six hundred. Early references by Dostoyevsky to the planning of the novel, and also the evidence of the Notebooks in which he shaped these plans on paper, show that he at first conceived *Crime and Punishment* as a shorter work, to be written in the first person and to embody the confession of a murderer about his crime. His later decision to switch from the first to the third person is significant of his move away from excessively introspective inspiration, such as had been carried to its logical conclusion in the 'I' novel, *Notes from Underground*.

Superficially, however, Raskolnikov does seem to be yet another 'dreamer'. He lives in a miserable 'corner', a small room with a low ceiling and peeling wallpaper at the top of a tenement in the brothel area of St. Petersburg. Into these coffin-like quarters he has 'retreated from everyone like a tortoise into its shell', having 'squashed himself up into his corner like a spider'. Even as a student he had been almost without friends and had 'avoided everyone'. Now he has left the University without completing his course, being without money and in debt to his landlady, who has cut off his food supplies. The bout of introspection in which he has 'plunged inside himself' also unites him with earlier dreamers, but its upshot, the murder, shows him in a different light. Previous dreamers had been incapable of exploding into action.

Dostoyevsky knew that he was now on a new road, and gives notice of this on the first pages of the novel, explaining that his hero is not 'cowardly and downtrodden, indeed quite the opposite'. Raskolnikov's appearance also marks him off from his more cringing forebears. 'He was remarkably good-looking, with beautiful dark eyes, of dark auburn colouring, being above middle height, slim and well-built.' He may have been a dreamer, but he was no underdog.

Raskolnikov's reason drives him to murder and rob, once fate has put in his path an ideal victim, the grasping old pawnbroker who lives nearby, tyrannizing her inoffensive half-sister and exploiting her clients. Raskolnikov thinks that he can found his future on the proceeds of his projected crime, calculated at about three thousand roubles of the old woman's savings. He will return to the University and start a career in which a hundred benefactions will wipe out a single evil deed. He also needs the old woman's money to rescue his beloved mother and sister from poverty, his decision being clinched by the news that his sister has just agreed to marry the scoundrel Luzhin in the hope of helping her brother with Luzhin's money. Thus Raskolnikov is driven to murder by the motive of philanthropy.

This philanthropic motive-stream is later intertwined with a different complex of motives, deriving from Raskolnikov's view that humanity consists of two types: a majority of feeble nonentities, and a minority of powerful figures such as Napoleon. These figures tower so high above the herd that crime means nothing to them, and their strength entitles them to commit evil to attain their aims. They have the right to transgress any moral or legal code, and do so without even giving any thought to the matter. Thus Raskolnikov commits murder in order to become a Napoleon and also (which is not quite the same thing) in order to prove to himself that he is a Napoleon.

The superman-motive, involving as it does Raskolnikov's desire to raise himself above humanity, conflicts with the philanthropic motive of helping humanity. But this is no accidental inconsistency in Raskolnikov's character, for it is precisely this inconsistency on which Dostoyevsky repeatedly insists. Raskolnikov is yet another Dostoyevskian oscillator between two contradictory positions, the inconsistencies in his character being worked out with especial subtlety. His oscillations are no longer up and down the 'humiliation slot' of the Underground Man and previous oscillators, for he is relatively free from the obsession with status which had dominated them. His oscillation swings between helping his fellowmen and turning his back on them, opposing tendencies which correspond to the philanthropic murder-motive and the superman murder-motive respectively.

Typical of this ambivalence is the incident where he is moved to pity by a young girl in a predicament of a kind familiar to Dostoyevskian young girls. Having just escaped from one debaucher, she is seen wandering the streets, hopelessly drunk, while another would-be seducer shadows her, hoping to take advantage of her helplessness. Raskolnikov calls a policeman and gives twenty copecks to help the girl. But as the policeman moves off with the girl a characteristic revulsion follows. Raskolnikov shouts: 'Leave her alone! Let him [the seducer] amuse himself.' And after they have gone he reflects angrily: 'Let them swallow each other alive—what do I care?'

Raskolnikov's ambivalence is analysed by his friend Razumikhin, who describes him as generous and kind, but sometimes cold and indifferent to the point of inhumanity, 'as if two opposite characters kept changing places inside him'. Dostoyevsky is thus again making a point already made in a different way about his Underground Man: human beings are perverse and inconsistent creatures. They are too perverse to be put in order by those Socialist or Liberal 'progressives' who had become to Dostoyevsky's mind so much the embodiment of evil that from now on much of his fiction and theoretical writing would be directed against them.

The main heresy of these ideological enemies consisted of attempting to organize human affairs 'by the mind alone'. This heresy is once more demolished in *Crime and Punishment*, a moral tale about a heretic who carries his reasoning to its logical conclusion and then acts on it, thus attempting to live 'by the mind alone'. This concept unites the seeming conflict between the two motives which led Raskolnikov to murder. Both as a would-be philanthropist and as a would-be superman he has committed the cardinal sin of behaving *rationally*, the words 'rational' and 'reasonable' having now become terms of abuse in Dostoyevsky's vocabulary.

The connection between the theory of 'rational egoism' (as Dostoyevsky sometimes describes the heresy of living by the mind alone) and murder is made explicit in *Crime and Punishment* where Raskolnikov first clashes with his sister's suitor, Luzhin. The latter, imagining that Raskolnikov (like many of his fellow-students) must be a typical 'progressive' of the period, attempts to ingratiate himself by airing progressive ideas. 'Science says: love yourself above all others, for everything in the world is founded on self-interest.' To this Raskolnikov retorts: 'Carry what you have just been preaching to its conclusion, and it will turn out that one may murder people.' This retort gains a powerful flavour of irony in its context, because this is what Raskolnikov has just done.

Among the subjects of early experiments put to effective use in
Crime and Punishment is the technique of suspense, hitherto chiefly
employed to usher in some semi-humorous Scandal. It is also used
in this way in minor scenes from *Crime and Punishment*, but comes
into its own in its impact on the central plot—the murder and its
consequences. Harnessed here to a serious and tragic theme, suspense
broods over the novel from the first page to the short epilogue at
the end. In the first of the six parts into which the novel is divided,
suspense centres in the murder, the plan for which is revealed
gradually and with great artistry from the first obscure hints of some
important 'deed' which Raskolnikov has in mind to the moment
where he makes his hazardous escape down the stairs of the tenement which is the scene of the crime.

The association of staircases with violence is intimate on Dostoyevsky's pages, especially in the breathtaking sequence of Raskolnikov's murder, an essay in suspense which was occasionally equalled
later, but never surpassed. It begins when he oversleeps the hour in
the early evening at which (as he happens to know) the victim will
be alone in her flat. After sewing a sling inside his coat to hold the
axe with which the deed is to be done, he steals downstairs, then
makes his way to the scene of the crime, where the victim has her
flat on the third floor. He kills her, but having forgotten to close the
flat door, is surprised by her half-sister, who becomes his second victim.

Now that the murder is accomplished, a new tension takes over
and is maintained in the remaining five parts of the book: will
Raskolnikov be detected? Having left no clues, he could have
escaped had it not been for his irresistible urge to betray himself.
Here the supreme exponent of reasoned logic runs true to Dostoyevskian psychology by becoming unreasoned and illogical. He seeks
out a police official in a restaurant and deliberately leads the conversation to the murder. 'What if', he asks at one stage, using a favourite
Dostoyevskian formula, 'What if it was I who killed the old
woman?' At first this is interpreted as a sign of his innocence, for
obviously no guilty man would talk in this way.

Later Raskolnikov seeks out Porfiry Petrovich, the police investigator, being drawn 'like a moth to a candle' by a desire to betray
himself. The three-stage duel with Porfiry Petrovich contributes
some particularly subtle writing, as the investigator, admitting that
he has no direct clues to the murderer's identity, explains to Raskolnikov that the unknown criminal will inevitably end by giving himself

up. Meanwhile why should he arrest him prematurely when this will only bring him relief? These scenes are marked by the use of irony, a device which Dostoyevsky had employed sparingly before *Crime and Punishment*, but which now becomes an important weapon.

In thus playing with fire Raskolnikov shows himself as an extreme sensation-craver. He extends his self-betrayal over several hundred pages, during which he commits himself more and more until he finally presents himself at the police station and confesses. His trial and eight years' imprisonment in Siberia are to follow, with the possibility of expiation through suffering.

*

As already mentioned, the main plot of *Crime and Punishment* is flanked by two sub-plots, the first of which to be considered concerns Raskolnikov's sister Dunya. Here six characters fall neatly into two trios, virtuous and evil. To the virtuous trio belong Dunya herself, her mother (Pulkheriya Aleksandrovna) and Raskolnikov's former fellow-student (Razumikhin). Evil, which (as is customary in Dostoyevsky) fields a stronger team, is represented by the nihilist Lebezyatnikov, and by two unsuccessful assaulters of Dunya's virtue: Luzhin and Svidrigaylov. Each trio contains two characters who are humorously described and one wholly serious character, so that the line-up may be expressed schematically in a way which emphasizes the symmetrical structure of the novel:

	Virtuous	Evil
Serious	Dunya	Svidrigaylov
Humorous {	Pulkheriya Aleksandrovna	Luzhin
	Razumikhin	Lebezyatnikov

In this sub-plot the virtuous team bears a light ideological load, for the main champion of Dostoyevskian Good is Sonya Marmeladova, who comes from the second sub-plot. But the virtuous trio headed by Dunya is of interest partly because all three characters are so convincingly realized, showing that Dostoyevsky could infuse life into figures who are not incarnate ideas. A new departure in Dostoyevsky's humour must also be noted. Hitherto, as has been remarked above, this had usually been aggressive and savage, but it is now linked with sympathy. Pulkheriya Aleksandrovna is an ineffectual and absurdly garrulous middle-aged woman who often appears in a comic light, but remains sympathetic, partly because her love for her son comes over so strongly. She is one of the least aggressive in the gallery of Dostoyevsky's middle-aged women.

A significant minor role is played by Razumikhin. This jolly, back-slapping extrovert corresponds to an image in which Russians like to see themselves, as creatures of broad, generous impulses with their 'soul unbuttoned' (*dusha naraspashku*). Razumikhin's inability to conceal his feelings (notably his love for Dunya, written on his face from the moment when he first meets her) is successfully used to place him in a good-humouredly comic light. Razumikhin is also interesting because of affinities with a more important later character, Dmitry Karamazov, also an ebullient 'Russian' figure, but one who carries a load of sin, from which Razumikhin is free.

R.zumikhin also shares with Dmitry Karamazov an experience denied to other Dostoyevskian heroes by participating in a love-affair which is more than an arid catalogue of love-hate oscillations. Dunya Raskolnikova is one of Dostoyevsky's least complicated heroines, a warm-hearted, honourable and intelligent girl. In portraying her Dostoyevsky is again found achieving something which students of his previous work might have considered outside his range.

Razumikhin is granted an honour denied to the other members of the virtuous trio in which he figures, being allowed some ideological load. This is shown, for example, when he takes part in a theoretical discussion on crime, speaking out against the 'progressive' theory that crime is to be viewed exclusively as a protest against bad social conditions, and that it would disappear if society came to be organized 'normally'. He also attacks the idea of a rationally organized society in language like that of the Underground Man.

Svidrigaylov heads the camp of Evil in *Crime and Punishment*, but the two lesser devils, Luzhin and Lebezyatnikov, are also fascinating figures. Luzhin represents the only large-scale attempt to portray the character-type against which the Underground Man had inveighed, the so-called 'man of action'. He is the most fully fledged specimen of the bourgeois on Dostoyevsky's pages, and carries all the stigmata of his creator's most blistering hatred, being repeatedly described by the two strongest condemnatory epithets in the Dostoyevskian vocabulary of abuse—'solid' and 'respectable'. He has built up a substantial capital by thrift and the successful promotion of his career, something unforgivable in Dostoyevsky's writings where the possession of money is always suspect. True, a man may

come into a windfall by a legacy or gambling without compromising his integrity. But the careful saving of money earned by a man's own efforts, excusable in a German (who could not be expected to know better), was intolerable in a Russian.

This recalls another paradox in Dostoyevsky's complex nature. Though a pillar of extreme political conservatism, he was an ultra-Bohemian in many ways: his debts, gambling, weird love-affairs, unwillingness to strike roots and intellectual originality. His attitude to two conservative sections of the community, 'high society' and the bourgeoisie, was contemptuous. Such was his contempt for the successful bourgeois that after Luzhin he did not even bother to describe the type again, except in a few minor figures.

It is, accordingly, the old savage humour, not the new sympathetic comedy, which surrounds Luzhin in *Crime and Punishment* in three memorable scenes, each leading to his discomfiture. The first is his interview with Raskolnikov shortly after the murder, the scene which ends with Raskolnikov's threat to throw him 'head over heels downstairs'. Attempts to revenge himself by maligning Raskolnikov to his mother and sister lead to another quarrel in which Dunya breaks off her engagement. Finally, his plan to frame Sonya, and thus revenge himself on Raskolnikov, by planting a hundred-rouble note on her and then accusing her of theft, is thwarted by Lebezyatnikov in the riotous celebration which follows Marmeladov's funeral.

Of all Dostoyevsky's characters Luzhin seems to be the one most hated by his creator, who almost trips over himself in doing Luzhin down. As the novel progresses Luzhin becomes less and less convincing, ending almost as a villain of melodrama. It is curious that Dostoyevsky did not betray such personal hatred when portraying representatives of ultimate Evil like Svidrigaylov. The reason for this may be that Svidrigaylov was at least ideologically engaged, if on the wrong side, while Luzhin's ideological engagement begins and ends with considerations of his personal comfort.

Dostoyevsky's conception of 'comfort' is important to the idea-structure of *Crime and Punishment*, since this word belongs, like 'reasonable', 'solid', and 'respectable', to the vocabulary of abuse. Here again Razumikhin acts as the mouthpiece. For example, he accuses Dostoyevsky's political opponents (the 'rational egoism' school) of reducing all human problems to the question of comfort. The theme also occurs in Razumikhin's tirade to a minor character, the comfort-loving young doctor Zosimov, whom he advises to cultivate Raskolnikov's landlady, noted as a purveyor of creature-comforts.

> Here is the principle of the feather-bed. . . . This is the world's end, an anchor, a quiet harbour . . . the essence of pancakes and pies with plenty of fat, of a samovar in the evening, quiet sighs and warm, fur-trimmed jackets and warm couches—just as if you'd died, but are alive all the same.

As this passage indicates, the condemned principle of comfort is opposed to the approved principle of 'life'. Here one is reminded of Dostoyevsky's comment on his courtship of his first wife—'I may have suffered, but I've lived'—for the concept of 'life' was closely bound up with the other approved concept of suffering. A man should not step outside the battles of life, with their attendant sufferings, to anaesthetize himself with the living death of comfort. Thus Raskolnikov, despite his crime, is ultimately justified by his involvement in 'life', whereas Luzhin, too prudent and comfort-loving ever to bang an old woman on the head with an axe, is ulti-mately condemned. Accordingly when the investigator Porfiry Petrovich advises Raskolnikov to confess and accept his punish-ment, he pays him the highest compliment by remarking: 'You're not one to pine for comfort—you, with your heart.'

Lebezyatnikov, the second character from the camp of Evil to be discussed, is a minor figure, but of some importance as the first fully developed nihilist on Dostoyevsky's pages. From now on nihilists were to be a permanent ingredient in his fiction, figuring in each of the four long novels after *Crime and Punishment*.

Lebezyatnikov is the most comic figure in *Crime and Punishment* because he preaches ideological heresy in and out of season and persists in applying his superficial formulae to the profound prob-lems of the major characters. This is seen at its most comic where he discusses Sonya Marmeladova who has heroically taken up prostitu-tion to support a dying stepmother with three young children. In doing so, Sonya, according to Lebezyatnikov, is making legitimate use of her 'capital, of which she has the full right to dispose'. He looks on her way of life as an 'energetic . . . protest against the organization of society', for which he deeply respects her.

As a true nihilist, Lebezyatnikov supports the principle of free love—to such an extent that if he should ever marry he would not

D*

merely permit his wife to take a lover, but would insist on it. ' "My darling," I'd tell her, "I love you, but I also want you to respect me." ' He enunciates a basic creed in nihilist faith by claiming the cleaning of cesspits to be 'much more noble, for example, than the activity of some Raphael or Pushkin because it is more useful'. Although he does not know any other language, Lebezyatnikov cannot express himself in decent Russian. This taint, symbolic of estrangement from the Russian soil and of the foreign origin of nihilist ideas, would later be given to other heretics.

For all the scorn poured on Lebezyatnikov's ideas, Dostoyevsky does not express equal contempt for him as a person, having a soft spot for the young and ardent. Even if the young nihilists of the period were backing the wrong ideological horse, it was at least to their credit that they had placed a bet. So Dostoyevsky gives Lebezyatnikov an important role in unmasking Luzhin, who lacks the redeeming qualities of youth, ardour and ideological zeal.

Arkady Ivanovich Svidrigaylov, the senior representative of Evil in *Crime and Punishment*, is the second in the line of Dostoyevskian Bogeymen which begins with Prince Valkovsky in *Insulted and Injured*. Like other Bogeymen, Svidrigaylov receives a build-up in which the reader is primed with crimes, misdeeds and acts of violence committed in the period before the novel begins. The build-up proceeds in an atmosphere of mystery, hints and half-statements. Was Svidrigaylov guilty, for example, of driving to suicide a four-teen-year-old deaf and dumb girl? Was the 'cruel insult' which led to the suicide rape? Had he also driven his servant Filipp to his death 'from torments' six years previously? Did he poison his wife, Marfa Petrovna? Not all these points are cleared up by the end, but the reader is clearly invited to give a mental verdict of 'guilty', though the only fully substantiated item on the list of Svidrigaylov's misdemeanours is the minor charge of insulting Dunya with a 'disgusting proposal' when she was a governess in his household.

The vital point about Svidrigaylov is that he belongs to the class of Napoleonic supermen which Raskolnikov proves to weak too join. He is like the 'strong personalities' which Dostoyevsky had described in *The House of the Dead*, figures of such strength of character that they could commit crimes without a hint of remorse.

Svidrigaylov's chief addiction is the cultivation of lust, and here his main target is Dunya. Having overheard Raskolnikov's confession of his murder to Sonya (this eavesdropping theme is a hang-over from earlier and less successful works) he uses this as a lever to trap her in a locked room. But unluckily for him Dostoyevskian seductions are only permitted to be carried out in a build-up phase. Though frequently foreshadowed and projected, they are never permitted to take place when they form part of the main narrative. After Dunya has twice fired a revolver at him unsuccessfully, he permits her to depart unscathed in a melodramatic scene, the weakest (as has often been remarked) in the novel.

Dostoyevsky could create a monster of wickedness, but, as the example of Svidrigaylov shows, often did not know what to do with him once created. Paradoxically enough, Svidrigaylov's impact on the action is philanthropic, when he settles money on the orphaned Marmeladov children and assists Sonya to give up prostitution and follow Raskolnikov to Siberia. The paradox may have been intended to make a point not brought out in the novel, but already an implicit article of Dostoyevsky's faith: a person's acts are not important, but his state of mind is. This is demonstrated by the contrast between Sonya (the saint who engages in prostitution) and Svidrigaylov (the wicked man who does good).

The most memorable scene associated with Svidrigaylov is that of his suicide. This, the first big Dostoyevskian suicide, was later followed by other impressive suicides, those of Kirillov, Stavrogin and Smerdyakov. But none of these makes such an impact as the scene of Svidrigaylov's death, in which Dostoyevsky chills the spine with an emphasis on trivial squalor set in contrast with the awfulness of the deed. On the previous night Svidrigaylov takes a room in a sordid suburban hotel, where he passes a few restless hours beset by nightmares—about a mouse which gets inside his shirt, about the young girl whom he had driven to suicide, about another girl, aged five, whose face assumes the expression of a prostitute, thus reviving the pervasive theme of infantile sexuality. Between nightmares he wakens and, hearing the cannon which warns the inhabitants of the city that flood water is rising in the Neva, thinks of rats floating out of the flooded cellars. He finds flies buzzing round a plate of veal which he had ordered the previous night, and after trying in vain to kill one, walks out into the thick mist of the St. Petersburg dawn and shoots himself by the side of a policeman.

In keeping with the mystery surrounding Dostoyevskian Bogeymen no clear indication is given of the motive for the suicide. But the reader is expected to draw a lesson along the following lines. As has been indicated above, Svidrigaylov is the strong figure into which Raskolnikov vainly sought to turn himself, for Svidrigaylov has repeatedly been found capable of that unique act of strength which had been beyond Raskolnikov: the casual crime not followed by regrets or agonized self-questioning. But instead of leading to the grandiose career of a Napoleon, this very strength had only brought intolerable boredom and triviality. This becomes clearer when one compares Svidrigaylov with his near relative, Stavrogin in *The Devils*, who combines supreme strength of will with supreme boredom in terms which are made more explicit.

Like Stavrogin, Svidrigaylov is a non-ideological figure of evil, being free from the political and social heresies which Dostoyevsky pillories in Lebezyatnikov. Here *The Devils* reproduces in more developed form the pattern of evil in *Crime and Punishment* by providing a representative of ideological evil in Pyotr Verkhovensky and a representative of non-ideological evil in Stavrogin. Svidrigaylov's indifference to ideology is not put forward as a reason for his suicide in the text of *Crime and Punishment*, but the idea was in Dostoyevsky's mind as is shown by a passage from the Notebooks in which he planned the novel: 'Svidrigaylov. If I had been a socialist, then of course I'd have gone on living, because there would have been something to do.'[2]

Recognizing in Svidrigaylov one pole of his own oscillatory nature, Raskolnikov is both fascinated and repelled by him. They are both 'berries off the same field', as Svidrigaylov tells him on one occasion, using a common Russian idiom. Among the complex of motives leading to Raskolnikov's confession is that he must be punished or himself turn into a second Svidrigaylov. 'Either a bullet in the forehead or the road to Vladimir' (the first stage of the journey on which convicts were sent to Siberia) is the form in which the predicament presents itself to him.

＊

At an early stage in the planning of *Crime and Punishment*, Dostoyevsky had in mind two separate works, one to be called *The Drunkards* (presumably with Marmeladov as the main hero) and the other to be a murderer's confession. The two plans eventually coalesced in *Crime and Punishment*, where the second of the two sub-plots revolves around the misfortunes of the Marmeladov family. Here structural symmetry is again preserved, since this sub-plot has three major characters, of whom two (Marmeladov and Katerina Ivanovna) have comic elements, while the third (Sonya) is serious. Thus the character trio in the Marmeladov sub-plot reproduces the pattern of each of the two character trios which perform in the Dunya sub-plot.

The Marmeladovs belong to the 'Poor Folk' strain in Dostoyevsky's work. Marmeladov, the head of the household, takes the reader back in spirit to Russian literature of the eighteen-forties, the heyday of the poor clerk as a fictional hero. He is thus a descendant of Dostoyevsky's first hero, Makar Devushkin, with whom he shares distinguishing marks. He holds the same grade in Government service, that of titular councillor, by common consent among Russian authors and readers the most comic and pathetic grade in the 'table of ranks'. And the buttons of his coat, like Devushkin's, tend to hang by a thread.

Unlike Devushkin, Marmeladov has a compulsive vice—drunkenness—the motive-force behind his drinking being of interest as a comment on his creator. Marmeladov drinks, not to drown his sorrows, but to increase them. 'I drink because I wish to suffer doubly.' As a true Dostoyevskian character he opts for intensified, not for dulled, sensation.

Marmeladov is used to drive home the lesson that man is a wayward creature who refuses to act in the mechanical way dictated by rational egoism. Rational egoism would have kept Marmeladov slogging away at his titular councillor's desk, where he might have earned enough money to support his consumptive wife, Katerina Ivanovna, and his wife's three children by a former marriage. He could also have kept Sonya, his own daughter by a former marriage, off the streets. But Marmeladov is a human being, not a piece of mechanism. Obtaining employment as a clerk after a period without work, he has not long brought home his first month's salary in triumph to his wife, before he has stolen the money from the trunk where she has hidden it and disappeared on a drinking bout during which he pawns his civil servant's uniform. He is even base enough to go to Sonya, after running through this money, and to borrow some of her immoral earnings to spend on the 'hair of the dog'. It is not callousness, but a desire to revel in his own degradation which causes him to behave in this way.

Marmeladov's obsession with his own baseness leads him to buttonhole Raskolnikov and explain his history in public in the tavern scene at the beginning of the novel. Here the 'chorus reactions' of the audience are typical concomitants of a Dostoyevskian Scandal. It is characteristic that two disreputable youths behind the bar should 'emit a snort of laughter' at the crucial moment where Marmeladov tells how his daughter has been compelled to 'go on the yellow ticket' (to take up prostitution).

Wishing to be humiliated before an audience, Marmeladov persuades Raskolnikov to accompany him to the home where he has not been seen since disappearing on his drinking orgy several days previously. Marmeladov falls on his knees and the frenzied Katerina Ivanovna drags him into the room by his hair, while he screams 'I enjoy this as well.' This is Marmeladov's only appearance except for the scene where, misfortune-prone to the last, he is involved in a street accident and trampled to death by horses' hooves.

Katerina Ivanovna is a fitting mate for Marmeladov, being equally misfortune-prone, though her misfortunes are less self-induced. Like Marmeladov, she poses some unanswerable questions about Dostoyevsky's humour. To stress unduly the comic elements in this grotesque couple would seem callous, while to deny their presence would be ridiculous. The pair represent the *reductio ad absurdum* of the hackneyed Russian critical formula, 'laughter through tears'. Whatever else may be said about the Marmeladovs and similar Dostoyevskian 'Poor Folk', it is impossible to accept the contention, sometimes expressed in Russian interpretations, that these figures represent an attempt at social criticism in which Dostoyevsky 'unmasked' an unjust system. Perhaps it is best not to attempt a final explanation of these nightmare figures, but to accept them as an explosion of Dostoyevsky's fertile imagination.

Katerina Ivanovna presents the fullest study of mental derangement since *The Double*. Prominent in the build-up of her insanity are her memories of youth and of the great event of her life when, as a schoolgirl, she had been invited to dance in front of a Provincial Governor, receiving for this a gold medal and a 'certificate of merit'. This certificate tends to turn up in the Scandals in which she is involved, heightening the absurd effect. Then there are her delusions of retiring to the country and starting a boarding-school for daughters of the nobility.

Katerina Ivanovna plays her part in the polemic against 'rational egoism' by her irrational decision to spend money given to her by

Raskolnikov (the only funds in her possession) not on food for her starving children, but on giving her husband an unnecessarily respectable funeral which turns out not respectable at all. She decides to follow convention by holding a 'commemorative banquet' (*pominki*) after the interment, and thus sets the scene for the only large-scale Scandal in the novel, an episode in which the grotesque and the pathetic appear in potent combination.

The episode begins in a manner typical of the Scandal, with a roll-call in which the identity of the main participants is indicated. One pathetic feature of the occasion is that Katerina Ivanovna has prevailed only upon the more disreputable of her fellow-lodgers to do honour to her husband. So the list of guests begins with a 'miserable little Pole' (*polyachok*), always an indicator of improprieties to come, especially as this one brings in his train two gatecrashers, also 'miserable little Poles'. Then there is a 'disgusting little chancery clerk . . . in a grease-stained tail-coat, covered with blackheads and with a repulsive smell'. Other guests include a drunken retired Lieutenant and a 'certain personage', who actually appears in a dressing-gown and so has to be thrown out before the proceedings have begun. The guests also include Katerina Ivanovna's absurd landlady, with whom she is in permanent feud and who is continually threatening to throw the family out of the flat. Thus the expulsion theme is already prominent before the fur has even begun to fly. The landlady (Amaliya Lippewechsel) is a German, so that both the Polish and the German element are represented in the roll-call phase, a rare combination, and an indication to those attuned to the niceties of the Scandal that a particularly rich recipe is being put to simmer.

The roll-call concludes with the characteristic formula: 'Such a beginning did not presage a good end.' Nor did it. The ensuing Scandal is both painful and comic. It begins to warm up as a drunken guest makes indecorous reference to Marmeladov's drinking habits and to Katerina Ivanovna's custom of dragging him about by his hair. The deranged woman tries to defend her husband, pointing out that he may have been drunk at the time of his accident with the horses, but a gingerbread cockerel had been found in his pocket, showing that he had not forgotten the children. The 'certificate of merit' is produced and goes the rounds among the tipsy guests, while Katerina Ivanovna develops her fantasy about starting a boarding-school. Her proposal to give Sonya a post on the staff produces a typical 'chorus reaction': 'Someone at the end of the table gave a snort.'

As the improprieties thicken, the absurd landlady once more orders the family to vacate the flat and begins collecting the silver spoons from the table. But this is only the beginning, for it is Dostoyevsky's custom to pile crisis on crisis in his Scandal scenes. A familiar formula makes its appearance: 'At that moment the door opened . . . ' It is now that Luzhin appears (this being one of the moments at which the two sub-plots of *Crime and Punishment* cross) and accuses Sonya of having stolen a hundred-rouble note, an episode which has already been discussed. The Scandal of the funeral feast has an even more painful sequel, for the German landlady actually does turn Katerina Ivanovna out of the house. The poor mad-woman puts her three children into improvised fancy dress and tries to make them sing and dance on the street in order to collect money from passers-by. A rumour that she is using a frying-pan as a percussion instrument to accompany the performance turns out to be unfounded.

The sequence ends with Katerina Ivanovna's death. On her death-bed she refuses to see a priest: 'I have no sins. God must forgive me anyway. . . . He knows how I have suffered! . . . And if he doesn't forgive me it doesn't matter.'

As the senior representative of Good in the novel, Sonya Marmela-dova is not given the farcical aura which surrounds her father and stepmother, but is portrayed as a serious figure. To the principle of ultimate self-assertion represented by Svidrigaylov she opposes ultimate self-abasement. She confronts Svidrigaylov's atheism with a fervent belief in God, now a prominent axiom of Dostoyevskyism.

In attempting to embody the ideal of Christian meekness in Sonya, Dostoyevsky set himself a problem which he was not yet equipped to solve. He did succeed in making her convincingly meek, but meek to the point of anaemia. It was not until his last novel that he at last hit on a successful technique for the portrayal of the Dostoyevskian Good, free from the sickly timidity which he laid on Sonya with a trowel.

Sonya also suffers from an atmosphere of theatricality in her dealings with Raskolnikov. This is found in the first of their dia-logues, in which he bows down and kisses her foot, an act to which Dostoyevsky seems to have attached special significance, to judge from the frequency with which it is recorded in his fiction and biography. The over-theatrical atmosphere of the scene is emphasized in a comment which follows the reading of a passage from the Gospels : 'The candle-stub had long been dying in the twisted holder, dimly illuminating in this miserable room the murderer and the prostitute, strangely united in their reading of the eternal book.'

In the same spirit is the demand which Sonya makes of Raskolnikov after he has confessed to her that he is a murderer. 'Go to the cross-roads, bow down to the people, kiss the earth . . . and say aloud to the whole world: "I am a murderer!" ' Attempting to carry out these instructions, Raskolnikov does get as far as kissing the earth, but refrains from making his public confession after a youth, standing nearby, has uttered a colloquial comment for which the nearest English equivalent might be: 'Cor, 'e's pickled!' This is one of the moments when Dostoyevsky the moralist and Dostoyevsky the artist clash, for the moralist was always showing signs of taking wing and needed to be brought back to earth by some similar natural touch.

A less skilful artist than Dostoyevsky might have spoiled *Crime and Punishment* by allowing Sonya to convert Raskolnikov too easily. But this is not what happens, as is revealed in the passages where Raskolnikov harangues her about his crime. The main point is that he remains unrepentant. He is prepared to follow Sonya's teaching by confessing and expiating his crime, but this does not mean that he has abandoned his theory of the superman who is entitled to commit crimes. It only means that he has discovered that he himself does not happen to be such a superman. Nor can he even bring himself to regard the murder of the pawnbroker as a crime.

'Crime! What crime?' he shouted in a sudden access of fury. 'The fact that I killed a loathsome, pernicious louse, that wretched old pawnbroker, a creature of use to nobody, whose killing merits the forgiveness of forty sins, who sucked the juice out of the poor—and you call that a crime!'

When discovered in the Epilogue a year and a half later and with nine months of Siberia behind him, Raskolnikov is still unrepentant. 'Oh, how happy he would have been if he could have blamed himself!' But he cannot. However, towards the end of the Epilogue Dostoyevsky begins to indicate a transformation which will eventually end Raskolnikov's isolation from the human community. This isolation had been especially marked by his inability in prison to make contact with the common people (*narod*), the class to which most of his fellow-prisoners belonged. Instinctively recognizing him as an opponent of Dostoyevskyism, the common people hate him, condemning his crime on sociological grounds. Raskolnikov belongs to the privileged upper classes, so what does he mean by usurping the privileges of the *narod* and going round waving an axe? They also condemn his atheism in terms which, whether intentionally comic on Dostoyevsky's part or not, show how easily outrageous elements could occur in his conception of Christianity: 'You don't believe in God! You ought to be killed!'

Finally, on the last two pages of the novel, intimations are given of Raskolnikov's 'resurrection'. The common people, sensing his conversion to Dostoyevskyism, now no longer hate him. 'Instead of dialectics, *life* had begun.' The novel concludes:

> But now begins a new story, the story of the gradual renewal of a man, the story of his gradual rebirth, of his gradual passage from one world to another, of how he got to know a new and hitherto entirely unfamiliar reality. This could form the theme of a new story—but our present story is ended.

CHAPTER SIX

'THE IDIOT' AND 'THE ETERNAL HUSBAND'

BY the middle eighteen-sixties Dostoyevsky's inability to look after himself seemed to have increased. Tormented by frequent epileptic fits (which sometimes left him prostrated for days), juggling with his debts to dozens of creditors, often reduced to writing humiliating letters asking for loans, and now in the grip of his new addiction to gambling—he apparently faced a future in which these involvements would overwhelm him entirely.

In fact, however, his ill health and incompetence in practical affairs concealed vast resources of courage and resilience, so that inability to take care of himself did not prevent from from trying to care for others. He nursed his sick wife Marya devotedly in the final stages of her disease, and looked after his stepson Pasha, now a feckless youth in his middle 'teens, to whom he unsuccessfully directed much sound advice on the advantages of an orderly and sensible life.

With the sudden death of his brother Mikhail, Dostoyevsky's responsibilities had increased. He took over his brother's commitments and the care of the bereaved family, thus further increasing his debts. His letters of the period often express the fear of being sent to the debtors' prison.

It is at this stage in his life that he at last weakens in his role as a seeker of sensation by looking for a second wife among young women of less anguish-provoking character than his first wife or Apollinariya Suslova. The search was at first unsuccessful, and two candidates had turned down his proposals of marriage before, in October, 1866, he met Anna Grigoryevna Snitkina.

The meeting was the happiest accident of his life, and typical of the switchback progress of his fortunes in being the result of a particularly menacing crisis. He had signed an absurd contract with an unscrupulous publisher on terms which obliged him to produce a new short novel by 1st November, 1866, on pain of relinquishing all rights over his work, past and future, for nine years. Casual as ever, he ignored this threat until the beginning of October, when he suddenly realized that he must produce a story of some two hundred pages in about four weeks. This seemed an impossibility until the idea was put to him that he might make use of a new-fangled invention called shorthand. The novel—*The Gambler*, which was discussed in Chapter Four—was completed on time, and it was early in the following year that Dostoyevsky married Anna, the stenographer whom he had engaged to help him.

Anna was twenty-five years younger than her husband, which might have seemed a poor augury for the marriage, and not the only one. Together with Dostoyevsky she also married his crises of emotion, bad health and debts, being compelled to become by turns nurse, mother, child, lover, accountant, secretary and business-manager.

The marriage was given an inauspicious start by the attitude of the groom's stepson and of his new dependants, the widow and children of his brother Mikhail, who felt that their financial support should have first claim on Dostoyevsky's energies. They went out of their way to set him against his young bride, and with some success because he was not a difficult man to impose on. Dostoyevsky and Anna hoped to escape from family quarrels, and also from his creditors, by going to live abroad, a plan which his relatives tried to thwart by claiming what little ready money he could lay his hands on. Anna helped to solve the problem by selling furniture and clothes which she had brought as her dowry, and in April, 1867, she and Dostoyevsky left Russia, beginning a period of over four years' residence in Germany, Switzerland and Italy.

Anna might have been sent by providence to bring into Dostoyevsky's life as much order and emotional stability as he was capable of sustaining. As is shown by his letters to her (since published, but certainly not intended for publication) and by her memoirs, theirs was a union of physical and emotional love which continued to grow closer during their fourteen years' life together.

Her importance to Dostoyevsky was as his beloved wife and the mother of his children, but she also had an influence on his literary evolution. A new rhythm of creative work was evolved, whereby Dostoyevsky planned at night and dictated to his wife during the day, all his remaining novels being written in this way. She eventually turned herself into his publisher, thus saving him from the exploitation which had commonly been his lot. In the end she even managed to tidy up some of his financial involvements after a long series of running battles with his creditors.

Anna Dostoyevskaya survived her husband by nearly forty years (she died in 1918), and after his death devoted herself to cultivating his literary memory. Her own memoirs and the memoirs of Dostoyevsky which she encouraged others to write, together with the preservation of his Notebooks and her work on his bibliography, have helped to salvage much information which would otherwise have been lost. Like most cults this was allowed to get out of hand, as when she erased in indelible ink the numerous passages in Dostoyevsky's letters to her where he used the intimate language of the bedroom. But her services to Dostoyevskian scholarship outweigh this unfortunate result of her natural modesty.

She was an unimaginative and ordinary person, no intellectual mate for Dostoyevsky and little concerned with the battle of ideas which raged inside his head. Her tact and business sense were well above average, but were commonplace qualities beside his towering genius. However, her very ordinariness helped to make her an ideal complement to him.

*

To the four years (April, 1867–July, 1871) spent in Western Europe belong *The Idiot* and *The Devils*, of which the latter was completed on Russian soil, although the greater part of the work was done abroad.

Like their predecessor, *Crime and Punishment*, these two novels were published in the Moscow monthly *Russky Vestnik*, of which the proprietor was the well-known conservative publicist M. N. Katkov. It was on advances from Katkov that Dostoyevsky chiefly depended to meet his living expenses during his four years' stay abroad. He was sincerely grateful to Katkov for making these advances against work which (as was not difficult to predict) would inevitably be completed long after the promised date. No other editor showed such patience, and Katkov was rewarded by becoming the first to publish Dostoyevsky's four greatest novels, for *The Brothers Karamazov* was later added to the previous three masterpieces.

Katkov's patience must have been tried during this period, especially at those moments when Dostoyevsky came close to blackmailing him. 'I'll write to Katkov at once and ask him to send me another 500 roubles . . . ' Dostoyevsky wrote to his wife in May, 1867. 'He will frown of course, but he'll give it to me. Having already given me so much (3,000 roubles), he won't refuse this. In fact he hardly can refuse—for how on earth can I finish my work without money?'[1]

It will be remembered that Dostoyevsky had depended on such advances almost from the beginning of his career as an author. The system was disadvantageous to him financially (as he himself continually claimed), since he could have obtained better terms for work already completed, but it is seriously arguable that his creative powers were somehow liberated by the atmosphere of debts and deadlines in which his work was written.

In demanding advances Dostoyevsky conformed with a code of honour. 'When I've received money in advance I have always sold something existing, i.e. I've only sold myself at a point when the poetic idea has already been born and has ripened as far as possible. I have not taken money in advance *for a blank space*, i.e. in the hope of *thinking up* and *composing* a novel by a given date.'[2]

However many advances he might receive, and however much his young wife's common sense might now be helping to put his affairs to rights, Dostoyevsky's financial history during his four years' stay abroad continued in an atmosphere of crisis. He sometimes even had to pawn his underclothes and trousers. Although it was more bad management than actual poverty which caused these crises, he had long come to regard himself as a 'literary proletarian', contrasting himself with more fortunately placed writers among his contemporaries, such as Tolstoy, Turgenev and Goncharov, who had financial means which freed them from dependence on advances.

Some interesting passages in his correspondence are devoted to this theme, especially one where, in the summer of 1870, he discusses a new novel which he then planned—*The Devils*. 'I know that if I had two or three years' [financial] security for my novel—like Turgenev, Goncharov or Tolstoy—then I too would write the sort of thing that people would still be talking about in a hundred years' time!'[3] This passage is one among many which remind one of Dostoyevsky's continuing humility about his position in the Russian literary hierarchy. He tended to regard himself as a writer of the second grade who might possibly have reached top rank if only external circumstances had been more propitious. This modesty about his literary achievement contrasts with the hint of arrogance often present when he made pronouncements in the sphere of politics, religion or sociology. He thus made extravagant claims for himself in precisely those areas where his achievement was least impressive, while remaining diffident about his supreme achievement.

Gambling continued a major preoccupation during his four years in Western Europe. He often left his wife behind when he went on gambling expeditions, taking the train to some distant town which possessed a casino. Soon he would be writing to say that he had lost all his money. Would Anna please send money for his hotel bill and train fare? Then he would be writing again to say that the new money had no sooner been received than it too had been lost in another orgy at the tables . . . but that he had at last learned his lesson and proposed to give up gambling.

When this ritual was repeated at Wiesbaden in the spring of 1871, and Dostoyevsky once more wrote to Anna that he had finally conquered the obsession which had tormented him for close on a decade, she can have had no more reason to believe him than on previous occasions when such protestations had been made. But Dostoyevsky was, as ever, unpredictable, this time keeping his word. He never gambled again. This marks the second important step away from the Bohemianism of his youth and early middle-age, the first having been his marriage to Anna Grigoryevna. Financial self-torment was now going the way of sexual self-torment.

During this period Dostoyevsky was permanently homesick. He felt himself an exile, believing that his Russian creditors would have him thrown into prison as a debtor if he should cross the Russian frontier. It was his constant hope during his stay abroad to earn enough money from his writings to meet these Russian debts, and thus to make it possible for him to return. But his return was repeatedly held up, while all the time he found Western Europe 'worse than Siberia', and felt as if he and his wife were marooned on a desert island. Their life was indeed solitary, for they not only avoided local society, but also shunned their own compatriots.

Dostoyevsky also found his creative impulses stifled by long absence from Russia. Like all the great Russian fiction-writers, he was chiefly interested in portraying his own country in a contemporary setting. Hence the prevalence during his four years' exile of such complaints as: 'There is no Russian life, there are no Russian impressions around me—and for my work this is always necessary.'[4] 'I have absolutely got to return to Russia. Here I shall even lose my capacity for writing, not having to hand my perpetual and essential material for writing—that is, Russian reality (which provides me with ideas) and Russian people.'[5] He tried to make Russian newspapers a substitute for his native land, but found them unsatisfactory.

> *Every day* I read *three Russian newspapers down to the last line* and I take two magazines. But I shall be left behind by the *living stream of life*—not by the idea, but by its flesh, and that has a terrific effect on artistic work.[6]

•

The Idiot was begun in Switzerland in 1868 and finished in Italy in early 1869. It contrasts with Dostoyevsky's preceding master-piece, *Crime and Punishment*. Having there taken a firm hold on the technique of tightly knit construction, Dostoyevsky now slackens his grip, for *The Idiot* is a string of episodes rather than a unified work of art. But Dostoyevsky is here found penetrating further into his own peculiar territory, so that by comparison with the best parts of *The Idiot* even the extraordinary *Crime and Punishment* seems ordinary. Clearly *Crime and Punishment* is the better novel. But it is not quite so clear that it is the greater achievement.

The hero of *The Idiot* is Prince Myshkin, to whom all the other characters are foils and who presents a fascinating problem. Like its predecessor, *The Idiot* is a one-hero novel, for just as Raskolnikov had been present in almost every scene of *Crime and Punishment*, so Myshkin is almost everywhere present here.

Raskolnikov had been one of Dostoyevsky's 'sinners', capable of redemption, this point being touched on in the Epilogue to the novel, where Dostoyevsky said that 'it might form the theme for a new story, but our present story is finished'. He had devoted over six hundred pages to Raskolnikov's crime but less than six lines to his moral rebirth. To an author who was now setting up as a moralist this emphasis might seem a poor advertisement, implying that he was more interested in evil than in good and more concerned with diagnosis than with cure. Such considerations must have led him to conceive the hero of *The Idiot*, in contrast to Raskolnikov, as a 'positively good man', though it was not until a late stage in the planning that this conception became prominent. Because of it *The Idiot* can be regarded as the 'new story' to which Dostoyevsky refers in the last sentence of *Crime and Punishment*.

When he decided to create a good man, Dostoyevsky was not the first writer of fiction to have found himself portraying negative characters, whether criminal or merely vulgar and trivial, more successfully than positive figures. In English literature the example of Dickens suggests itself. Among Russian writers, Gogol had actually driven himself mad by trying to create virtuous characters, while it seemed that his pen could only describe the grotesque and vulgar.

Would Dostoyevsky succeed where Gogol had failed? He knew that he had taken on a difficult task.

> The main idea of the novel [he wrote in a letter of January, 1868] is to depict a positively good man. There is nothing more difficult in this world, and especially at the present time. All writers—not only ours, but even all European ones—who have set themselves to depict the *positively* good have always given up. . . . Of good figures in Christian literature the most perfect is Don Quixote. But he is good only because he is also ridiculous at the same time. Dickens's Pickwick (an infinitely weaker conception than Don Quixote, but nevertheless an immense one) is also ridiculous—and that is the only source of his appeal. Pity is aroused for the Good which is mocked and does not know its own value, and the reader's sympathy is consequently also awakened. It is this evocation of sympathy which constitutes the secret of humour. Jean Valjean is also an impressive attempt, but he arouses sympathy by his terrible ill-fortune and by the injustice of society to him. I have nothing like this [in *The Idiot*], absolutely nothing, and so I am terribly afraid of an out-and-out failure.[7]

Here Dostoyevsky suggests that his own 'good man', in contrast with those of Dickens and Cervantes, was not conceived as a comic figure. This agrees with the findings of the many critics who have seen Myshkin as a serious character, and as a serious presentation of an ethical ideal. To mention this is to be reminded of the wide variety of interpretations to which Dostoyevsky lends himself, and it also reminds one that there are few concepts in literature more controversial and elusive than humour. The view which will be put forward here is that Myshkin is a comic figure. As for the suggestion sometimes made that he represents a serious ethical ideal, this is perhaps the richest piece of comedy about him. However, it would be wrong to overstate the case. To suggest that Myshkin is wholly comic would be as mistaken as to claim that he is wholly serious. It is not possible to determine the exact degree of admixture of these two elements in Myshkin, a fact which is partly responsible for the fascination of the problem. But that Myshkin does contain at least some humorous elements seems difficult to deny. These have perhaps never been better illustrated than by the suggestion that, in a film version of *The Idiot*, the ideal interpreter of Myshkin would be Charlie Chaplin.[8]

The interpretation of Myshkin as a humorous character has the important defect that it contradicts Dostoyevsky's own intentions for his hero, as implied in the letter quoted above and also in his rough notes for the novel. In these he again claims that Pickwick and Don Quixote succeed 'because they are comic'. As for Myshkin, 'if he is not comic, he does have another sympathetic quality—he is innocent'.[9] Though Dostoyevsky here expresses himself hypothetically ('*if* he is not comic'), it is clear that he did not in fact regard the matter as hypothetical. Myshkin was intended as a serious figure.

That the comic interpretation of Myshkin clashes so directly with Dostoyevsky's own conception of his hero is a less serious objection than such a conflict would be in the case of many other authors. For Dostoyevsky was so often at cross-purposes with himself. Although he often sought to adopt an attitude of unmixed reverence, such an attitude was not easy for him to sustain. Sooner or later involuntary promptings led him to stick pins in his own idols, to 'put out his tongue', as Prince Valkovsky had been made to say in *Insulted and Injured*, at the Good and the Beautiful.

In Myshkin, Dostoyevsky did his best to embody an ethical model, even a sort of reincarnated nineteenth-century Christ, but Myshkin might have been a less impressive creation if this attempt had been sustained. A novelist never treads a more slippery path than when he tries to provide models for his fellow-men to follow. Novelists who have attempted this, such as Socialist Realist writers of the Soviet period with their idealized portraits of 'Soviet Man', have usually made themselves and their model men look equally ridiculous. Dostoyevsky, like most great writers, seems to have been born to provide exceptions to literary rules, and later trod even this dangerous territory, providing a model more acceptable than Myshkin when he created Alyosha Karamazov. But Alyosha is a less effective literary character than Myshkin.

It is instructive to compare Myshkin with Alyosha Karamazov and the other figures who complete the gallery of six Good characters in the novels of Dostoyevsky's maturity. Myshkin had been preceded by Sonya Marmeladov in *Crime and Punishment*, and was to be followed by Shatov in *The Devils*, Makar Dolgoruky in *A Raw Youth* and Father Zosima, who in *The Brothers Karamazov* runs in double harness with Alyosha as a representative of the Good. All these characters are serious in conception and execution, though it is hardly possible to take one of them (Makar Dolgoruky) very seriously. But though each of them has an important part to play, none of them is as dominant as Myshkin. None of them is present, as Myshkin is, on almost every page of the narrative.

This is why Dostoyevsky was able to treat his other five Good characters seriously, while placing Myshkin in a comic light. Dostoyevsky the artist, who so often had to jog the elbow of Dostoyevsky the moralist, knew that seven hundred pages of undiluted goodness would be altogether too much. Some relief was essential, and what more natural to the irreverent Dostoyevsky than to turn to ridicule which at times masks the original edifying intention? How far this was a matter of conscious policy is another point. The tension between the edifying surface Dostoyevsky and the irreverent submerged Dostoyevsky was one of the important springs of his art.

Before the beginning of the action Myshkin had spent four to five years in a Swiss sanatorium. Now cured of the 'idiocy' from which he had suffered all his life, but still subject to epileptic attacks, he is first discovered returning to Russia by train. He falls into conversation with two chance travelling companions and quickly shows one of his most important characteristics by giving polite and untroubled answers to comically impertinent questions about his personal life. He thus reveals himself in a different light to that class of Dostoyevskian heroes whose extreme representative is the Underground Man. These habitually took offence and were often quick to offend others when they got the chance, but Myshkin exists apart from this world of grievance, insult and injury. He operates outside the 'humiliation slot'.

Myshkin is naïve and apparently lacking in self-respect. He seems only partially aware of his surroundings and has no normal reticence, being capable of admitting to a stranger that he has no knowledge of women because of his illness. While waiting to be received in General Yepanchin's house he does not sit down quietly like a respectable guest until the General is ready to see him, but addresses the butler with a tirade on the horrors of capital punishment, and further offends against the proprieties by asking permission to smoke his pipe. As these early scenes show, his manner remains unaffected whether he is talking to a General or a servant, an attitude unusual anywhere, but particularly so in nineteenth-century Russia.

Though Myshkin's simplicity occasionally repels at first, even creating the impression that he may be a confidence trickster, no one can long resist him. He captivates in quick succession the Yepanchins' butler and General Yepanchin himself together with his wife and three beautiful daughters. These scenes give Dostoyevsky the opportunity to indulge in delightful comedy, as at the lunch table where Madame Yepanchina, previously warned of her guest's eccentricity, insists on treating him as a combination of small child and harmless lunatic, nodding in unison with his every word and even offering to tie a napkin round his neck. At this point, early in the novel, the conception of Myshkin as a serious figure is already wearing thin.

Myshkin lacks ordinary discretion. He is always ready to translate thought into word and to blurt out secrets entrusted to him because of the automatic confidence which he inspires. He is childlike and a lover of children, calm and imperturbable, but capable, inevitably on the most inappropriate occasion, of excited, prophetic utterance. Awkward in society, but with a strange authority over others, he possesses a curious clairvoyance, as when he foresees the murder of Nastasya Filippovna by Rogozhin. He is spontaneous, quick to laugh and gregarious, but often longs for solitude. These qualities combine to make him one of Dostoyevsky's weirdest creations. He is not completely convincing as a human being, but those who wish to emphasize his significance as a symbol of goodness can claim that this remoteness from humanity effectively underlines his function as the embodiment of an ideal, a person 'not of this world'.

As has been pointed out, Myshkin's physical features derive from the model of Christ. With his blond hair, sunken cheeks, and thin, pointed, almost completely white beard, he resembles the traditional representation of Christ in Russian ikons. Other features also derive from the Gospels—his habit of 'turning the other cheek', of 'not judging' (except in an occasional outburst such as that against Catholicism to which reference will be made below) and associating with sinners and the moral equivalent of Biblical publicans.

Less attention has been paid to another ingredient in Myshkin,

Dostoyevsky himself. Myshkin's 'idiocy' before his removal to the Swiss sanatorium corresponds to Dostoyevsky's involvement with the socialist and atheist ideas of Belinsky and the Petrashevsky circle, ideas now branded by him as a form of 'idiocy'. Myshkin's four or five years of exile in the Swiss sanatorium tally with Dostoyevsky's four years in Omsk gaol, now reconstituted in his mind as a kind of spiritual rest cure. Dostoyevsky attributes to Myshkin his own disease of epilepsy, makes him speak feelingly about a man condemned to death (without attributing this experience of his own to his hero) and puts into his mouth ideas of his own about Russia and the West.[10]

Dostoyevsky also attributed to Myshkin his own awkwardness in society, but in other respects—Myshkin's lack of irritability and his ability to get on with other people—created something quite un-Dostoyevskian. Among the other figures, all foils to Myshkin, Rogozhin (his rival in love) is savage, jealous and lustful, while Myshkin is mild and chaste. General Yepanchin and Totsky are worldly, sensual and financially successful, while the spiritual Myshkin cares nothing for material things. Ippolit Terentyev, like the fatuous nihilists who surround him, is an irritable and cynical atheist, whereas Myshkin is simple and saintly. Lebedev intrigues and squirms while Myshkin is straightforward and transparent. Other characters, such as Ganya, Varya and Ptitsyn, differ from Myshkin because (a point which is given mysterious emphasis in the novel) they are 'ordinary people'. Above all, these other characters are active, pursuing erotic and financial ambitions, quarrelling, murdering, fornicating, seducing, stealing, attempting suicide, spitting in or slapping people's faces and uttering derisive guffaws. Myshkin is passive. Despite his formula 'positively good man', what Dostoyevsky in fact created was a negatively good man. Like interconnected cogwheels the other characters move in frantic but futile revolutions. Myshkin remains unengaged.

But is he really less futile? Judged by ordinary standards, certainly not. He achieves neither material nor spiritual gain for himself or his associates. When the novel closes Nastasya Filippovna lies murdered by the hand of Rogozhin, who is to be condemned to hard labour in Siberia. A fate worse than death, judged by strict Dostoyevskian standards, overtakes Aglaya Yepanchina, who sinks to marrying a Pole and (even worse) goes over to the Catholic faith. Myshkin himself, seven months and as many hundred pages after his original departure from Switzerland, has lapsed into gibbering idiocy and is taken back to his original sanatorium, where the doctor now believes him incurable.

This harsh dismissal of the hero agrees with the aura of ambiguity around Myshkin. Some interpreters have claimed that, the more spectacular Myshkin's failure by ordinary standards, the more triumphant the demonstration that he is not to be judged by ordinary standards and that his kingdom is 'not of this world'. Others may wish to attribute Myshkin's relapse to one of Dostoyevsky's recurring gusts of disbelief in his own creed, but it is not so much the truth or falsehood of either view as the tension between them which makes Myshkin.

*

The plot of *The Idiot* is complicated and in parts obscure, centring on interlocking financial and amatory intrigues. Two devastatingly beautiful women, Aglaya Yepanchina and Nastasya Filippovna, compete for Myshkin's love, one odd feature of this triangular relationship being that Myshkin is apparently impotent. His admission at the beginning of the novel that, owing to his illness, he has no knowledge of women is reinforced by his later statement to Ganya Ivolgin: 'I can't marry anyone. I am unwell.' This feature of Myshkin, taken in conjunction with the hectic love intrigues in which he is involved, contributes to the halo of absurdity which surrounds him.

Other suitors compete for Aglaya and Nastasya, extending the love intrigue beyond the triangular, and the other love relationships are almost all tainted by money, an effective contrast with the unmercenary Myshkin being achieved. Rogozhin bids for Nastasya's favours, quickly raising his offer from eighteen thousand to a hundred thousand roubles at a hint of opposition, and does so in the presence of Ganya Ivolgin, Nastasya's potential fiancé. Ganya has his own financial interest since he has been promised seventy-five thousand roubles by Nastasya's former seducer if he is prepared to marry her.

These intrigues are tedious, but are justified by the grandiose Scandals in which they periodically erupt. The riotous scene in which Rogozhin bids for Nastasya has a worthy sequel in her flat, where she accepts Rogozhin's hundred thousand roubles, only to throw them on the fire, saying that Ganya can have them if he will pull them out with his bare hands. These are the first two of the five notable Scandals which are the best scenes in *The Idiot*.

Nastasya Filippovna is modelled (like Polina in *The Gambler*) on Dostoyevsky's former mistress, Apollinariya Suslova. She has been seduced several years previously by the wealthy 'connoisseur' of young girls, Totsky, whose 'solidity' and love of comfort evoke some passing sarcasms from Dostoyevsky. Nastasya fastens upon the injury done to her, out of which she extracts rich emotional dividends. Her interest in Rogozhin's hundred thousand roubles is not financial but in the fact that it enables her, by accepting the money in the presence of her original seducer, to parade as a 'woman of the streets'. It is Myshkin, alone of those present, who, with his intuitive understanding, knows that she is really nothing of the sort. She in turn loves him because he is the only man whose attitude to her has no element of self-seeking. She repeatedly oscillates between Rogozhin and Myshkin and after several of these switches allows herself to be carried off by Rogozhin, who murders her. She reverts to Rogozhin because she wants to save Myshkin from involvement with a fallen woman and to continue enjoying the contemplation of her lapsed virtue.

Myshkin's feelings for Nastasya Filippovna are left somewhat vague, but there are indications that he feels pity for her rather than love. Perhaps his attitude towards Aglaya Yepanchina comes closer to that of a lover. But his marriage to her is made impossible by his continued obsession with Nastasya, and also, on a more mundane level, by his social ineligibility, dramatically revealed by the finest Scandal in the novel, the Chinese vase incident.

*

The incident occurs at a reception held by General Yepanchin and his wife to introduce Myshkin to their social set. Myshkin has not actually become betrothed to their daughter Aglaya. But she has spent so much time making fun of him and saying that she does not intend to marry him that her parents, well attuned to the laws of Dostoyevskian perversity, have come to regard the match as inevitable. Myshkin holds a respectable and ancient title and has now come into a large inheritance, but his strange manners make him a dubious proposition as a son-in-law. It is felt, however, that he might just be acceptable if only he can survive the ordeal of the reception without behaving eccentrically.

Hardly has the idea of the reception been mentioned when Dostoyevsky, following normal practice in his great Scandal scenes, has injected into a situation already pregnant with absurdity many extra suggestions of impending doom. Myshkin himself realizes that the Yepanchins are afraid of the impression which he might produce, especially after he and Aglaya have taken part in the following exchange:

> Aglaya: Will you be capable of taking and drinking a cup of tea respectably when everyone's making a point of watching you?
> Myshkin: I think I shall be capable of it.
> Aglaya, heavily sarcastic: That's a pity. Otherwise I might have had a laugh. Do at least break the Chinese vase in the drawing-room. It's an expensive one. Please break it. It was a present. Mother's so fond of it that she will go out of her mind and burst into tears in front of everyone. Make some sort of gesture such as you are always making, hit it and break it. Make a point of sitting near it.
> Myshkin: On the contrary, I shall try to sit as far away as possible. Thank you for the warning.

Aglaya further warns him that if he does start his usual gesticulating and if, as she is ready to predict he will, he begins holding forth on something like capital punishment or the economic state of Russia, then he must never dare to show himself in her presence again. To this Myshkin replies: 'Well, now you've made it inevitable that I shall start a harangue and even perhaps break the vase.'

After this interview Myshkin spends the whole night in a fever. Quite apart from the danger of knocking over the Chinese vase, what if he should have an epileptic fit?

The reception begins with that characteristic preliminary of the Scandal, a roll-call. In listing the important persons present in the Yepanchins' drawing-room, Dostoyevsky expresses his satirical attitude to high society. The social level of *The Idiot* is higher than that of previous novels, where only an occasional titled person or successful professional man intrudes upon the world of the poor and downtrodden. Dostoyevsky emphasizes the emptiness of such society by contrasting it with Myshkin, too good-hearted to have realized what a viper's nest he had entered.

> The charm of exquisite manners, straightforwardness and apparent sincerity was almost magical. It couldn't even occur to him that all this simplicity of heart and nobility, wit and high sense of personal dignity were perhaps only a magnificent external embellishment. In

spite of their imposing exterior, most of the guests consisted of pretty trivial people.

The company includes Madame Belokonskaya (an old lady who patronizes the Yepanchins) and an influential elderly man who is considered the 'protector' of the Yepanchins. There is also a very 'solid' army general, an 'administrator on an Olympian level' and General Yepanchin's superior in the service. Lesser personages are also listed, down to one who calls forth Dostoyevsky's most corrosive sarcasm in a passage where he pays off snubs administered to himself as a writer and introduces one of those wretched little foreigners who are the seasoning of a Scandal. 'Finally there was even a certain literary man, a poet of German extraction, but a Russian poet, a person moreover of complete propriety so that he could be introduced without any qualms into good society.'

By insisting on the importance and pomposity of the company, Dostoyevsky has made careful preparation for catastrophe, but characteristically does not spring his trap straight away. Contrary to the reader's fears, Myshkin at first behaves sensibly. 'He spoke little and then only to answer questions; finally he grew completely silent and sat listening.' But soon he is drawn into conversation with an important elderly man who, it turns out, had met Myshkin when he was a boy of ten or eleven. The old man is able to give information about two elderly ladies who had at that time acted as the boy's guardians, and this news has a strong emotional effect on Myshkin. 'The Prince listened to him with eyes shining with ecstasy and emotion. . . . The Prince even quivered all over.' Belokonskaya directed an angry look at him and pursed her lips. Everyone stopped talking and listened.

Worse is to come, for the old gentleman goes on to claim that Myshkin's benefactor Pavlishchev (who had paid for his treatment in the Swiss sanatorium) had, shortly before his death, become a convert to Catholicism. These were fighting words to use to a representative of Dostoyevskian Good. 'The Prince was beside himself. "Pavlishchev . . . Pavlishchev . . . went over to Catholicism? Impossible!" he screamed in horror.' Pavlishchev had been a true Christian, so how could he submit to a faith which is un-Christian? 'Catholicism is nothing more or less than an un-Christian faith.'

Speaking with extraordinary emotion and not scrupling to contradict the gathering in a manner 'disproportionately brusque', Myshkin warms to his theme.

E

Roman Catholicism is even worse than atheism itself. Atheism only preaches nothing, while Catholicism preaches a distorted Christ. . . . Antichrist! Roman Catholicism believes that without universal state power the Church cannot maintain itself on earth. . . . The Pope seized the earth and took the sword. To the sword they added lies, intrigue, deceit, fanaticism, superstition, evil-doing . . .

Typical chorus reactions follow. The old gentleman laughs openly, while a certain unnamed Prince takes out a lorgnette and stares at Myshkin through it. Then—something which Dostoyevsky had been saving up—'the wretched little German poet crawled out of his corner and moved nearer to the table, smiling a baleful smile'. Meanwhile Myshkin is proceeding to an appeal for the regeneration of all mankind and its resurrection by the 'Russian idea, the Russian God and the Russian Christ'. Hardly a suitable topic for drawing-room conversation.

Now, in the middle of a sentence, comes the snap of the spring, heralded by the typical formula: 'There suddenly occurred a certain incident and the orator's speech was interrupted in the most unexpected fashion.' Myshkin suddenly stood up . . .

gave a careless swing of the arm and a general shout broke out. The vase shook, at first as if in indecision as to whether it should fall on the head of one of the old gentlemen, but it suddenly veered in the opposite direction towards the little German—who, horrified, only just managed to jump out of the way—and then crashed to the floor.

It is characteristic that, in the midst of this absurdity, there should be indications of something even more absurd (the vase actually falling on someone) which might have happened, but did not. This common device adds a touch of convincingness to a far-fetched scene, but Dostoyevsky had not finished with Myshkin yet. The tirade continues, being cut short by a second climax, again subconsciously awaited by the reader. Myshkin has an epileptic fit. Thus his three forebodings, that he would 'start haranguing', that he would break the vase, and that he would have a fit, all came true. Having loaded the situation with these explosive potentialities, Dostoyevsky touches them off with superb timing.

What lends this scene particular interest and makes it stand out even among the other Scandals is the audacious introduction into Myshkin's mouth of some of Dostoyevsky's own beliefs—on the bankruptcy of Catholicism, on the 'Russian Christ' and so on. These theses are brought in with such comic effect that the untutored reader would not deduce from the context that they were actually Dostoyevsky's own. It is a defect of *The Idiot* that in other parts of the novel similar chunks of Dostoyevskyism are sometimes included irrelevantly. But here they are part of the dramatic pressures of the scene.

This is a different thing from literary dissociation as practised by Chekhov, a writer of more modest temperament, so averse from preaching to his readers that, when he introduced a character intended as a mouthpiece of his own views, he usually endowed him with some absurd characteristic such as continually losing his galoshes. No such sensibilities trouble Dostoyevsky. His readiness to pillory his own beliefs in the person of Myshkin is part of the mystery of his personality. The only explanation which suggests itself is that he both believed and did not believe in these things at the same time. Whatever the reason, the artistic effect—one of relief from excessive didactic impact—is the same as in Chekhov.

•

Of the five Scandals which are the main delights of *The Idiot* the two which have not yet been mentioned are concerned with nihilists, a term which will be studied more fully in the following chapter. For the moment it may be said that nihilists differ mainly from Dostoyevsky's other non-approved groups (socialists, atheists Catholics, liberals and so on) in being younger, noisier, dirtier and more vociferous defenders of what they consider to be their rights. The fury with which Dostoyevsky attacks this type derives, as do his associated attacks on atheists and socialists, from the fact that he was stamping on his own past—on the period when, as a member of the Petrashevsky Circle, he had been temporarily led astray by atheism and socialism.

What more natural than that Dostoyevsky should decide to show a particularly unruly group of nihilists gradually softened by con- tact with his positively good man? This he does in the scene where a group of nihilists pass off one of their number as the illegitimate son of Myshkin's benefactor Pavlishchev, and on the basis of this try to extort money from Myshkin.

It is often hard to determine how many characters are present at a Dostoyevskian Scandal. In the scene under discussion the number seems to be about twenty. The nihilists themselves number only four and as soon as they appear on the already crowded stage they are described in normal roll-call manner. The first to attract attention is older than the rest, being about thirty years of age, a retired lieutenant. Then comes the young man who has convinced himself that he is Pavlishchev's son. He is described as:

> poorly and untidily dressed, in a frock-coat with sleeves so greasy that they shone like a mirror, with a greasy waistcoat . . . with unwashed hands . . . with an extraordinarily pimply face, and if one may use the expression, a look of innocent impudence. Not a trace of irony, not the slightest reflex was expressed on his face—on the contrary, there was a blind intoxication with his own rights and at the same time something which approached a strange and unrelenting need to be and feel himself constantly injured.

Though of Russian descent he pronounces his words as if he were a foreigner—the trait so often given by Dostoyevsky to non-approved characters. The third nihilist is Lebedev's nephew who plays little part in the novel, and the fourth is Ippolit Terentyev who, some might think, plays too large a part.

To the unraveller of the threads in Dostoyevsky's fiction Ippolit is of interest, being a representative of the 'Poor Folk' strain as well as a nihilist, so that in him Dostoyevsky combines what he usually treated as two distinct breeds. Aged about eighteen, Ippolit is in the last stages of consumption and has only a few weeks to live. The consumptive Ippolit follows the line of the consumptive student Pokrovsky in *Poor Folk*.

The scene under discussion provides Dostoyevsky with a wonderful opportunity of delineating *naglost* (brazen impudence). These nihilists have caused to be printed a slanderous article expressing their claim against Myshkin in insulting terms, an article which shows Dostoyevsky as a master of comic parody. The falseness of their claims is easily demonstrated, but Myshkin proposes, despite the insulting article and the indignation of his friends, to make the pretended son of Pavlishchev a large money present. However, the touchy young man stands on his dignity and refuses the gift, leaving Myshkin to regret his own tactlessness in not having found a more acceptable way to offer the money. This scene effectively brings out the contrast between the unworldly Myshkin and the other characters. Yepanchina indignantly comments, after the gift has been refused, that 'This idiot [Myshkin] will already be trotting off to them tomorrow to offer them his friendship and his money.' But whatever Yepanchina and Myshkin's other well-wishers may think, he has soothed the irritation of the nihilists by turning the other cheek and won over at least two of them to be his devoted friends.

Ippolit, whose attitude to Myshkin remains ambivalent to the the end, is one of Dostoyevsky's most macabre and puzzling characters. Superlatively Dostoyevskian is his sudden irritated invitation to General Yepanchin: 'Your Excellency, I have the honour to invite you to my funeral, if you will deign to confer such an honour on me.' Notable too is much of the material in the second Scandal connected with the nihilists, which revolves round Ippolit's 'Confession'. This curious document, much of it written in the tortuous manner associated with the earlier Underground Man, is read out from his sick-bed by Ippolit to a miscellaneous group of persons, many of them drunk, in the small hours of the morning. It contains a curious amalgam of material—dreams and visions, including a nightmare (Ippolit imagines himself pursued by a writhing, scorpion-like insect which oozes white when crunched in the teeth of a Newfoundland dog); a long anecdote about a doctor and his family who were saved from the direst straits of poverty by Ippolit's intervention; reference to a downtrodden man called Surikov whose many calamities included the freezing of his small son to death, the sight of the baby's corpse causing Ippolit to produce an 'unintentional guffaw'; a long description, full of cruel detail, of Holbein's picture of Christ taken down from the Cross.

Dostoyevsky could hardly write anything which does not repay consideration, and even this hotch-potch of scrapings from the floor of his subconscious is compelling in patches, though serious students of his work have been known to admit themselves incapable of reading it to the end. Since Dostoyevsky pushed the frontiers of imaginative writing into so many unexplored regions, it is not surprising if he occasionally trespassed into nonsense. There is a danger that the uncritical reader may solemnly take parts of the Confession for something more significant than they are.

The later part of the Confession includes more effective writing, as Ippolit recounts the reasons which have brought him to suicide, the only act of free will open to him since he will die anyway in a few weeks' time. As the thought dawns on the reader that Ippolit's suicide is actually planned to take place at the moment when he has finished reading his Confession, the emotional temperature of the scene rises. The dreariest of sermons would gain in interest if the preacher could persuade the congregation that he was about to shoot himself at the end of his peroration.

It is not completely clear how Ippolit is to be interpreted. He is obviously meant to be, like Rogozhin, some sort of opposite to Myshkin—compare, for example, his attack on *smireniye* (humility or submissiveness), one of Myshkin's most outstanding characteristics. Some of his rhetoric on the futility of life and on his own predicament is indeed moving. It seems that Ippolit, as the young and innocent victim of a fatal disease, embodies the idea of a 'revolt' against God's world which was to receive more powerful treatment in the mouth of Ivan Karamazov. And it seems safe to say that Myshkin and Ippolit stand opposed to each other as symbols of two opposing poles in Dostoyevsky's split outlook just as Alyosha and Ivan Karamazov stand opposed, though in *The Idiot* this opposition is less effectively realized.

Particularly noteworthy is Myshkin's inability to offer Ippolit effective comfort in meeting his death. At one point Ippolit asks him: 'Tell me, how can I best die? So that it should happen as . . . virtuously as possible.' Myshkin's reply ('Pass by us and forgive us our happiness') has been described by one critic as 'one of the great answers in literature'.[11] Ippolit's own reaction, which this commentator does not quote ('Ha! ha! ha! Just as I thought. I knew you'd say something like that') suggests that to him this was far from one of the great answers in literature. Dostoyevsky's mouthpiece Myshkin proves as incapable of obtaining moral ascendancy over his anti-Dostoyevskian opponent Ippolit as Alyosha Karamazov was to prove in conflict with his brother Ivan.

The sequel to the Confession provides a particularly gross example of macabre comedy when Ippolit, whether accidentally or on purpose is characteristically never made clear, fails in his attempt to shoot himself because he has forgotten to load the pistol. Dostoyevsky could not allow even this painful scene to pass without running true to form by introducing that most typical of all chorus reactions to Scandal, the guffaw. 'The initial fright of the onlookers quickly began to give way to laughter. Some even emitted guffaws.'

*

Linked with Ippolit, because the youth's mother is his mistress, is another and more successfully portrayed character, who also belongs to the 'Poor Folk' strand in Dostoyevsky's work—General Ivolgin. The humour which surrounds Myshkin cuts much deeper and is an elusive affair, the roots of which cannot all be satisfactorily traced. No such ambiguity attends the comic elements in Ivolgin.

The General is the most extreme example in Dostoyevsky's fiction of the practitioner of *vranyo*, a special Russian form of activity not always appreciated by foreigners. The word *vranyo* is sometimes crudely translated as 'lying', but its nearest English equivalent (which still does not come close enough to the exact meaning) is 'blarney'. *Vranyo* consists of putting forward fantastic pieces of invented verbal embroidery, and in order to understand this particular brand of deceit it is helpful to remember that among Russians the lie has been developed into an art form to be practised for its own sake—perhaps an oriental trait which contrasts with the Western habit of lying only in order to gain some specific advantage.

Ivolgin's *vranyo* may first be illustrated by an experience which he recounts as having happened to him in a railway train. He tells how he was once sharing a compartment with a woman who was travelling with her lap-dog. Objecting to his cigar, she snatched it from him and threw it out of the window, upon which Ivolgin took his revenge by throwing the lap-dog after the cigar. Unfortunately a member of Ivolgin's audience, unsympathetic to *vranyo*, breaks the conventions by pointing out that this incident has recently been reported in a Belgian newspaper, and that General Ivolgin was not concerned in it at all.

This is a relatively simple example of *vranyo*, a concept which comes truly into its own in a magnificent passage from Book Four of *The Idiot* where Ivolgin relates to Prince Myshkin an imaginary story about his supposed experiences during the Napoleonic Campaign of 1812. Ivolgin claims that Napoleon appointed him his page during the occupation of Moscow, and the high-point of the *vranyo* is reached when Napoleon is actually described as having decided to order the French retreat on young Ivolgin's advice. ('Clear off home, General.') But the main point is that Ivolgin tells his story not merely for the pleasure of practising a special skill, but also to test the extent to which Myshkin is willing, in spite of the *vranyo*, to respect him as a person. He repeatedly comments on the expression on Myshkin's face. ('. . . . "You are smiling, Prince. You are looking at my face" . . . he squinted mistrustfully at the Prince' and so on.) After Ivolgin has left, his Victim 'had a premonition that he

[Ivolgin] belonged to that category of liars who, although they lie to the point of sensual self-indulgence and even to a condition of trance, nevertheless suspect that they are not being believed and cannot be believed'. Myshkin had manfully contrived to listen to Ivolgin's absurdities with a fairly straight face, and thus (as he hoped) to minister to the General's self-respect. But he had not done well enough, for he received a note from the General that same evening breaking off all relations.

Ivolgin is certainly a comic figure. But it would have been contrary to Dostoyevsky's methods to create a character on this scale in whom the element of comedy was not mixed with something more serious. Like other comic figures—Marmeladov in *Crime and Punishment*, Stepan Trofimovich Verkhovensky in *The Devils* and Captain Snegyryov in *The Brothers Karamazov*—Ivolgin also has his tragic side, being one of those 'laughter through tears' characters which figure so commonly in Dostoyevsky's writings. All these buffoons in their different ways belong to the type of the Pagliaccio who weeps behind his greasepaint as he puts on the motley.

The serious side of Ivolgin's character emerges towards the end of the novel where he becomes the victim of the sadism practised by that tortuous character Lebedev. The incident develops out of the cunning use made by Lebedev of the latest example in the long series of Ivolgin's lapses from the standards of an officer and a gentleman, the theft of Lebedev's pocket book containing four hundred roubles.

Lebedev is a character so devious that it is doubtful if he will ever receive his full due in criticism. It is in describing the consequences of the theft of his pocket book by General Ivolgin that Dostoyevsky most fully develops Lebedev's complex character, but to do full justice to the incident one would have to quote it at greater length than space permits. The essence of the episode, which is unrolled in two interviews between Lebedev and Myshkin, is as follows.

During the unruly and drunken night of Ippolit's Confession, Lebedev, as he explains to Myshkin, lost his pocket book. The evidence (so Lebedev chooses to pretend) points at a minor character called Ferdyshchenko as the culprit. It is true that General Ivolgin also had the opportunity to abstract the wallet, but he of course, so Lebedev claims, is above suspicion. The more Lebedev protests to Myshkin that the General is innocent, the clearer it becomes that Lebedev knows him to be guilty. Lebedev develops his sadism with fantastic ingenuity when he persuades the General (who now suspects that he has been found out) to join him in an attempt to bring the theft home to Ferdyshchenko. And Lebedev goes one further by confiding the details of this intrigue to Myshkin, who is so fond of the absurd old General that he suffers as much as if he had himself been the thief.

At the second interview with Myshkin, Lebedev reveals, without actually saying so, that the General has been making clumsy attempts to return the wallet. First it mysteriously appeared on the floor of Lebedev's room, under the table, but Lebedev refused to notice it despite the General's efforts to draw his attention to it unobtrusively. It next turned up in the lining of Lebedev's coat, but he has been pretending not to notice that it is there. Eventually Myshkin, making one of his few successful incursions into the world of action, intervenes on General Ivolgin's behalf and persuades Lebedev to call off his elaborate persecution. He is too late, however, for the shame of the incident helps to bring on the stroke which afflicts the poor old General in the street and leads to his death. Dishonourable, drunken and in every way ridiculous, the General nevertheless sets a high value on his own self-respect, and not mistakenly in Dostoyevsky's scheme of things. On his pages a thief may be a man of honour —in fact he is more likely to be a man of honour than someone who is unwilling to get caught up in the sin-confession cycle.

The two interviews between Lebedev and Myshkin are instances of an important device which is prominent in Dostoyevsky's later work and may be termed the 'barbed duologue'. Such duologues represent a variant on the confrontation of Predator and Victim so common throughout Dostoyevsky's work, and are built upon the fact that the Predator is in possession of knowledge which threatens the Victim's peace of mind. It is a feature of the barbed duologue that the Predator withholds the damaging information in his possession, while allowing the Victim and the reader gradually to guess what he knows from a series of hints and denials. The Predator operates with such subtlety that the Victim cannot even be sure that he is really being 'got at' until the eventual moment of the showdown, which is delayed by every possible means so as to keep him on the hook as long as possible. Elaborate professions of goodwill and confidential sniggers accompany the cruel probings of the Predator, the interjection 'tee-hee-hee' (in Russian *khe-khe-khe*) being one of the regular embellishments of the barbed duologue.

E*

The first notable example of such duologues had been the sequence of three interviews between Raskolnikov and the police investigator Porfiry Petrovich in *Crime and Punishment*. But these, magnificently developed though they are, seem relatively straightforward compared with the duologues in which Lebedev takes part. Most important among the barbed duologues in Dostoyevsky's subsequent work are the clashes between the husband and lover in *The Eternal Husband*, which will be discussed shortly, and the series of interviews in *The Brothers Karamazov* in which the lackey Smerdyakov gradually reveals to Ivan Karamazov, again using the technique of death by a thousand cuts, how it was that Fyodor Pavlovich Karamazov lost his life.

The barbed duologue is a difficult thing for the non-Russian to understand, since he is not usually schooled in this particular brand of deviousness. But it would not be fanciful to claim that a close study of the barbed duologues in Dostoyevsky could form a valuable introduction to an aspect of the Russian character which often eludes the foreigner, who is not necessarily more straightforward and kindhearted than the Russian, but is often a great deal less subtle. It is fascinating to find similar duologues cropping up in the work of the Soviet novelist Leonid Leonov, a writer deeply influenced by Dostoyevsky. In a short study of Leonov by the present author, the handling of these duologues in a Soviet setting is described as follows:

> Various features of these duologues—the atmosphere of cat playing with mouse, the tortuous hints, the blackmail, the sarcasms parading as polite inanities, the threat of denunciation to the Security Services—are in keeping with Leonov's addiction to the oblique approach. He leaves his master Dostoyevsky behind, both in the incidence of such barbed duologues and in the fabulous ingenuity, slipperiness and elusiveness with which they develop.[12]

If *The Idiot* contained no other characters besides Myshkin, Ivolgin and Lebedev, it would have special claims on the admiration of readers because of the profundity and subtlety of the characterization. But it also has a wealth of other original and superbly sketched characters. The violent Rogozhin is another variant of the Bogeyman, and comes over as a potent and demoniac figure, though yielding in interest to other major Bogeymen because Dostoyevsky has not endowed him with the tendency to self-analysis which is an important quality in Svidrigaylov and his successors. But Rogozhin remains the only really interesting specimen of the non-intellectual Bogeyman. Kolya Ivolgin is also worth mentioning as a successful portrait of a child.

As is usual in Dostoyevsky, the female characters in *The Idiot* make less impact than the male. For all the sound and fury which attend their doings, Nastasya Filippovna and Aglaya Yepanchina do not fully succeed in sweeping the reader off his feet as Dostoyevsky clearly intended that they should. On the other hand, a less important figure—Madame Yepanchina—does everything which Dostoyevsky could have wished for her and is a notable portrait of a domineering, but good-hearted and slightly comic middle-aged woman.

It is on such points of detail—the genius of the characterization, the excitement of individual scenes and Dostoyevsky's elusive use of humour (more prominent here than in any other work except *The Devils*)—that the high reputation of *The Idiot* must rest. The enigmatic status of the hero, of which a tentative explanation has been attempted here, will probably continue to puzzle readers, its very mysteriousness being perhaps the greatest single feature of the book. *The Idiot* serves as an object lesson of how great can be the satisfaction afforded by what is in so many ways—shapelessness, over-complexity, poor construction and pursuit of irrelevancies— an offence against any conceivable theory of how a novel ought to be put together.

*

The short novel *The Eternal Husband* (1870) is built on a situation of permanent fascination to Dostoyevsky, the relationship between two men who love the same woman. Being sensation-cravers, the two rivals do not avoid each other, but are drawn together by mutual fascination. They are involved in the kind of love-hate duel which continued to interest Dostoyevsky after he had withdrawn from personal participation in such situations into happy marriage with a faithful wife.

The two rivals of *The Eternal Husband* are fortunate in being able to devote their entire attention to their mutual relationship, undistracted by interference even from the woman whom they both love, since at the time when the action begins she has already been dead for a few months. She was Natalya Vasilyevna Trusotskaya, 'one of those women who seem to have been born in order to be unfaithful wives'. Her husband, Trusotsky, belongs to 'the type of husbands whose sole function consists exclusively in corresponding to this feminine type. . . . It is impossible for him not to be a cuckold.' Trusotsky is the eternal husband of the title, while the third part in the triangle is taken by Velchaninov, the eternal lover.

Nine years before the beginning of the action Natalya Vasilyevna had been Velchaninov's mistress. As was her practice with her numerous lovers, she had suddenly 'discarded him like an old shoe' and sent him packing from the provincial town in which she lived. According to Natalya Vasilyevna her husband had known nothing of the liaison, which was in any case 'none of his business'.

Now, nine years later, Trusotsky turns up in St. Petersburg, where Velchaninov is living, and the duel between husband and lover begins. Suspense is created by the fact that neither the reader nor Velchaninov knows how much Trusotsky knows about Velchaninov's former relation with the wife. Nor will Trusotsky declare his hand, proceeding instead to make ominous hints which allow both protagonists to exploit their relationship as a source of inflamed sensation. Their conversations follow the lines of a 'barbed duologue' as already developed with great subtlety in *Crime and Punishment* and *The Idiot*. The tormenting of Velchaninov by Trusotsky echoes the tormenting of Raskolnikov by the investigator Porfiry Petrovich, and of Ivolgin and Myshkin by Lebedev.

Trusotsky is able to put on the screw particularly hard when it turns out that he has arrived in St. Petersburg with a charming little girl, eight years old, called Liza. Is Velchaninov Liza's real father, as Trusotsky hints, with oracular references to the chronology of the nine-year-old liaison? Velchaninov believes that he is, and later developments show that he is not mistaken. But Liza knows nothing of this and loves Trusotsky as her father, thus placing him in the strong position of being able to torment Velchaninov by tormenting her.

The tormenting of children was one of Dostoyevsky's most persistent obsessions. It was connected with his interest in the evil potentialities of human nature since he held the opinion, from which it is difficult to dissent, that nothing could be more wicked than to torture a child. On his pages such ill-treatment is normally physical, whether it takes the form of rape (*Crime and Punishment*, *The Devils*), tossing Bulgarian babies on Turkish bayonets (*Diary of a Writer* and elsewhere) or setting a pack of hounds on a small boy (*The*

Brothers Karamazov). Trusotsky proceeds by more subtle means, telling Liza that he intends to hang himself and even preparing a noose in her presence so that she shall understand what he has in mind.

Velchaninov rescues Liza from the monster, but she falls ill and dies a few days later. The man whom she believes to be her father remains cruel to the end, refusing to visit her sick-bed.

The duel now proceeds in a new milieu when it transpires that Trusotsky has decided to marry again. Faithful to the predilections of Dostoyevskian middle-aged men, he has picked out an innocent fifteen-year-old girl called Nadya, whose father favours the match because Trusotsky is a man of means. Now Trusotsky insists that Velchaninov shall accompany him on a visit to his fiancée's household, though the logic of the situation makes it inevitable that the young girl should prefer the Eternal Lover to the Eternal Husband. Here Trusotsky preserves a true Dostoyevskian sense of priorities by opting for the heightened sensation involved in exposing his fiancée to Velchaninov's charms in preference to his prospects, dim in any case, of a happy married life. So impatient is he to resume the duties of an Eternal Husband that he cannot even wait for the marriage ceremony before introducing the Lover.

Some amusing scenes take place at the country villa where Nadya is staying with her family. Though she does fall under Velchaninov's spell, she does not desert Trusotsky for Velchaninov, since she has all the time been in love with a penniless nineteen-year-old nihilist. Like all Dostoyevsky's later fiction, *The Eternal Husband* has its nihilists, but here Dostoyevsky's mockery is particularly gentle and sympathetic, and he is more concerned to portray the ardour of youth than to denounce ideological heresy. The scene in which Nadya's suitor imperiously demands that Trusotsky should renounce all claim to the girl is one in which Dostoyevsky demonstrates that his humour need not inevitably be savage.

In a sense the confrontation of Velchaninov and Trusotsky reproduces the confrontation of Predator and Victim familiar in Dostoyevsky's early work. But the relationship between the two protagonists is more complex than that between earlier Predators and Victims. Velchaninov possesses all the distinguishing marks of the Predator, being handsome, charming and socially successful, while Trusotsky, miserable and downtrodden, is clearly cast for the role of Victim. However, in practice, each protagonist oscillates between the two roles. Trusotsky successfully torments Velchaninov, but repeatedly appears in the role of Victim, especially in the scene where he becomes the butt of the happy young people at the country villa. Velchaninov too is portrayed as a split personality in his attitude to the basic theme of humiliation, as in the reveries described at the beginning of the novel, where he alternates between memories of scenes in which he inflicted and received humiliation.

Original and stimulating as a further development of basic ideas in Dostoyevskian psychology, *The Eternal Husband* is also well constructed, although Mochulsky exaggerates when he describes it as 'from a formal point of view perhaps the most perfect of Dostoyevsky's works'.[13] The element of suspense is also handled with skill. However, in spite of all these virtues, there is something disappointing about the novel, which makes too skeletal an impression. The main defect lies in the characterization. While endowing his two rivals with a wealth of subtle psychological traits, Dostoyevsky somehow forgot to give them flesh. The novel rubs home a lesson which is emphasized again and again the more one considers Dostoyevsky's work: he needed a violent crime to bring his talents to full fruition. It is therefore significant that the main crisis of *The Eternal Husband* is that in which Trusotsky, having exhausted all other possibilities of his relationship with Velchaninov as a source of inflamed sensation, attempts to stab him with a knife, but fails. Murders which are projected, but do not come off, seem to have been the sign of Dostoyevsky's own dissatisfaction with his work. His dissatisfaction with *The Eternal Husband* is recorded in his letters, where he describes his work on the novel as 'hard labour' and says that he 'conceived a loathing for this disgusting story from the very beginning'.[14]

CHAPTER SEVEN

'THE DEVILS'

THE years 1871 and 1872 saw the publication of *The Devils*, also known in English as *The Possessed* because of the choice of that title by early translators. *The Devils* has commonly been ranked below others in the chain of Dostoyevsky's greatest novels, but its claims to be regarded as his supreme masterpiece are worth considering.

The qualities of the novel include its destructive ferocity, its use of suspense, the range of its humour and the impact with which a complicated plot is brought to bear on the main theme. An audacious amalgam of comedy and tragedy, it reaches the peak of Dostoyevskian humour in the Scandal of the Fête, and in the moving account of Shatov's murder sounds the depths of Dostoyevskian tragedy. Above all *The Devils* excels in creating, as every good novel must, a world of its own, in this case a world peopled by characters even more grotesque than those in Dostoyevsky's other novels.

This is the most sanguinary and crime-ridden of his works. Four of the main characters are murdered and two commit suicide. Together with assassination and arson go minor misdemeanours including scenes in which the chief hero pulls an elderly member of the respectable local club across the floor by his nose and bites the ear of the Provincial Governor. There are also several essays in sacrilege which include the introduction of a live mouse into the case containing an ikon, the insertion of pornographic literature into the bundle of Gospels carried by an itinerant bible-seller, and reference to a scene where a holy man pelts a visitor with boiled potatoes. All this takes place in an atmosphere of gossip, rumours, threatening letters, blackmail, spying and denunciation to the police. But the novel is remarkable not so much for its whirling extravagancies as for the way in which Dostoyevsky, deploying a number of now familiar devices, makes these things convincing to the reader.

This is the only novel of Dostoyevsky's in which politics are the dominant concern. The main theme is one which has already been traced in his work, but which nowhere else in his fiction receives such exhaustive treatment—nihilism. After firing some ranging shots on this target in the persons of Lebezyatnikov and his associate Luzhin in *Crime and Punishment*, Dostoyevsky had brought down more concentrated fire on Ippolit Terentyev and his group in *The Idiot*. But these were merely premonitory rumblings in comparison with the deadly barrage which now plastered more innocent victims as well as legitimate military objectives. For Dostoyevsky does not confine his attack to nihilists even in the widest sense of this by no means stable term.

Nihilism in its narrowest use refers to a social type prominent in Russia of the eighteen-sixties. The nihilists consisted mainly of young people, often students, who rejected traditional religious and moral beliefs. They were rude and outspoken, wore strange clothes and were accused of not washing. The men had long hair, while the women kept theirs short and often sported blue spectacles. They practised, and even more frequently preached, free love. They were atheists, and though not necessarily active conspirators, could be presumed in sympathy with revolution. Unlike Dostoyevsky, who placed God in the centre of his philosophy, they put their central emphasis on man, and as a subject of study attached overriding importance to science.

Like other militant conservatives, Dostoyevsky tended to extend the range of nihilism as a convenient term of abuse and to apply it to all who held left-wing views. Thus in *The Devils* he hits out hard at nihilists in the stricter sense, but groups them with what may be termed the fellow-travellers of nihilism—political oppositionists of a milder and more liberal hue.

The novel is therefore a heresy-hunt against Russian political opposition. Its blows fall on such various, overlapping and often mutually hostile groups as liberals, progressives, radicals, socialists, communists, revolutionaries and Westernizers. Dostoyevsky thought the disease so virulent that he did not care whether his opponents had it in mild or severe form. All were germ-carriers and he lumped them together. In the passage from St. Luke's Gospel which he chose as a text for the novel, he equated these heretics with the Gadarene swine, into whom there entered 'devils' which sent them plunging to destruction.

In effect Dostoyevsky was attacking the whole Russian intelligentsia. This term, which was first used in the eighteen-sixties, had in the late nineteenth century a narrower application than that which it has since come to receive, for it did not usually include intellectuals and members of the professions, except in so far as these were politically oppositionist. Hence Dostoyevsky himself, though one of the supreme examples of a Russian intellectual, was not, strictly speaking, a member of the Russian intelligentsia. As a political conformist he was in fact one of its main enemies. In his *Diary of a Writer* the words 'intelligentsia' and *intelligent* (an intellectual) belong to the vocabulary of abuse.

A work of literature tended to stand or fall by its rating with the intelligentsia, so that by attacking the people who were to make or mar its reputation *The Devils* got off to a bad start. This is one reason why it has received less than its due in criticism. The intelligentsia, ever since the rise to prominence of its forerunners in the days of Belinsky, had tended to assess a writer's quality as an artist by the degree to which his books could be interpreted to imply political opposition. For a work which actually dared to attack the opposition no forgiveness could be expected. Other contemporary right-wing Russian writers and critics, including Leskov (less fortunate than Dostoyevsky, who suffered mainly in respect of this one work), also found themselves neglected for similar reasons.

The intelligentsia was even less disposed to forgive the attack because of the novel's outrageous unfairness. That Dostoyevsky was unfair to Russian political opposition and to the growing revolutionary movement cannot be disputed, and many commentators have spoken as if this bias detracted from the novel. In fact one of its main delights lies in this very quality. Swift was equally unfair when, in one of the few satires in world literature of comparable force, he equated the human race with his Yahoos. One does not have to agree with Swift's presentation of the human race to appreciate *Gulliver's Travels* any more than one has to agree with Dostoyevsky's political diagnosis when assessing *The Devils*.

That extreme bias can go hand in hand with high literary achievement may be illustrated by comparing *The Devils* with Turgenev's *Fathers and Children*. Turgenev's novel, which had appeared a few years previously, is free from bias. But it is a greatly inferior work to *The Devils* despite its many virtues.

Fathers and Children was the novel in which the term nihilist was first widely publicized. Turgenev treats his 'Fathers' (the liberals of the forties) and his 'Children' (the nihilists of the sixties) as two opposed groups, each meriting sympathy, whereas Dostoyevsky lumps them together as equally pernicious. Another study of nihilism, equally celebrated in Russia of the eighteen-sixties, was the novel *What is to be done?* by Dostoyevsky's main ideological opponent, Chernyshevsky, who was in Siberian exile at the time when *The Devils* was written. This was no objective study of the subject, but its bias lay in the opposite direction, since it was the gospel of the nihilists and as such anathema to Dostoyevsky. Almost comically lacking in literary merit, *What is to be done?* is nevertheless a fascinating document of the period and provides a foretaste of the Soviet Socialist Realist novel. Incidentally, disparaging reference is made in the text of *The Devils* both to *Fathers and Children* and to *What is to be done?*—quite apart from the fact that one of the minor characters in *The Devils* is a vicious caricature of Turgenev.

Besides irritating the intelligentsia of Dostoyevsky's day, *The Devils* has also been an embarrassment to Soviet critics because it preaches a reactionary point of view, and contains so much material which clamours to be interpreted as a prophetic satire on Soviet practices. For example, Dostoyevsky's nihilist theoretician, Shigalyov, advances a system of ideas in which 'proceeding from unlimited freedom I end with unlimited slavery'. Even more telling is Stavrogin's comment on the nihilists: 'because of their incompetence they are terribly fond of accusing people of spying'. During the Second World War, Soviet critics made the most of the novel as a prophecy of Fascism, presumably hoping that everyone would be too busy to notice that it could also be made to point nearer home. But this attempt at a revival of *The Devils* did not last long.

What about the failure among non-Russian readers to give *The Devils* its due? Can this have been due to ignorance of the historical background? Despite their admitted 'Russianness', most of Dostoyevsky's works are not so closely attached in detail to the Russian scene as he himself sometimes pretended. But *The Devils* does demand a feeling for social and political pressures in Russia of the middle and late nineteenth century unless much of it is to remain unintelligible. Too unintelligible in this respect for some non-Russian readers, the novel is in other ways perhaps too disappointingly intelligible. For in spite of some pretentious reasoning put into the mouth of Kirillov, it has not given much scope for that preoccupation with ultimate profundities which has tended to attract attention away from other aspects of Dostoyevsky's work. This also helps to account for its relatively low assessment by Russian critics

of the early twentieth century. But now that the 'Russian Soul' is increasingly regarded as a farcical conception, the time has come when
The Devils can receive its true rating.

*

In this exposé of what he regarded as the supreme heresy, Dostoyevsky shows how his nihilists effect the moral disintegration of an
unnamed provincial town.

By making his provincial 'our town' the centre of the action, he
was following a practice familiar in the works of other Russian
fiction-writers and was deserting St. Petersburg for the first time
in a major work. He also adopted what was for him a technical
innovation and one which had an important effect on the tone of the
novel. Hitherto some of his fiction had been written from the 'omni-
scient author' point of view, as in *Crime and Punishment* and *The
Idiot*. Alternatively and less commonly it had been written, as in
Insulted and Injured and *The Gambler*, in the first person, in the name
of a narrator who himself participates in the action. *The Devils* falls
between these two techniques. It has a narrator, but one who
scarcely participates in the action.

This device enables Dostoyevsky to envelop his action in a
characteristic aura of vague portentousness by the use of such
formulae as 'none of this was clear at the time', 'only later, when the
full story came out was it revealed that . . . ' Above all Dostoyevsky
makes full use of this semi-participating narrator to inject the note
of impending doom, the feeling that 'all is not well', so brilliantly
used in *The Devils*.

Though accused at one point by Shatov (Dostoyevsky's own
mouthpiece in the novel) of the awful crime of bring a 'moderate
liberal', the Narrator adopts towards the nihilists an attitude of
indignant condemnation which may be identified with that of
Dostoyevsky himself. His greatest indignation is reserved for the
leading nihilist and conspirator of the book, the evil and glib Pyotr
Stepanovich Verkhovensky. Like his associate, Stavrogin, the other
chief character of the novel, Pyotr Stepanovich makes a late appearance, about a quarter of the way through, after the reader has been
prepared for him by 'build-up' material. He has just spent four
years abroad, mainly in Switzerland. In this he resembles other
characters in *The Devils*—Shatov, Kirillov and Stavrogin—and also
recalls Myshkin from *The Idiot*. It seems likely that the habit of

exiling his characters for this particular period was due to an echo in Dostoyevsky's mind of his own four-year imprisonment in Omsk.

At this time Russian revolutionaries were active in Switzerland, so that it was natural to represent Pyotr Stepanovich in the oblique manner of *The Devils*, as having been in touch during his stay abroad with a mysterious revolutionary centre. Among the Russian revolutionaries then active in Switzerland were Bakunin and his notorious young associate, Sergey Nechayev. It was on Nechayev that Dostoyevsky modelled Pyotr Stepanovich to whom he regularly refers as 'Nechayev' in his preliminary notes.

The leading feature of Nechayev's character was an extraordinary capacity for bluff, intrigue and make-believe. He had a talent for inventing 'political societies of which he was the commander-in-chief, and of which the rank and file scarcely existed outside his own imagination'.[1] His practice was to set up in Russia revolutionary 'cells' consisting of five members, and as none of these cells had any contact with any of the others except through Nechayev, he was able to impress his dupes with imaginative stories which none of them could verify about the size of the whole organization.

In all these respects, as well as in his personal ascendancy over his victims, Pyotr Stepanovich is copied from Nechayev. Moreover, the murder of Shatov reproduces in its essentials the murder of the Moscow student Ivanov, organized by Nechayev and carried out on 21st November, 1869—the incident which served as Dostoyevsky's initial inspiration for *The Devils*. Like Ivanov, Shatov was a member of a 'cell'. Like Nechayev, Pyotr Stepanovich organized a collective murder by other members of the cell on the pretext that the victim was likely to denounce them to the police, but actually in order to bind them all together in common guilt and thus to place them more completely in his power. Other features of Ivanov's murder reproduced by Dostoyevsky were the placing of the body in a pond and the panic which overtook the murderers, with the exception of their ringleader, at the scene of the crime.

As a predator preying upon a flock of victims, Nechayev was a character bound to fascinate Dostoyevsky, in whose fiction the relationship had always been so prominent. But Pyotr Stepanovich is a new and brilliant variation on the theme of the predator. He possesses to a greater extent than any of Dostoyevsky's other heroes the quality of *naglost* (brazen impudence), which he brings to bear on the members of his own revolutionary cell and on more respect-

able members of society, such as the Provincial Governor, the
Governor's wife and his own father. Since Dostoyevsky's oppressors
and humiliators easily tend, owing to the characteristic oscillatory
process, to assume an opposite role, it is not surprising to find
Pyotr Stepanovich cringing in front of the strong man of the novel,
Stavrogin.

Pyotr Stepanovich is represented as constantly on the move. He
lives in a whirl of intrigue, much of which is merely hinted at in
the novel, and is shown as constantly 'running errands'. For some
reason, perhaps in order to stress his materialism, Dostoyevsky
shows him as fond of eating and drinking—he is often ready to
pause in the middle of some sinister errand to eat a beef steak, or
to drink a glass of wine or cognac.

By dressing fashionably, though without excessive elegance, he
departs from the nihilist tradition, as he does by his ability to affect
the manners of respectable society rather than the bluntness of
Turgenev's nihilist Bazarov. It is this feature which enables Pyotr
Stepanovich to extend his ascendancy into circles—the Provincial
Governor's household for example—which might have rejected a
more traditional nihilist. His social charm enabled him to 'get to
know everyone in our town in a flash'. Yet nothing is more memorable about him than his capacity, while maintaining outward forms
of politeness, to adopt a tone of sneering rudeness outside the range
of his more pedestrian nihilist associates.

While creating Pyotr Stepanovich, Dostoyevsky found him 'to
my own surprise turning out as a semi-comic character'.[2] This
comment illustrates how difficult it sometimes is to accept Dostoyevsky's own estimates of his characters, particularly where the
element of humour is involved. A contrasting example is his conception of the semi-comic Prince Myshkin as a wholly serious figure.
Pyotr Stepanovich remains a monster of repulsiveness in whom it
is difficult to detect any comic element whatever, though it must be
admitted that his cruelty and *naglost* are constantly provoking comic
scenes.

The other nihilists of the novel include the preposterous members
of Pyotr Stepanovich's revolutionary call. Among these is the
official Virginsky, who has so thoroughly absorbed nihilist teaching
on the absurdity of conventional sexual morality that when his wife
takes the impossible Captain Ledyadkin as a lover and sends him
into 'retirement', he is alleged to have told her: 'My dear, hitherto I

have only loved you. Now I respect you.' (This joke had already been made at least once—by Lebezyatnikov in *Crime and Punishment*.) Another and more odious cell-member is Liputin, a 'congenital spy' who makes a point of blurting out confidential information in the quarter where it can do most harm and is a more objectionable variant on the type of Lebedev in *The Idiot*. No less horrible is the little Jew, Lyamshin, renowned for his party tricks, such as his realistic imitation of a woman in childbirth followed by the cries of the new-born baby, renowned also for his unsavoury practical jokes, for it was he who put a mouse in an ikon case and foisted pornographic pictures on a bible-seller. The last two members of the cell, the theoretician Shigalyov and the blindly obedient Erkel, are portrayed more sympathetically. Despite his stupidity Erkel reflects the sympathy which Dostoyevsky often showed for idealistic youth marching eagerly along the wrong ideological road.

In one memorable scene Dostoyevsky groups his cell-members in Virginsky's house together with a host of minor satellites. This is one of the three main Scandals in the novel. It begins with a roll-call in which the presence of the 'flower of the very brightest red liberalism in our ancient town' is recorded. The company includes Virginsky's wife, whose habit of committing adultery 'on principle' is again noted; her thirteen-year-old sister, 'a creature taciturn and poisonous'; Virginsky's sister who was a student; an eighteen-year-old schoolboy with an air of injured dignity; and several school teachers and officers, together with a Major who liked 'foregathering with extreme liberals' and who, being politically neutral, serves Dostoyevsky as a foil to the others.

Pyotr Stepanovich puts on a great display of *naglost*, showing his contempt for this gathering of dupes by yawning and asking the hostess if she has any playing cards. He calls for brandy, though everyone else is drinking tea, and then demands a pair of scissors to cut his long and dirty nails in the midst of some further quarrelling and an attempt to settle whether the gathering constitutes a 'meeting' or not. This point is only decided after some unsuccessful attempts to vote on the matter, during which in the general confusion no one seems clear whether a raised hand is to be interpreted as for or against the motion.

After the confusion has subsided the theoretician Shigalyov, is allowed to make some points on revolutionary theory from a book of ten chapters which he has written on the subject, though his offer to spend ten evenings reading the entire work to the assembly evokes general laughter. This is the book in which, reaching a conclusion diametrically opposite to his initial idea, Shigalyov, 'proceeding from unlimited freedom', ends with 'unlimited slavery'. As emerges from later discussion, Shigalyov foresees the division of humanity into two unequal parts. Ten per cent are to have freedom and unlimited powers over the remaining ninety per cent, whom he regards as a herd. Such are his prerequisites for a paradise on earth, which foreshadow the precepts of the Grand Inquisitor in *The Brothers Karamazov*. One of the most telling points in this parody of revolutionary theoreticians is Shigalyov's dogmatic assertion that his system constitutes an inexorable law of historical development. So inescapable does he claim it to be that he advises his hearers, if they are unwilling to listen to him, to go away, the men to serve the state and the women to work in the kitchen, activities which any self-respecting revolutionary would regard as the lowest form of moral depravity.

It is characteristic of Pyotr Stepanovich that he is not interested in Shigalyovism or any other theory. After stating that he has not come along to take part in discussions, he proceeds to his real purpose by compromising the lapsed revolutionary Shatov (whom he has lured to the meeting against his will) as a potential informer, thus paving the way for his murder.

*

Most prominent among the 'fellow-travellers' of nihilism who become Pyotr Stepanovich's victims is his own father, Stepan Trofimovich Verkhovensky, one of the best examples of characterization in Dostoyevsky's work. The father-son relationship is of symbolic importance because, as indicated above, Dostoyevsky was especially concerned to emphasize the links between 'liberals of the forties' such as Stepan Trofimovich and 'nihilists of the sixties' like his son. This did not imply any harmony in their personal relations, for Pyotr Stepanovich treats his father with patronizing impudence which on one occasion causes Stepan Trofimovich to chase him out of the house with a stick. On another occasion, in a scene of particularly cruel humour in the Dostoyevskian tradition, Pyotr Stepanovich claims to be not Stepan Trofimovich's son at all, but the son of a 'wretched little Pole' with whom his mother (as Stepan Trofimovich had confided) had at one time been involved.

This was not the first occasion on which Pyotr Stepanovich had deliberately blurted out secrets confided in him by his garrulous father, for a similar indiscretion forms the basis of the notable Scandal scene with which the action proper begins.

Stepan Trofimovich is an object of gentler satire than that which Dostoyevsky pours over his nihilists. He is portrayed as a weak and fairly contemptible character but his faults and absurdities only help him to win the affection of the reader. He is a variation on the 'laughter through tears' type, but differs so much from the previous most notable example of this type in Dostoyevsky's work—General Ivolgin in *The Idiot*—as to serve as an object lesson of the way in which Dostoyevsky could deal in 'types' without repeating himself. He is a less extravagant character than Ivolgin, sharing with him, but in a milder degree, his financial improvidence, talkativeness, capacity for self-deception and tendency to drink too much.

Before his early retirement to 'our town' as the tutor to Stavrogina's son, Stepan Trofimovich has been a university lecturer engaged in desultory research into subjects as various as Arabian history and the importance of the town of Hanau between 1413 and 1428. Priding himself on his liberal views, he has for a brief moment become sufficiently important to be mentioned in the same breath as such celebrated mouthpieces of liberal oppositionist ideas as Chaadayev, Herzen, Belinsky and Granovsky. The last-named, a less well-known figure than the other members of this quartet, had been a 'Westernizing' historian prominent in his day and it was upon him that the character of Stepan Trofimovich was originally modelled, his name preceding that of Stepan Trofimovich in Dostoyevsky's preliminary notes.

Stepan Trofimovich is an emotional poseur, and no one in his senses would consider him a revolutionary, but he has fallen under official suspicion at a time of extreme political oppression, presumably towards the end of Nicholas I's reign. This has given him an excuse to retire from the public arena and retreat to what he prefers to regard as exile in 'our town'. He likes to stress his imaginary status as an exile and to believe himself under police supervision because of his 'dangerous views'. Nothing could be more insulting to him than the suggestion that he is in fact not dangerous at all. The posture of political martyr and persecuted tribune of the people flatters his self-esteem and gives him an alibi for not attempting serious work. He likes to think of himself as a 'standing reproach' to the abuses in Russia of his day, but, as is pointed out, Stepan Trofimovich is too easily visualized as recumbent to carry off this posture successfully. A typical Russian 'man of the forties' in his emotionalism, addiction to elevated sentiments and romantic attitude to life, he stands in comic contrast to the brusque matter-of-factness of the succeeding nihilist generation. He is well qualified to function as one of Dostoyevsky's victims.

The friendship between Stepan Trofimovich and the good-hearted but tyrannical Stavrogina provides one of the most comic confrontations of victim and predator in Dostoyevsky's work. Of their relationship the comment is made: 'there are strange friendships in which each of the friends is almost ready to eat the other one alive. They keep this up all their lives, yet cannot bring themselves to part.' More domineering than her nearest predecessor in Dostoyevsky's work, Madame Yepanchina in *The Idiot*, Stavrogina has placed Stepan Trofimovich on a pedestal in her mind as an eminent man of letters, which does not prevent her from nagging, bullying and organizing him in every sphere outside this supposed speciality of his, or from accusing him of surrounding himself with human 'scum', of having grown flabby, of being unable to do without wine and cards, of spending all his time gossiping and of spluttering when he speaks. Characteristic of Stavrogina are her 'venomous hiss' and 'irritable screech'. So addicted is she to organizing other people's lives that, not content with projecting a marriage between Stepan Trofimovich and her ward Dasha (neither of whom wants to marry), she even offers at one stage to accompany them on their honeymoon. Despite her overbearing nature, wealth and high position in society, even Stavrogina falls to some degree under the spell of the nihilists, though she does not become one of their more abject victims.

To this more abject class belongs one of the most interesting minor figures of the book, the writer Karmazinov, who (being one of the 'Fathers' of the novel) in his impact on the theme in many ways repeats the points made in the person of Stepan Trofimovich, except that he is not given any endearing characteristics. One of Karmazinov's chief claims to attention is the fact that he is a deliberate caricature of Turgenev. The story of the quarrel between the two authors has been told many times. They had been on bad terms since the eighteen-forties, when Turgenev had formed the habit of teasing the over-sensitive Dostoyevsky, and the ill will which Dostoyevsky conceived for Turgenev was increased by the envy of a writer of plebeian origin for an aristocratic contemporary who was usually able to command a higher fee. In the eighteen-sixties Dostoyevsky came to dislike Turgenev particularly strongly for two cogent reasons: he had come to disapprove of Turgenev's political views and he owed Turgenev money which he was for many years unable to repay.

Whatever the rights or wrongs of this quarrel, Dostoyevsky fully avenged any fancied injury received from Turgenev when he created Karmazinov. He gave Karmazinov a different physical appearance, making him a small man whereas Turgenev was large. But in most other respects, including his 'petulant' voice, Karmazinov was a recognizable, but maliciously exaggerated, likeness. Constantly referring to Karmazinov by the sarcastic phrase 'great writer', Dostoyevsky's Narrator points out that he was in fact a mediocre talent and not the genius for which he had been taken. He stresses Karmazinov's conceit and the importance which he attaches to his connections in high society.

Karmazinov is brought into line with the theme of the novel by the emphasis laid on his estrangement from Russia—for example in the remark which he makes about being more interested in the drainage system of Karlsruhe, his chosen place of residence, than in the fate of his own motherland. Even more significant as a barb aimed at Turgenev is the accusation of adopting a sycophantic attitude towards the nihilists:

> The great writer was pathologically scared of modern revolutionary youth, and imagining from ignorance that they held in their hands the keys of Russia's future, ingratiated himself with them in a humiliating way, mainly because they paid no attention to him whatsoever.

The 'fellow-travellers' of the older generation also include the Provincial Governor, Von Lembke, and his wife, who become two of the most pathetic of Pyotr Stepanovich's victims. The Governor, a harmless and well-meaning nonentity, happier when making model trains out of paper than when wielding the rod of authority, is finally driven out of his mind. The tragedy of Von Lembke is mixed with the farce usual with such 'laughter through tears' characters. Especially moving is his appearance, carrying a bunch of flowers which he has absent-mindedly picked, in the middle of some peacefully demonstrating workers, whom, already deranged in mind, he orders to be flogged. No less absurd and tragic is the Governor's wife, Yuliya Mikhaylovna, whose pathetic wish to see herself the centre of an adoring society of young people and faith in her ability to restrain nihilist youth by kindness help Pyotr Stepanovich to accomplish the moral disintegration of 'our town'.

•

Yuliya Mikhaylovna's illusion that she is the centre of an adoring group of young people is finally removed in the first two chapters of Part Three of the novel wherein is described the Scandal which took place on the occasion of the Fête organized by her in aid of 'the poor governesses of our province'. The Fête scene represents the finest piece of sustained humour and possibly the finest piece of sustained writing in Dostoyevsky's works, as well as providing the best sample of that undiscovered Dostoyevsky who is the subject of the present study.

Nowhere in Dostoyevsky's Scandals are the notes of coming doom sounded in more sinister fashion. Many of these go back to points earlier in the narrative, so that by the time the Fête begins almost everyone knows that it will end in a fiasco. The only real interest is—what form will the fiasco take? 'The Fête took place in spite of all confusions', Dostoyevsky's Narrator explains at the beginning of Part Three, adding that Yuliya Mikhaylovna has by now become so obsessed with her plans that she would not have cancelled them even if her husband had died in the night. Meanwhile, in expectation of crisis, many are 'rubbing their hands in advance' for, as the Narrator explains: 'a Russian takes incredible delight in every kind of scandalous public upheaval.'

As in all transitional periods (the Narrator regards this as a transitional period, adding the typical comment, 'from what or to what our transition was, I do not know') various forms of human scum have floated to the surface. Rumours are in circulation, including one to the effect that Karmazinov (who is among the scheduled speakers) intends to deliver his much-publicized Farewell to his Readers dressed in the costume of a governess of the province. Many people, not knowing that Yuliya Mikhaylovna has decided on an austerity Fête in order to bring in more money for her governesses, have been talking of a free champagne lunch, which seems reasonable in view of the high price of the tickets. The more disreputable section of those who are expecting some sort of 'Belshazzar's Feast' fall into an ugly mood when they find that there is not even to be a bar during the afternoon session.

The celebration is to fall into two parts—a session of literary readings in the afternoon and then, after a long interval, a ball in the evening. Before the afternoon session has even started, things have already begun to go wrong. A tremendous crush develops outside the entrance. Inside the hall a colossal, pock-marked retired Captain 'drunkenly demanded to be directed to the non-existent bar and had to be dragged out'. Unruly shouts come from the public seated in front of the stage on which the reading is to take place: 'Perhaps we don't want any readings. . . . We've paid our money. . . . The public's been taken in. . . . We're the bosses, not the Lembkes.' The Lembkes arrive late and are greeted by an absurd flourish from the orchestra arranged by the nihilist and practical joker Lyamshin, whom Yuliya Mikhaylovna has inadvisedly accepted as master of ceremonies.

Further devices step up the pressure. So much has the Fête captured public imagination that, it transpires, many of the poorest officials have pawned their underclothes, sheets and very nearly their mattresses to 'our Jews', so as to be able to buy tickets and dress their ladies suitably. The magnificent hall which has been lent for the occasion, the silks, velvet and jewellery of the wealthier women, which 'shone and burned on all sides', and the decorations worn by the more reputable menfolk contrast with the guffaws and catcalls of the hooligans who have also gained admission, and ensure that the final calamity shall be on the most spectacular level.

The ceremonies consist of five absurd episodes of uneven length which illustrate many features of Dostoyevsky's comic and satirical genius. Among these are his mastery of the unexpected, the range of his variations on the ridiculous, the breathless, seething atmosphere so splendidly sustained by the style, and above all his ability to go one better, and, at the very moment when one staggering blow has been struck, to strike another and yet more staggering blow.

The first reading is one which had not been on the programme at all. On to the stage—a complete surprise to all except the nihilist conspirators who have put him up to it—staggers the preposterous Captain Lebyadkin, red in the face, wearing a white tie and tailcoat. 'He raised his hand, wiped his forehead with it, shook his shaggy head and with an air of one who has come to a desperate decision took two paces forward and suddenly emitted a snort of laughter, laughter not loud, but overflowing, long and happy which made his whole corpulent bulk shake and his little eyes screw up.' Greeted with answering laughs from half the public and claps from the more solid citizens, he is escorted off the stage.

Liputin now appears and explains that Lebyadkin, moved by 'humane and lofty aims', had written an ode in honour of the poor governesses which, in response to shouts from the audience, he proceeds to read aloud. As might have been predicted, Lebyadkin's ode turns out to be in the worst of taste, contrasting the former lot of the governess (who while teaching 'snivelling children' was so desperately keen to get married that she was even ready to 'wink at the sexton') with her present good fortune, now that, equipped with a dowry as a result of the present Fête, she will be able triumphantly to spit in everyone's face—literally 'spit at everything and triumph'.

Liputin's *naglost* in reading this absurd ode is one of the signs, of which more are soon in evidence, that the nihilists have come out into the open and are no longer even bothering to disguise their intention of wrecking the Fête. Into this atmosphere of mounting rowdiness Dostoyevsky injects the victim of his satire whom he treats most savagely of all, Turgenev in the character of Karmazinov.

Karmazinov is greeted respectfully, for Dostoyevsky realizes that the time has now come to decrease the tension momentarily. Ignoring the law whereby even an arch-genius cannot hope to entertain the public unpunished with a literary reading of longer than twenty minutes, Karmazinov proceeds at great length to deliver a piece of mystical, obscure and romantic balderdash, studded with references to obscure plants which have never been heard of outside botanical reference works and dealing, in so far as it can be understood at all, with a love affair of his early youth. It is not easy to take parts of Turgenev seriously again after reading this viciously telling parody. The episode ends with an undignified argument between the 'great writer' and disrespectful nihilist members of the audience, during which the expression on Karmazinov's face seems to say, 'I'm not the sort of person you think. I'm on your side. Only praise me, praise me more, praise me as much as possible. I like it awfully. . . .'

Now that the tradition of public argument with the audience has been established, things go even harder with Dostoyevsky's next victim, Stepan Trofimovich Verkhovensky, who has chosen to treat this as an occasion on which his fate would be decided. He

proceeds to challenge nihilism in the name of the aesthetic ideals
associated with Russian 'men of the forties', claiming that Shakespeare and Raphael are more important than socialism or chemistry.
Various people rush towards the stage and shout insults. Stepan
Trofimovich bursts into hysterical tears and a further push is given
when one of the interrupters accuses him of having many years
before sold the escaped convict Fedka (who now wanders round the
town cutting throats) into the army as a recruit in order to pay his
card debts. Amid general screams, tears and applause, Stepan
Trofimovich raises both hands above his head and curses the
audience.

After the disappearance of Stepan Trofimovich, Dostoyevsky has
by no means finished. 'Suddenly the final catastrophe burst.' The
third reader (a maniac, whom the Narrator has earlier noticed re-
hearsing his speech off stage to the accompaniment of powerful
swings of the fist apparently destined to pulverize some imaginary
opponent) rushes on to the stage and delivers an impassioned
harangue on the theme 'never has Russia reached such a depth of
shame as at the present day'. This is greeted with wild applause.
'That's the stuff! Hurray! This is better than aesthetics!' Dostoyevsky's Narrator comments: 'Russia was being publicly dishonoured,
so how could one fail to roar with delight.' Dragged off by a group
of officials, the maniac somehow bursts free and rushes back for one
final cry of 'But never has Russia sunk . . .' before he is finally
removed.

It now remains for a nihilist girl student, another speaker not on
the programme, to mount the platform: 'Ladies and gentlemen,
I have come to tell you of the sufferings of the unhappy students
and to arouse them everywhere in protest.'

These last two episodes are brief, but it is difficult to exaggerate
their comic impact, coming as they do at a point when Dostoyevsky
seems to have exhausted all the possibilities of comedy. They owe
much of their effect to a device which may be called 'loading'. The
maniac had been introduced to the reader before the speeches of
Karmazinov and Stepan Trofimovich were recounted. His prose
style and habit of smashing down his fist are already known, but,
having been temporarily forgotten during the excitement which
follows, impinge all the more effectively because they are already
familiar. Similarly loaded is the girl student's obsession, which has
already been conveyed in an earlier chapter, with the fate of the poor

students. This device of loading was later to contribute much to the effectiveness of Father Ferapont's outrageous irruption into the vigil over Father Zosima's dead body in *The Brothers Karamazov*.

The first part of the Fête is now over. The ball which takes place in the evening proceeds in an atmosphere of even greater disorder, but here, despite certain absurd episodes such as the 'literary quadrille', Dostoyevsky has most suitably chosen to tone down the comedy. A more sombre atmosphere is cultivated as the reader observes the tragic derangement of Von Lembke, who in his insanity orders Yuliya Mikhaylovna herself to be arrested. The sequence ends with a dramatic finale entirely free from humour when it is learned that a whole suburb of the town, where many of the guests have their homes, is on fire. The nihilists have done their work. In the remaining section of the novel leading up to and including Shatov's murder, there is no place for the riotous absurdities of the 'literary reading'.

One might search the whole of fiction in vain for a finer scene than Dostoyevsky's Fête.

*

Nikolay Stavrogin is probably the most challenging and elusive character in the whole of Dostoyevsky's fiction, and dominates *The Devils* to a greater extent than any other single figure, as it was Dostoyevsky's intention that he should. 'Everything is contained in the character of Stavrogin', he wrote in his notes for the novel. 'Stavrogin IS ALL.'[3]

As Dostoyevsky's letters and Notebooks show, the idea of Stavrogin arose at a late stage in the planning of the novel and compelled him to rewrite a great deal of his text. In its first conception the book had been intended as a simple 'pamphlet novel' directed against political heresy and based on a conflict between Evil (as personified by Nechayev = Pyotr Stepanovich Verkhovensky) and a Dostoyevskian Good man who is called Golubov in the drafts, being a recognizable preliminary sketch for Shatov.

While planning *The Devils* in this relatively crude form, Dostoyevsky was also brooding on something which he regarded as entirely separate and more important—a whole cycle of novels, to be grouped together under the title *Life of a Great Sinner*. This cycle, which was never written, served him as a pool of ideas on which he drew when planning all his three last novels, and it was out of this pool that

Stavrogin arose, began to take on a life of his own and irrupted into *The Devils* to steal the role of chief villain from Pyotr Stepanovich Verkhovensky.

Eventually Stavrogin turned into a formidable embodiment of outward self-sufficiency which concealed inner coldness and emptiness, but when he was first conceived—as an unnamed 'Prince'—he was a more pliable figure. There are references to his 'impressionable . . . shy soul', and he is to be found submitting wholeheartedly to the teachings of a Dostoyevskian holy man about the religious vocation of Russia. These early descriptions of Stavrogin, recorded in Dostoyevsky's notes, show how much the character changed before the novel found its final form. By then Stavrogin had developed along more satanic lines, so that it was no longer he who submitted to others, but others who submitted to him.

Stavrogin has always been recognized as a mystery man, but the irreverent suggestion arises that one of the chief mysteries about him is what he is doing in the novel at all. His connection with the main theme (the moral disintegration of 'our town' under nihilist influence) is so apparently slight that it has been natural to discuss many important aspects of *The Devils* in the preceding pages while scarcely mentioning his name.

However slight Stavrogin's seeming connection with the main theme, there are plenty of threads linking him with the plot, and most of these run through Pyotr Stepanovich. As already mentioned, Stavrogin is the one figure whom Pyotr Stepanovich respects. Impressed by Stavrogin's self-control, power and prestige, Pyotr Stepanovich attempts to involve him in the revolutionary movement as an influential figurehead, because as he says, 'this democratic scum with its cells is poor support. What is needed here is a single magnificent despotic will.' With this in view Pyotr Stepanovich spreads nets of blackmail and flattery, attempting to get Stavrogin in his power in various ways. Stavrogin neither accepts nor rejects Pyotr Verkhovensky's attempts to groom him as a nihilist superboss, but seems to tolerate them because they are mildly amusing, a quality of importance to him since the keynote of his character is boredom.

There has been much speculation about Stavrogin's origins and among the models thought to have contributed to his character are figures as various as Steerforth in Dickens's *David Copperfield*, Dostoyevsky's well-known contemporary Bakunin and another less well-known Russian revolutionary, Speshnyov. One source is the Byronic tradition of the lonely and picturesquely disillusioned superman, a tradition which had been given its own special twist in Russian literature and had found its most notable representative in Pechorin, the central figure of Lermontov's *A Hero of our Time*.

Like Pechorin, Stavrogin is very attractive to women and makes an impression on the ladies of 'our town' with his elegant manners and handsome appearance, and also because he is known to have killed a man in a duel. Four of his marital or extra-marital adventures have a close bearing on the plot. His liaison with Dasha Shatova serves as one of the hidden pressures in the scene of Stepan Trofimovich's humiliation over his projected marriage. The night spent with Liza Tushina at the end of the novel serves to demonstrate finally Stavrogin's inability to feel strongly and hence prepares his suicide. His involvement with Shatov's wife results in her arriving in 'our town' just in time to bear Stavrogin's baby before Shatov is murdered. Finally, his marriage with Marya Timofeyevna provides a blackmail lever for Pyotr Verkhovensky and Marya Timofeyevna's brother, the odious Captain Lebyadkin, while the murder of Marya Timofeyevna and Captain Lebyadkin (actually carried out by the escaped convict Fedka) is, to an extent which characteristically cannot be determined, Stavrogin's own moral responsibility. As these involvements show, Stavrogin, if not closely linked with the main theme of the novel, is at least closely woven into the plot.

Stavrogin has clear affinities with at least two preceding Bogeymen in Dostoyevsky's fiction—Prince Valkovsky of *Insulted and Injured* and Svidrigaylov in *Crime and Punishment*—though he outshines both as a product of Dostoyevsky's creative talent. He shares with Valkovsky, Svidrigaylov and many others that propensity for debauchery in low haunts about which Dostoyevsky loves to cast sinister hints. He also shares their general air of mystery and unpredictability, their supreme arrogance and self-confidence, together with an addiction to criminal eccentricities which seem to spring rather from a desire to experience strong sensations than from any essential criminality, for it is a feature of this type that its capacity for experiencing normal sensations has become atrophied.

It is characteristic of the eccentricities committed by his Bogeymen that Dostoyevsky avoids giving any authoritative explanation of them in his capacity as author. Stavrogin's motives are often made

F

the subject for speculation by other characters in the novel, but it is deliberately not made clear how far such explanations are to be believed. For example, an explanation is offered of his marriage to the crippled girl when Kirillov tells him: 'You deliberately picked the lowest of creatures, a cripple, a woman doomed to eternal disgrace and beatings, knowing what's more that this creature was dying of a comic love for you, and suddenly began deliberately to make a fool of her purely in order to find out what would happen next.' The absurd marriage to the crippled girl is also an example of another theme common in Dostoyevsky's work, the act knowingly and deliberately committed by a man in flagrant defiance of his own interests.

Stavrogin receives a bigger preliminary build-up than any other character in Dostoyevsky. This is spread over the first quarter of the novel, during which he does not actually appear on the stage. By the time he does appear the reader knows of him as a pale, thoughtful, quiet, physically strong and strikingly handsome young man who had been forced to resign from his cavalry regiment for taking part in two duels. Reduced to the ranks by court martial, he had served with distinction in the Polish troubles of 1863—a reference such as rarely occurs in Dostoyevsky to a contemporary historical event—had been decorated and recovered his officer's rank. Though he had been received everywhere in society he had given rise to 'rather strange rumours' and was regarded as a bully who offended people for the mere pleasure of giving offence, while remaining calm and immeasurably self-possessed.

A brilliant section of Stavrogin's build-up is the passage describing his stay in 'our town' at a period preceding the beginning of the main narrative by several years. Having already created a monster of mysterious unpredictability in the reader's mind, Dostoyevsky immediately shows what is—except to those who have closely studied his methods—his own unpredictability by making him behave mildly, a common manœuvre which may be designated as the 'sag'. Thus Stavrogin did not begin his stay in 'our town' by committing outrages. On the contrary he lived there for six months 'apathetically, quietly and rather sullenly. He appeared in society and with unflagging attention adhered to all our provincial etiquette.' Characteristically, however, the sag is soon followed by further foreboding: 'suddenly the beast showed his claws'. It is by skilful alternation of sag and foreboding, of anti-climax and climax, that

Dostoyevsky builds up pressure, blowing up a balloon which must eventually burst.

The next in-stroke in the build-up of pressure around Stavrogin is a short Scandal scene. Pyotr Pavlovich Gaganov, a respected elderly member of the local club to which Stavrogin also belonged, had the innocent habit of remarking on every possible occasion, 'No, sir, you cannot lead me by the nose.' He had once made this favourite remark to a group of by no means undistinguished fellow-club members, when Stavrogin, who had been standing nearby, suddenly went up to him and, unexpectedly seizing him firmly by the nose, pulled him two or three paces across the floor. The 'two or three paces' are again a typical manœuvre—here termed the 'softener'—whereby Dostoyevsky when describing some preposterous episode makes it convincing by toning down some of the details, for a less controlled author might have made Stavrogin drag the unfortunate Gaganov right across the floor. Also contributing to the flavour of this preposterous episode is a richly typical comment to which it is worth drawing special attention, for it is precisely by such unobtrusive touches that Dostoyevsky manages to carry off his wilder episodes: 'People said afterwards that he [Stavrogin] at the actual moment of carrying out the operation, looked rather thoughtful.'

The uproar which followed this incident evoked public sympathy for Gaganov, and Dostoyevsky takes the opportunity to execute another technical flourish. It turns out that a subscription dinner was planned in Gaganov's honour, and that the idea was only abandoned at his own earnest request and 'perhaps because it at last dawned on people that the man had after all been pulled by the nose, so that there wasn't really very much cause for celebration'. Such reference in Dostoyevsky's more absurd scenes to something even more absurd which might have happened—but in fact did not —is, as noted previously, a staple feature of his method. The really impressive thing about these absurd scenes is less their actual absurdity than the technical mastery whereby Dostoyevsky makes them convincing, walking, as it were, on a tightrope between the idiotic and the humdrum, or—if one wishes to employ terms which have become threadbare in the criticism of Russian authors— between fantasy and realism.

Having burst one balloon, Dostoyevsky at once follows through by inflating and bursting another in the scene where Stavrogin, summoned to account for his behaviour by the kindly Provincial Governor (Von Lembke's predecessor) makes as if to whisper confidentially into the Governor's ear, but then seizes the upper part of it between his teeth and holds on to it for several paragraphs. Pressure is again built up by foreboding and sag. Finally, but only after Stavrogin has been put under arrest, Dostoyevsky provides an explanation of his conduct—after he has had some sort of seizure three doctors proclaim that during the whole period of these eccentric happenings he had been in a state of delirium and not responsible for his actions. But this is made only a half-explanation, for, as the Narrator says, 'some of us remained convinced that the scoundrel had simply been laughing at everyone and that his illness had nothing to do with it'.

Stavrogin's manner when he appears after the beginning of the action proper is once more courteous and restrained, though with a suggestion of coldness, indifference and apathy. He performs no further outrages, apart from his suicide which concludes the novel. Rather does he seem anxious to atone for his misdeeds. He accepts without retaliation Shatov's violent blow on his face, though he is a man who might be expected to avenge such an insult by killing his opponent on the spot without bothering to challenge him to a duel. He fights in an actual duel—with the son of Gaganov of the pulled nose—and fearlessly withstands his opponent's fire without attempting to shoot him in return, because, as he says, he has already shed enough blood. He also publicly admits the shameful truth about his marriage to the cripple girl, whom he has supported financially and will continue to support. It will be remembered in this connection that unmentionable villainies off stage and kind actions on stage were characteristic of Stavrogin's forerunner Svidrigaylov.

It soon becomes doubtful whether these kind deeds of Stavrogin are due to anything so mundane as repentance or a wish to make reparation. For example, Kirillov points out that Stavrogin, far from wanting to make amends, is 'seeking a burden' with which to saddle himself, and Stavrogin's kind deeds are later explained as a trial of his own strength, inasmuch as all demanded superhuman control of the nerves. 'I tried my strength everywhere [he writes to Dasha shortly before hanging himself at the end of the book]. I endured your brother's blow; I publicly admitted my marriage . . . I tried debauchery on the grand scale . . . but I do not like and did not want debauchery. . . . Do you know that I even looked upon our iconoclasts [i.e. the nihilists] with anger, through envy of their hopes?' Contrasting his own emptiness with the faith of Shatov (Dostoyevsky's mouthpiece, who insists that a man can have no aim in life if he loses the 'link with his own soil'), Stavrogin laments that 'nothing has come from me but negation, without magnanimity and strength. Even negation has not come.' This suicide note, which concludes the novel, is the nearest thing to an authoritative diagnosis of Stavrogin's disease offered by Dostoyevsky.

A further complication in the consideration of Stavrogin is created by the notorious 'banned chapter' entitled 'At Tikhon's' and omitted by Dostoyevsky from the published version of the novel because his publisher found it obscene. Here Stavrogin is made to confess to Tikhon, a Dostoyevskian holy man who does not appear in the novel proper, how he had once sexually assaulted a little girl. This is Dostoyevsky's most extreme treatment of the theme of sexual relations with a minor with which he flirted on more than one occasion. The closest foreshadowing of the incident occurs in *Crime and Punishment*, where the catalogue of misdemeanours attributed to Svidrigaylov had included the rape of a fourteen-year-old girl who had committed suicide as a result of the experience.

The crime which Stavrogin confesses in the banned chapter is essentially the same as Svidrigaylov's, but is described in greater detail and its revolting nature is intensified by lowering the age of the victim, here an eleven-year-old, and also by the fact that Stavrogin did nothing to prevent her suicide, though he was in a position to do so. Dostoyevsky's intentions in conceiving this scene were especially complex. Amongst other things he had set himself the task of improving on Svidrigaylov by creating in Stavrogin an even more extreme example of the satanic superman whose strength lay in his ability to commit crimes without any twinge of conscience. It seems to have been the lack of regret rather than the crime itself which Dostoyevsky most wanted to emphasize, and in order to put this over with the greatest possible force he decided to attribute to Stavrogin the most appalling deed which he could conceive—the offence against a child.

The offence was conceived as the culminating item in the catalogue of Stavrogin's misdeeds, as is made explicit in the banned chapter. 'Who knows,' the Narrator says, 'perhaps all this—that is, these sheets of paper and the intention of publishing them [the reference is to the printed version of his confession which Stavrogin proposed to make public] were nothing else than the bitten Governor's ear all over again, only in a different form.'

Is Stavrogin's proposal to circularize his Confession intended (a) as yet another demonstration of his strength? or (b) as an act of repentance? The tension between these two possible explanations is the essence of the 'banned chapter' and indeed of the whole conception of Stavrogin. Explanation (a) is of course the nearer to the truth, but Dostoyevsky refuses to commit himself to it explicitly, since to do so would be to decrease the enigmatic quality which was the most important thing to him in his conception of Stavrogin. So explanation (b) could be held in reserve to tantalize the reader.

Since Dostoyevsky was never satisfied until he had realized all of his characters' ultimate potentialities, it is easy to understand that he found *The Devils* incomplete without Stavrogin's Confession. When Katkov (the editor of *Russky Vestnik* in which the novel was appearing) refused to print the offending chapter, Dostoyevsky went to Moscow to persuade him to change his mind. Failing in this, he rewrote the chapter, toning it down to 'satisfy the chastity of the editorial office'.[4] But Katkov still refused to print it, and Dostoyevsky took no steps to have it inserted when, later on, *The Devils* was printed in book form. It was eventually published posthumously in 1923.

The question therefore arises whether the banned chapter is to be regarded as an integral part of *The Devils* or not. Here the verdicts of individual scholars are at variance. Mochulsky describes the banned chapter as Dostoyevsky's 'supreme artistic creation' and calls it the culmination of Stavrogin's tragedy, the second of these two points being easier to accept than the first.[5] Dolinin also regards it as the culminating point of the novel. Other interpreters, including Komarovich and Bem, have taken the opposite point of view.[6]

The main lesson to be drawn from these disagreements is not that either side is necessarily right or wrong, but that art, and especially Dostoyevsky's art, is so frequently ambiguous, its function often being to set puzzles rather than to solve them. In the case of Stavrogin it was Dostoyevsky's own explicit intention that this should be so. In his preliminary notes he had written: 'The Prince [Stavrogin] continually fails ever to reveal himself to anyone. . . . The essence of the tone is not to explain . . . the Prince.'[7]

Such warnings against being over-dogmatic are salutary, but it would be absurd to allow them to prevent one from expressing an opinion on such an important point as whether the 'banned chapter' does or does not belong with the rest of the novel. On the whole it does belong, and not least because it increases the weighting of Stavrogin in the novel as a whole to a point where the Stavrogin theme balances the nihilist theme.

The apparent conflict between these two themes, to which reference was made earlier, is in fact no conflict at all. Where the nihilists represent Dostoyevskian heresy on a social and political level, Stavrogin represents the same heresy embodied in an isolated individual with no political and social axe to grind. Whether political or non-political, Man-without-Dostoyevskyism is demonstrated as equally bankrupt. The same pattern may be traced in *The Brothers Karamazov*.

Novel	Representative of social and political evil	Representative of individual evil
The Devils	Pyotr Stepanovich	Stavrogin
The Brothers Karamazov	The Grand Inquisitor	Ivan Karamazov

Had Dostoyevsky himself once committed Stavrogin's crime? Rumours were current during his lifetime that he had once violated a little girl, brought to him (according to one version) when he was taking a bath. In her *Reminiscences*, written after her husband's death, Anna Grigoryevna Dostoyevskaya rejects this story, offering the curious argument that such a debauch would have been extremely expensive and therefore beyond his means. It seems in any case almost certain that this story was a malicious invention, to which some colour is lent by Dostoyevsky's preoccupation with the rape of minors in his fiction. It is true that he was a man with many extreme weaknesses of character, but is there any recorded instance of him deliberately injuring another individual except with verbal malice or financial inconsiderateness? He was an exasperating enough man, but not at all an evil one. Despite all his surface weaknesses, inconsistencies and absurdities, he emerges from the immense amount of evidence contained in his works, letters and in the vast memoir material as a person with whom so detestable a crime cannot possibly be associated. The crimes which he committed in his imagination are another matter. But outside the confines of his own mind he was probably as little guilty of Stavrogin's crime as of the crime of Raskolnikov or of other Dostoyevskian murderers, rapists, suicides and blackmailers.[8]

*

The two remaining important figures in the book, Shatov and Kirillov, are each closely associated with Stavrogin. Since Shatov represents Dostoyevsky's own views, while Kirillov represents anti-Dostoyevskyism carried to what Dostoyevsky liked to think of as its logical conclusion in suicide, there is here a geometrical opposition of poles crudely similar to that presented in *Crime and Punishment* by the opposition Sonya: Svidrigaylov. In *Crime and Punishment*, Raskolnikov stood between these two conflicting forces. And to a minor extent a similar position in relation to Shatov and Kirillov is occupied by Stavrogin. But whereas, in *Crime and Punishment*, Sonya and Svidrigaylov seem to be pulling Raskolnikov in opposite directions while he oscillates between them, the pressure of these forces in *The Devils* is centripetal.

Unlike Raskolnikov, the stronger-willed Stavrogin is an influencer of others, not a subject for their influence. 'Remember what you have meant in my life, Stavrogin', Kirillov tells him. A page later, in the next section, Shatov, clearly by deliberate echo on Dostoyevsky's part, almost repeats these words, telling Stavrogin: 'You have meant so much in my life.' As Stavrogin is a man without faith of any kind it is not surprising that he influenced Shatov and Kirillov in diametrically opposite directions. For it emerges from one long and important conversation between Stavrogin and Shatov that Stavrogin had persistently injected Shatov, once a revolutionary, with—of all things—Dostoyevskyism. 'You remember [Shatov tells him] your expression "An atheist cannot be a Russian." . . . You said, "A man who is not a member of the Orthodox Church cannot be a Russian. . . ." You believed that Roman Catholicism is not Christianity . . . that Catholicism has proclaimed Antichrist.'

Stavrogin is one of those characters whom Dostoyevsky endowed with qualities which he himself conspicuously lacked. In addition to his superhuman self-control, good looks, high position in society, social ease and other minor desiderata, Stavrogin is shown (in his relations with Shatov) to possess another quality which Dostoyevsky coveted more than these—an ability to convert a revolutionary to Dostoyevskyism. But Stavrogin did not possess another quality which Dostoyevsky would have envied even more, an ability, not merely to preach Dostoyevskyism successfully, but actually to believe in it himself wholeheartedly. For it turns out that while Stavrogin was thus agitating Shatov he was bringing to bear an influence of a very different kind on Kirillov. Shatov tells Stavrogin how he has discovered that at 'the very time when you were planting in my heart God and Motherland, at the very same time, even perhaps on the very same days, you poisoned the heart of that wretched maniac Kirillov. . . . You confirmed the falsehoods and slanders in him and brought him to the brink of madness. Go and look at him now. He is your creation.'

It turns out in fact that Stavrogin's successful excursions into political and religious agitation were just another attempt to 'test his powers' in a way which reveals him as an expert in promiscuous multiple ideological seduction, providing a parallel with his similar prowess in the sphere of sex.

As the Good man of the novel, Shatov continues the tradition of Sonya Marmeladov and Myshkin, and foreshadows the Alyosha-Zosima partnership in *The Brothers Karamazov*. He differs from all these figures in bearing a relatively light ideological load, for though his opinions are thorough-paced Dostoyevskyism, he is not obtruded as a mouthpiece or example to the same extent as the others mentioned. A reader unaware from other sources of Dostoyevsky's social and religious views would probably not recognize him as a mouthpiece at all. No doubt Dostoyevsky, having exhausted so much ingenuity on Myshkin, decided to play down his Good man in *The Devils*. An awkward and strange person given to leaving the room without warning in the middle of a conversation, Shatov is nevertheless not endowed with Myshkin's comic qualities, though he does on one occasion knock over and break a valuable table belonging to Stavrogina, thus echoing the Chinese vase incident.

To a greater extent than any other figure in the novel, Shatov is a self-portrait of the author both in opinions and physically, with his blond colouring, broad shoulders and frowning forehead. So far as opinions go, Shatov voices undiluted Dostoyevskyism, and has also made the transition from political opposition to conformism. In view of all these parallels one particular exchange between him and Stavrogin may be especially significant.

> Stavrogin: Do you believe in God?
> Shatov: I believe in Russia, I believe in her Orthodox Church. I believe in the body of Christ . . . I believe that the Second Coming will take place in Russia . . . I believe . . .
> Stavrogin: But in God? Do you believe in God?
> Shatov: I . . . I shall believe in God.

F*

Is this passage to be taken (in view of the equation Shatov = Dostoyevsky) as a confession by Dostoyevsky of his own lack of religious faith? If so it was certainly not consciously intended as such. Any such interpretation would have been vigorously rejected by Dostoyevsky himself, all the more vigorously because on the whole he tried to protect his conscious mind from the doubts and conflicts which beset him at the submerged creative level from which his great fiction proceeded.

An effective counterweight to the savage humour found in so much of the rest of the novel is provided by the pathos of Shatov's murder. This is anticipated by several hundred pages with indications of impending doom like those which herald Dostoyevsky's more comic crises. These include Stavrogin's warning to Shatov that an attempt will be made on his life and the scene in which Pyotr Stepanovich compromises Shatov in front of the nihilists as a potential spy. When Shatov leaves to show the conspirators the hiding-place of the secret printing press (Dostoyevsky's use of the printing press echoing his own involvement with such a press during the Petrashevsky affair) the reader already knows that this will be his last act on earth. The pathos is heightened by the unexpected arrival of Shatov's runaway wife, whom he dearly loves, and by the nightmare scene where she gives birth to Stavrogin's child, treating Shatov with outward contempt which, as the reader gradually discovers, only conceals her awakening love for him.

The excitement of this scene serves to put Shatov off his guard, so that when he is summoned to his prearranged meeting-place with the conspirators, the preliminaries to which involve (as is usual with a Dostoyevskian murder) much play with staircases, he has no thought for his own danger and meets his death by the pond at the moment of his greatest happiness in life. The murder itself, in which the panic-stricken vacillations of the minor conspirators contrast so effectively with Pyotr Stepanovich's loathsome callousness, is a triumph of suspense and horror.

With regard to Kirillov, who bears the main burden of 'philosophizing' in the novel, the suggestion must be made that, like Ippolit Terentyev in *The Idiot*, he is one of Dostoyevsky's most overrated characters. Dostoyevsky was hardly capable of creating a nonentity, and Kirillov, with his black, lustreless eyes, his curious unidiomatic Russian (a symbol of his estrangement from the Russian soil) and the preoccupation with tea-drinking which serves as his *leit-motiv*, is not easily forgotten. But his arguments that, because God does not exist, he must prove that he himself is God by killing himself and such pseudo-profound statements as 'God is the fear of the pain of death' contribute some of the least interesting pages in *The Devils*. The main point of these reasonings is one hinted at elsewhere in the novels—that suicide is the only course open to anyone who totally rejects the tenets of Dostoyevskyism. It is not until until the passage describing this suicide, in which Dostoyevsky's craftsmanship reasserts itself, that Kirillov ceases to be the most tedious figure in the book.

CHAPTER EIGHT

'*A RAW YOUTH*'

THE eight years from 1865 to 1872, which cover the planning and completion of three great novels—*Crime and Punishment, The Idiot* and *The Devils*—were the most creatively productive of Dostoyevsky's life. Not less productive quantitively were the eight years which remained to him from 1873 to his death at the beginning of 1881, for they saw the publication of two long novels, *A Raw Youth* and *The Brothers Karamazov*, together with *The Diary of a Writer*. But of these three works only *The Brothers Karamazov*, recognized by many as Dostoyevsky's supreme achievement, can compete in importance with the three novels of 1865 to 1872.

It is perhaps no accident that the relative falling off in creativity during Dostoyevsky's last eight years coincided with a period of relative comfort and calm in his personal life. Dostoyevsky's creative talent seemed to thrive most when he was ill, uncomfortable and pestered by debts. These features of his life did not by any means disappear during his last eight years, but were reduced by his wife's care and increasingly effective management of his business affairs.

It is worth noting that as this period began Dostoyevsky is to be found using the word 'comfort', always a key term in his personal philosophy, in an entirely new way. Previously it had been a strong disapprobation-indicator, as in his attacks on socialists for trying to reduce human affairs 'to the question of comfort alone', and in the theoretical structure of *Crime and Punishment*.

Now, however, Dostoyevsky is to be found speaking with approval of this once despised comfort, as in a letter written in the summer of 1872, where he advises his wife on the choice of a flat for the family in St. Petersburg. 'You know my principle about an apartment: even if it's a bit dearer, let it be comfortable and quiet.'[1] The rot had set in.

During the last eight years of his life Dostoyevsky was based on St. Petersburg, with regular residence *en famille* during most summers in the provincial town of Staraya Russa, and regular yearly excursions on his own to take the waters at Bad Ems. There were also occasional visits to Moscow, one of which included the only really stirring event of his last years, the triumphant reception which he received at the celebrations in honour of Pushkin which were held in 1880 and will be described in the next chapter.

These years gave Dostoyevsky more calm than he had been able to enjoy previously, but brought about no abrupt change in his character. He remained irritable, both with his fellow-Russians and foreigners. His letters are full of stories about how he had just 'taken down a peg' (*osadil*) various people who had affronted him by jostling him in a crowd or pestering him on a railway journey. Typical of such testy references is one in a letter of 1876 to two Russians whom he had met in Bad Ems, 'dirty little routine liberals' who had sought his company while making it clear that they condemned him as a reactionary. 'Conceited creatures . . . these two reptiles take it into their heads to teach lessons to such a man as I.'[2]

Another common theme in his letters of the period is the thought of his own death, combined with a fear that he would not be able to leave sufficient money to his wife and children. These were his constant preoccupation during his last years, and a source of great happiness. There is no evidence that his love for his family was shot through with the hatred which so regularly goes with love in his fiction.

*

Opinions differ about the relative rating of *The Devils* and *The Brothers Karamazov*, but few will disagree about *A Raw Youth*, the intervening long novel which appeared in 1875. This is a lesser eminence, if not a depression or morass. Dostoyevsky was not the man to do any job, even the writing of a bad novel, by halves. So it is only by courtesy that *A Raw Youth* can be grouped in the great quintet of novels which begins with *Crime and Punishment*. However, if even the failures of genius are instructive, a failure as spectacular as *A Raw Youth* may be doubly so.

In its underlying message *A Raw Youth* belongs with the other four novels in depicting Dostoyevskian Evil locked in conflict with Dostoyevskian Good. The Evil of self-centredness, which may find expression both in frantic self-assertion and frantic self-abasement, is again contrasted with the Good of serene selflessness. Once more it is Evil which most interests Dostoyevsky, being manifested in a wide range of scoundrels, atheists, nihilists and other undesirables, while the Good is virtually confined to a single figure, the aged, white-bearded Makar Dolgoruky, the most irritating character on Dostoyevsky's pages.

It is interesting that the least effective novel of the great quintet is also the only one which does not revolve around a murder. The climax or attempted climax with which it ends does contain what is probably an attempted murder, of Madame Akhmakova by Versilov. But like so much else in the novel this fizzles out. Versilov does not manage to shoot Akhmakova, and when he turns the revolver on himself only wounds himself in the shoulder. It is tempting to say that one is here in the world of Chekhov's *Uncle Vanya* rather than of Dostoyevsky, except that this scene is no artistically contrived anti-climax or deliberately cultivated whimper, but a whimper which seems to have been conceived as a bang. The novel does contain a number of suicides, but these are artistically feeble affairs compared with the earlier suicides, so superbly described, of Svidrigaylov, Kirillov and Stavrogin. As if to compensate for this neglect, Dostoyevsky devotes greater attention in *A Raw Youth* than elsewhere to blackmail and seduction. The novel abounds in illegitimate children and towards the end treats of the miscarriage of an illegitimate baby by the illegitimate hero's illegitimate sister. But all this is half-heartedly done, not in the manner of the ferocious and free-swinging Dostoyevsky. It was in diluted venom that he dipped his pen when he wrote *A Raw Youth*.

The usual explanation of such faults relates them to the magazine in which *A Raw Youth* was published—*Otechestvennyye Zapiski*, an oppositionist organ which was able at the time to offer more favourable terms than the conservative *Russky Vestnik* where the earlier novels of the quintet had appeared. Letters written by Dostoyevsky during the composition of *A Raw Youth* reflect his anxiety not to offend his new editor, Nekrasov, by the inclusion of material offensive to the political opposition. Since Dostoyevsky's own opposition to this opposition was the very core of his faith, and since Nekrasov was not far removed from Dostoyevsky's idea of a nihilist, this choice of publisher was naturally hampering. Not that Nekrasov was likely to interfere with Dostoyevsky's work, for he was a good literary business man, and this was not the first time that he had opened his columns to an ideological opponent. Another writer might have thrived under the moderating influence of these conditions, but not Dostoyevsky to whom the air of moderation was unsuited.

No doubt the thought of Nekrasov breathing over his shoulder was responsible for the feebleness with which Dostoyevsky handles nihilism in *A Raw Youth*. Like the other novels in the quintet, *A Raw Youth* does have its nihilists—the so-called Dergachov Circle, originally based on the followers of a real-life revolutionary called Dolgushin. But the Dergachov Circle consists of colourless figures. The only member with any claim to interest is Kraft, who provides a new twist among the theories of Dostoyevsky's nihilists by his claim, based on a study of phrenology, craniology, and mathematics, that the Russians are a second-rate people, destined not to play an independent role but to serve as material to be used by some more noble race. Dostoyevsky could not have endowed anyone with views more odious to himself, though Kraft is not portrayed as an unsympathetic figure—indeed his character is so little realized that he hardly leaves any impression at all. His suicide occurs early in the book and is the logical conclusion of his ideas about Russia from which it follows that for him 'in his capacity as a Russian' there is no point in living.

Dostoyevsky may have watered down his nihilists in deference to Nekrasov's supposed wishes, but the feebleness of *A Raw Youth* affects all aspects of the novel, not merely those with political implications. Its main fault, which it shares with a much better novel, *The Idiot*, is the lack of a strong cohesive plot. The most important single intrigue in the book centres round a letter, written some time before the beginning of the action, to a lawyer friend by the beautiful young widow Akhmakova and relating to the 'old' Prince Sokolsky, her father. The old Prince had, at the time the letter was written, been thought to be mad and Akhmakova had expressed a wish to have him put under restraint, since he was in danger of squandering his large fortune. Should this letter come into the hands of the old Prince, now restored to something approaching sanity, he would be certain to disinherit Akhmakova. At the time when the action begins the letter, an important power-lever, has come into the hands of the main hero and Narrator of the novel, Arkady Dolgoruky, who makes incredibly inept use of it.

As this summary of a small section of the plot suggests, simplicity is no more a feature of *A Raw Youth* than of Dostoyevsky's other long novels. It may be that the plot of *A Raw Youth* is no more complicated than that of *The Devils* or *The Brothers Karamazov*, but in these novels a strong central situation helps to draw everything into focus. Since such a situation is lacking in *A Raw Youth*, many of its complications are irritating and of all Dostoyevsky's novels it is the only one which leaves no indelible impression. What happens in it? Many of those who have struggled to the end would be unable to answer this question at the moment when they lay it down, whereas the murder committed by Raskolnikov or the arrest of Dmitry Karamazov might remain in the memory throughout a lifetime after a single reading. This unfortunate impression is strengthened by gratuitous perversities. Not only does the novel contain an 'old' Prince Sokolsky. It also contains some other 'Princes Sokolsky' of whom the most notable is the 'young' Sergey, and who are not related to the old Prince except by way of a common ancestor at the time of Peter the Great. Another unnecessary blur is created by the existence of a second letter, which also comes into the possession of the Narrator and would also offer scope for one less inept in the practice of blackmail. This concerns a lawsuit between the 'Princes Sokolsky' (not to be confused with the 'old' Prince) and the Narrator's father, Versilov. It shows that the Princes have a moral claim to the inheritance which forms the subject of the lawsuit, and which is awarded to Versilov. Just when the fatigued reader has begun to grasp these details, this second letter is allowed to fizzle out.

These anti-climaxes are the more provoking in that they are preceded in some cases by a skilful build-up such as ushers in the grand crises of Dostoyevsky's other works. Nowhere, except perhaps in the grandiose anti-climax at the end, is this build-up technique used with more disastrous effect—partly because of its very success in arousing interest—than in the treatment of the Narrator's 'idea'. At the beginning of the novel the reader learns that the Narrator, a poor young man of low social origin, plans to 'become a Rothschild'—to turn himself into a multi-millionaire by superhuman thrift and disciplined financial speculation. Riches are important to him as a source of power, and power in turn as a source of freedom which consists, in his conception, of 'the solitary and calm consciousness of strength'. This would be sufficient reward in itself, for even as a multi-millionaire he would still wear old clothes and carry an umbrella. Eventually he would give all his millions away.

When reduced to its bald essentials, the Narrator's plan does not sound very interesting, but it is effectively developed by Dostoyevsky, who prepares his reader for a saga of dizzy financial success or spectacular failure. However, no sooner has the idea been expounded than it is immediately dropped and plays no part in the further development of the novel, though it is occasionally referred to. Far from turning himself into a Rothschild, the Narrator behaves as improvidently in money matters as Dostoyevsky himself. He borrows large sums of money, wears expensive clothes, keeps a carriage which he cannot afford, and, in some of the best pages of the novel, gambles recklessly, eventually being thrown out of a gambling house on suspicion of having robbed the bank.

It is in the character of the Narrator, Arkady Dolgoruky, that one of the novel's main claims to interest resides. This is the only work among the mature novels with a fully participating Narrator, a choice of method which was out of harmony with the plot. Since Arkady Dolgoruky has to be present during the whole of the action, excessive use is made of the favourite Dostoyevskian device of eavesdropping in order to include scenes in which he cannot participate. The novel also contains too many conversations between two people, a surprising fault from an author with such a talent for describing crowded scenes.

Arkady represents a throw-back to a type of hero common in the earlier Dostoyevsky, being an introvert, awkward in society and subjected to constant humiliations which he both enjoys and hates. There is also a revival of the 'corner', into which he likes to withdraw because he dislikes people. The circumstances of his parentage provide him with a ready-made grievance which he parades on every possible occasion, although technically not illegitimate (as he constantly proclaims) for at the time of his birth his mother was married to the elderly Makar Dolgoruky, his legal father. Both his mother and legal father had at that time been serfs belonging to the landowner Versilov, Arkady's actual father.

Arkady has been brought up almost as an orphan. He gives a bitter account of his days in a boarding-school, where his teacher treated him as a servant and the other boys made fun of him. However, just as the downtrodden Underground Man had sought domination as well as humiliation, so Arkady too has another side to his character, as revealed during one painful scene, a visit to the school by his mother. A simple 'woman of the people', she arrives with some titbits which Arkady haughtily refuses to eat on the grounds that the school food is good enough. He cuts short her tear-stricken leave-taking by pointing out that they can be observed through the school windows, but after she has gone he weeps bitterly, clutching the handkerchief which she has given him and in which she has tied a few coins.

Although Arkady belongs to a type long established in Dostoyevsky's work, it was not Dostoyevsky's way to repeat himself when creating an individual variant. Arkady is a less painful specimen of the underdog-despot than the Golyadkin twins and the Underground Man, his youth and healthy pink cheeks distinguishing him from these etiolated specimens. His humiliations are described with humour which lacks the cruelty of *The Double* and *Notes from Underground*.

One of the best scenes concerns Arkady's clash with his half-brother, who, in addition to the advantage of legitimate birth, is a tall, handsome and arrogant young man with connections in high society, and thus in every way qualified as a purveyor of Dostoyevskian insults. Arkady, who has never met this brother previously, is compelled to call on him to receive a sum of money sent by his father. He arrives in a state of nervousness after dressing carefully, a common preliminary to Dostoyevskian humiliation scenes. Obtaining admission to the hall, he hears laughter coming from his brother's rooms, a sign that guests are being entertained. The servant who answers the door, Arkady relates, 'looked at me strangely and, as it seemed to me, not as respectfully as he should'.

Five minutes pass, whereupon Arkady orders another servant to announce him. The man refuses. Then when Arkady is just thinking of leaving, the first servant returns with forty roubles in his hand. Not only has Arkady's brother refused to receive him, but he has not even bothered to send out the money on a tray or in an envelope. When Arkady shouts a protest, the inner door opens and his brother, who is wearing a magnificent red silk dressing-gown, stares insolently at him through his pince-nez with a smile all the more insulting because it is scarcely detectable, and then retires without speaking. The scene ends with a quarrel between Arkady and the three servants, who lean over the balcony watching him walk slowly downstairs as he tries to conceal his injured dignity.

This is one of the few good scenes in the novel, and is in keeping with many in which Arkady is insulted or injured by others. He must also hold the Dostoyevskian record for being thrown out of or escorted off various premises, usually as the result of some impulsive outburst. He is continually blushing, blurting out tactless remarks and behaving impertinently to his elders, but differs from most of the early Dostoyevskian underdogs in being likeable. The reader is also given to understand that, at the time the reminiscences (which constitute *A Raw Youth*) are supposed to be written, Arkady's character has developed out of the humiliation-despotism slot up and down which he oscillates throughout the action. But Dostoyevsky, who has little to say about Raskolnikov's reform in *Crime and Punishment*, is even more taciturn about the change which takes place in his Raw Youth.

The chief oscillator in a novel fuller of oscillation than any of Dostoyevsky's other works, Arkady reveals the despotic pole of his character in relation to his own family, particularly to his father, Versilov, and to the desirable Madame Akhmakova. Arkady both loves and hates Akhmakova, and depending on which passion is dominant at the moment is disposed either to use the blackmail letter mentioned above to rob and humiliate her, or else to hand it over to her so that she can destroy it. Since Versilov (towards whom Arkady's feelings also oscillate between love and hatred) himself stands in a similar oscillatory love-hatred relationship to Akhmakova, long before the end of the novel the reader has been subjected to so many switches of current on this triangular circuit that his powers of reacting to them have become paralysed. Arkady himself in a rare moment of insight refers to this tangled intrigue as a 'romantic muddle unworthy of the attention of any serious and right-thinking man'.

The clash between Versilov and Arkady is of some importance. So far the relationship between father and son had played little part in Dostoyevsky's work, but he had touched on it in *The Devils* when portraying Pyotr and Stepan Verkhovensky. It was later to form the backbone of his strongest plot in *The Brothers Karamazov*. But the Arkady-Versilov relationship bears little resemblance to anything in *The Devils* or *The Brothers Karamazov*. Brought up as an orphan, Arkady has met his father only once during his childhood and makes him the focus of romantic imaginings. When he first comes into close contact with Versilov, his chief concern is to get himself taken seriously, if only by making his father seriously angry. This is not easy, for though Arkady is a powerful enough irritant, Versilov's easygoing manner is not easy to pierce.

Versilov's character is more interesting than his tiresomely oscillatory relations with others might suggest. He belongs to the line of Dostoyevskian strong and wicked men, though less of a 'Bogeyman' than Prince Valkovsky, Svidrigaylov and Stavrogin. Versilov's points of contact with these predecessors are numerous, the most important being that he is mysterious. He is found living in poverty at the beginning of the novel, but has been used to wealth, has the social ease of a 'man of the world' and even in humble surroundings possesses an air of urbanity and self-sufficiency. However, this smooth façade may be broken at any moment by some unpredictable outburst, a spasm of maniac rage or act of quixotic generosity. Like Stavrogin, the handsome Versilov is an elegantly painted bomb which may go off at any moment. Unfortunately Dostoyevsky's realization of Versilov is less full-blooded than his portrayal of Stavrogin. Versilov might have been a preliminary sketch for Stavrogin rather than a later model.

Various minor facets of Versilov are of importance to those skilled in reading Dostoyevskian lore. He does his hair in French style, pronounces Russian with a French accent, is said to have been a Catholic (the point is not made entirely clear) and it is also hinted that he is a seducer of 'unfledged girls'. These are all indicators of Dostoyevskian Evil, as the result of which it is possible to trace in *A Raw Youth* a triangular structure, such as is found in *Crime and Punishment*:

Good figure	Central figure	Evil figure
Makar Dolgoruky	Arkady	Versilov

Dostoyevsky follows his usual technique in creating Bogeymen by attributing to Versilov unmentionable deeds off stage. He is one more frequenter of 'low dives' and 'cloacas'. Besides references to various anonymous victims of seduction, it is also hinted that he is responsible for the pregnancy and later suicide (by eating phosphorous matches) of Akhmakova's mad stepdaughter Lidiya. But when the monster appears on stage he surprises everyone (compare Svidrigaylov and Stavrogin) by behaving as a model of considerateness and kindness, his almost unfailing patience with Arkady being a case in point. Moreover, some of the charges against him are shown to be false. It was not he, for example, but Prince Sergey Sokolsky who was responsible for Lidiya Akhmakova's pregnancy. In conceding to the Princes Sokolsky the entire legacy which he has just won from them by a lawsuit, he behaves with spectacular generosity which even embarrasses the opposing lawyers.

Once the tension between surface propriety and latent unseemliness has been established, Versilov is allowed (as is said of Stavrogin) to 'show his claws', for example by sending a fantastically insulting letter to Akhmakova and by attempting to involve her fiancé, the arrogant and stolid Boehring, in a duel. Later on Versilov is the prime actor in the most memorable scene of the novel, which takes place after the funeral of Makar Dolgoruky. Versilov has promised Dolgoruky to marry Sofya (Arkady's mother) after Makar's death, in token of which Makar has bequeathed to him an ikon which he particularly prized. With the ikon in his hand Versilov makes an important speech relating to what he calls his 'Double'.

Do you know, I have the impression that the whole of me is, as it were split in two. . . . I am split mentally and am horribly afraid of it. It is as if you have your own double standing next to you. You yourself are intelligent and rational, but the double at your side insists on wanting to commit some absurdity, sometimes something very amusing. And suddenly you notice that it is you yourself who want to do this amusing thing.

As an illustration Versilov remembers a doctor who had given an irreverent whistle during his father's burial service and who eventually 'came to a bad end'. Similarly, Versilov confesses, he himself now feels a desire to smash the ikon left to him by Makar Dolgoruky. When there is reference in Dostoyevsky to the possibility of something being smashed, it is always probable that, like the Chinese vase in *The Idiot*, it sooner or later actually will be smashed. Not long after his exposition of Double psychology—just long enough to allow a Dostoyevskian 'sag'—Versilov leaps to his feet and dashes the ikon against a corner of the stove, breaking it in two. Disappearing without even bothering to say goodbye, he is next found proposing marriage to Akhmakova, and after being refused, allies himself with the villainous Lambert, who has purloined one of the blackmailing letters in an attempt to accomplish her ruin.

The smashing of a holy object, here portrayed as the result of an irrational evil impulse, and also as a symbol of Versilov's intention not to marry Arkady's mother, is one more product of Dostoyevsky's preoccupation with sacrilege and irreverence, of which examples have already been given. By equating the irrational evil impulse with his 'Double', Versilov further complicates the obscure but pervasive concept of 'dualism' and 'doubles', terms which are best avoided in Dostoyevskian criticism. It may be mentioned in passing that in *The Brothers Karamazov* the word *nadryv* (psychological strain or rupture), in consequence of which various characters in spectacular fashion desert the paths of rational self-interest, is used in a manner similar to that in which Versilov employs the word 'double'. Versilov was of course not the first Dostoyevskian character to surrender to irrational impulse. Dostoyevsky's work had abounded in figures who knowingly and suddenly act in a manner contrary to their own interests, even before the Underground Man had proclaimed an addiction to such acts as an essential part in the make-up of his 'conscious person'. But Versilov was unique in associating this addiction with the concept of the Double.

One curious feature of Dostoyevsky's method was to insert slabs of Dostoyevskyism into the mouths of various fictional characters. But in view of Versilov's association with such indicators of Evil as foreigners, Catholicism and atheism it is surprising to find him spouting views such as Dostoyevsky might more naturally have put into the mouths of Good characters. For example in a long tirade on the superiority of Russians to other Europeans Versilov says, 'I alone as a Russian was the only European in Europe. . . . They are not free, but we are free.'

Whatever may be Versilov's credentials as a representative of Dostoyevskian Evil, there was no equivocation about the way in which Dostoyevsky put forward Makar Dolgoruky, Arkady's legal father, as the embodiment of Dostoyevskian Good. Despite the emotional capital which Dostoyevsky had invested in the innate virtues of the Russian 'people' (*narod*), its representatives play only a minute part in his fiction. Makar Dolgoruky, the most fully portrayed 'man of the people', does nothing to make one regret the omission.

Makar's ideological position is clear. Like Myshkin in *The Idiot* and like Alyosha Karamazov and Father Zosima in *The Brothers Karamazov*, he is set in opposition to the humiliators and humiliated as one who lives in a serene atmosphere entirely apart from these vanities. But, unlike other representatives of Dostoyevskian Good, he is a failure as a fictional character. A saintly old man, he spends nearly a hundred pages dying, uttering from his death-bed a series of rustic saws, moral homilies, improving anecdotes and specimens of hedgerow philosophy couched in uneducated Russian heavily laced with biblical expressions and the language of folk poetry.

A tendency for Russian literature to throw up such homespun wiseacres was not confined to Dostoyevsky. Gorky and Tolstoy were among notable figures who also repeatedly erred in this respect. But though of small interest in his own right, Makar is important to students of Dostoyevskian patterns as a forerunner of Father Zosima in *The Brothers Karamazov*, particularly in his insistence on happiness, joy and tranquillity. He embodies Dostoyevsky's growing insistence of the importance of 'the heart' as opposed to 'the head', as indicated in his comment on one of the subjects of his anecdotes, a retired lieutenant-colonel turned hermit: 'He's got plenty of brains, but an unquiet heart; there are a lot of people like that nowadays.' And elsewhere, 'The more brains the greater the boredom'. Makar makes a great impression on Arkady, who compares him to an anchor and who springs to his defence when his doctor describes him as a religious tramp:

> I assure you that it is rather you and I . . . who are the tramps and not this old man, who still has something to teach you and me, because he has something stable in his life, whereas we . . . have nothing stable.

Makar Dolgoruky is by no means the only purveyor of anecdotes, for the novel is more freely sprinkled with them than any of Dostoyevsky's other works. Two of the less edifying concern birds, a theme which also tends to crop up from time to time in the rhapsodizings of Makar. ('Whether a little bird sings or the stars in all their concourses shine in the night—it is all part of the same mystery.') Similar material was later to figure in the teachings of Father Zosima. Very different is Versilov's story of the merchant who strode into a Moscow tavern in which a nightingale was singing:

'How much does the nightingale cost?'

'One hundred roubles!'

'Fry it and serve it up!'

After the bird has been served up the merchant comes out with the punch-line: 'Now cut me off ten copecks' worth.'

In a similarly un-Makar-like spirit is the story of Arkady's villainous school-friend Lambert, who, upset by the discovery that his mother was the mistress of an abbot, went out and bought a caged canary which he tied to the branch of a tree and destroyed by firing a double-barrelled shot-gun at it from close range. Some of these stories seem to come from the more perverse crannies of Dostoyevsky's brain and raise the problem of whether Dostoyevsky writing his fiction can be compared with a patient speaking on an analyst's couch. It is interesting to note that Dostoyevsky himself makes Arkady write at the end of the book: 'I have re-educated myself precisely by this process of reminiscence and writing down.' And since he later adds 'a new life has started for me', there is some suggestion that Dostoyevsky himself found the process beneficial.

The reader of *A Raw Youth* is not likely to receive any corresponding benefit. Fascinating though the novel is to those steeped in Dostoyevskian lore, it has little to offer the general reader. The characters, apart from the three main figures discussed above, are sketchily drawn. If all Dostoyevsky's later novels were like *A Raw Youth* it would be possible to endorse the mistaken and now largely abandoned stereotype of Dostoyevsky as a writer of limited technical resources, inferior both as a stylist—for the style of *A Raw Youth* is slipshod and uneasy—and as an architect of fictional construction, who somehow redeems all these faults by his 'genius'. Except that such genius as one may find flickering on the pages of *A Raw Youth* is a pale reflection of the powerful beams which play elsewhere in Dostoyevsky's work.

CHAPTER NINE

'THE DIARY OF A WRITER'

The Diary of a Writer, Dostoyevsky's most important non-fictional work, began to be published in 1873 as a regular item in the conservative journal *The Citizen* (*Grazhdanin*), which Dostoyevsky edited during that year, relinquishing his editorship early in 1874 owing to disagreements with the proprietor, Prince Meshchersky. After two years' interval, during which Dostoyevsky's main achievement was the production of *A Raw Youth*, the *Diary* was restarted, now as an independent monthly publication. It appeared throughout 1876-7, lapsed during the writing of *The Brothers Karamazov*, and made a brief reappearance in 1880-1. The *Diary*, which runs to some twelve-hundred pages of normal size, is Dostoyevsky's longest work, and its importance in providing clues to the great novels and to the mind of their creator is considerable.

Dostoyevsky himself gave conflicting accounts of his motives for publishing the *Diary*. On one occasion he said that he published it 'as much for myself as for others, from an irresistible need to have my say in times so interesting and full of character as these'.[1] He had previously written that: 'The main aim of the *Diary* has so far consisted in clarifying as far as is possible the idea of our national spiritual originality and of indicating it as far as possible among current facts which present themselves'.[2] Less grandiloquent was the motive which he gave to a correspondent in a letter of the same year, where he explains his immersement in current affairs as an essential piece of self-preparation for a 'big novel' which he hoped to write and which would be devoted to the younger generation and the modern Russian family.[3] The novel which he had in mind was *The Brothers Karamazov*.

The importance here attached by Dostoyevsky to the detailed study of contemporary events was not new. He had long been a keen reader of Russian newspapers, especially during his four years' stay abroad (1867-71), and often drew inspiration for his fiction from this source, particularly from the crime reports. He felt that his fiction was closely bound up with the contemporary Russian scene, and seems in some of his pronouncements almost to have regarded himself as a kind of documentary realist. Modern readers tend naturally to be impressed more by the range and sweep of his imagination than by any tendency in his fiction to give a sober reflection of the Russian life around him. But Dostoyevsky continually insisted in comments made in his letters that 'real life' was more fantastic than any fiction could hope to be. If he does not appear in his fiction as a sober chronicler of everyday life the reason (at least this is what he himself would have maintained) is that ordinary life, especially that in Russia, is not a sober subject.

The Diary of a Writer is a diary only in name. It offers, not a record of daily events, but a series of tirades often (though not always) sparked off by the events of the month in which a given chapter was being written. While purporting to describe the contemporary Russian and European scene, Dostoyevsky in fact charts the landscape of his own brain and uses his *Diary* more as a vehicle for the exposition of Dostoyevskyism than as a record of the world around him.

Obviously only a small proportion of Dostoyevsky's admirers will ever succeed in reading through the *Diary*, though the book has a fascination for the addict which outweighs its main disadvantage: the over-concentration of revealed truths expounded in the language of impassioned harangue. Indeed, for those with the patience to digest it, the book contains interesting lessons which do not all fall strictly within the confines of Dostoyevskian study. Amongst other important items, it contains the classic nineteenth-century expression of an attitude for which the world is still having to pay: the Russian inferiority complex directed towards Western Europe. Here Dostoyevsky expands ideas which were first expressed in his *Winter Notes on Summer Impressions*.

Dostoyevsky's attitude to 'Europe' (i.e. Western Europe) continues to offer the familiar mixture of love and hate. Under the heading of 'love' come his repeated assertions that Europe is the Russian's 'second motherland' and such ecstatic invocations of Europeans as the following, where an attempt is made in translation to preserve the almost delirious style of the original:

> Oh do you know, gentlemen, how dear to us—to us Slavophile dreamers, who, according to you, are haters of Europe—is this same Europe, this land of 'holy miracles'? Do you know how dear these

'miracles' are to us and how we love and honour—love and honour with more than brotherly intensity—the great races which inhabit it [Europe] and everything lofty and beautiful achieved by them? Do you know that we are tormented and moved to the point of tears and compressions of the heart by the fortunes of this dear and beloved land, and how we are frightened by the storm clouds which increasingly envelop its horizon?[4]

Such confessions of love occur several times in the *Diary*, but are nevertheless relatively rare, for when Dostoyevsky became involved in a love-hate situation it was usually hate which predominated over love. As one who enjoyed the feeling of being insulted by 'Europeans' (to this day a favourite Russian pastime), he was keenly on the watch for incidents, however trivial, which could be turned to good account in provoking the flow of Russian adrenalin. One of these was culled from the *Petersburg Gazette* which gave an account of the strange behaviour of an Englishman on a visit to the Russian front during the Russo-Turkish War of 1877-8. It was not clear whether the Englishman in question, who wore a topee and a pea-coloured overcoat, was a Member of Parliament, a correspondent of *The Times* or just a self-styled 'friend of Russia'. What was clear was that he was a purveyor of insults. Apart from his rudeness in remaining seated in the presence of a Russian Grand Duke, he had on one occasion requested a Russian officer to help him on with his pea-coloured overcoat, an offence which earned him two pages of closely reasoned denunciation in *The Diary of a Writer*. Why (Dostoyevsky asks) had the Englishman behaved in this inexcusable fashion? Could it be put down merely to the eccentricity which all Russians were taught from childhood to attribute to Englishmen? Dostoyevsky rejects this explanation, preferring, in a passage where he reproduces the Englishman's supposed thoughts at some length, to regard the coat incident as a carefully calculated insult:

I am an Englishman and you are only Russians. . . . I've heard that you are heroes and have come to have a look at you, but all the same I shall return with the conviction that I, as a son of Old England (at this point his heart quivers with pride), am nevertheless the first man in the world, and you are only people of the second grade.[5]

The point here is not that the Englishman did not behave badly— he probably did—but that it was Dostoyevsky's habit to over-react to proffered slights as well as to imagine them when they were not really present at all.

Dostoyevsky's touchiness, as revealed in the exaggeration of this incident, is one of the dominant features of the *Diary*, and is directed as much against his fellow-Russians as against Europeans. The most amusing example of this is his treatment of an anonymous abusive letter to himself, with which he deals at length in the May–June, 1877, issue of the *Diary*. This leads to a long fantasy about the imaginary fate of the author of the letter, involving all kinds of shame and humiliation including being kicked in the face by a General. Here Dostoyevsky reveals himself as the psychological twin of his own earlier Underground Man in his determination to extract the last drop out of any situation in which he can, reasonably or unreasonably, imagine himself to have been humiliated. Part of the unconscious humour of the *Diary* lies in the contrast between such paranoiac pettiness and sweeping philosophical disquisitions about man's destiny or the nature of the Russian soul.

One of Dostoyevsky's main charges against Western Europeans was the support which, according to him, they gave to Turkey in suppressing the independence of the Balkan Slavs. Turkish atrocities play a big part in the *Diary*, one of the most notable and sarcastic passages of all being devoted to the supposed effect of these atrocities on Disraeli who, being both an Englishman and a Jew, was to Dostoyevsky an especially important focus of emotion. Dostoyevsky imagines Disraeli's thoughts as he retires to his comfortable bed one night, shortly after receiving the news of how two Orthodox priests had been crucified by Turkish 'bashi-bazouks'.

'What about those black corpses on crosses?' thinks Beaconsfield. 'H'm! well, of course . . . But then the State is not a private individual. It cannot sacrifice its interests out of sentimentality. . . . But perhaps I'd better go to bed. . . . H'm! . . . It was their own fault for turning up. After all, they might have hidden themselves somewhere . . . under a sofa. *Mais, avec votre permission, messieurs les deux crucifiés*, I've got completely bored with your stupid adventure, *et je vous souhaite la bonne nuit à tous les deux*.' And Beaconsfield falls asleep, sweetly and tenderly. He dreams about being a Viscount, surrounded by roses and lilies of the valley and beautiful ladies.[6]

The main elements in Dostoyevsky's attitude to Europe are as follows. Russia owes an immense debt to Europe for guiding her along the path of civilization, but the 'European period' of Russian civilization has now come to an end. Russia, a young country, now represents the future, while Europe represents the past, her doom being prophesied both collectively and in individual passages, such as 'France has had her day', 'If not we, then our children, will see how England will end up.'

Europeans, according to Dostoyevsky, are constantly sneering at Russians, whom they regard as 'barbarians' and as an alien people unworthy to be treated as fellow-Europeans. They look on Russians as their enemies and as the future destroyers of European civilization. At the same time they are completely ignorant of Russia, an ignorance which contrasts with the educated Russian's intimate knowledge of Europe, and which is surprising. 'One always had to wonder that such enlightened people took so little interest in studying a nation which they so much hate and which they constantly fear.'[7]

In this connection Dostoyevsky was continually pointing out the extent to which Western European literature was known in Russia, and contrasting this with the total ignorance of Russian literature to be found in the West.

> It seems to me [he wrote] that all our great talents are fated to remain —for a long time perhaps—unknown to Europe. It will even be the case that, the bigger and more original the talent, the less recognizable it will be. Meanwhile we, I am convinced, understand Dickens in Russian almost in the same way as the English—even, perhaps, including all shades of meaning. It is even possible that we love him not less than his fellow-countrymen do.[8]

Elsewhere he wrote: 'It will be a long time before people read our [writers] in Europe, and when they do read them it will be a long time before they understand and appreciate them.'[9] Events have proved this one of the less wild prophecies embodied in *The Diary of a Writer*.

Less successful as prophecy were Dostoyevsky's musings on revolution, which he believed likely to attack the states of Western Europe, while Russia, preserved by her spiritual integrity, remained immune from it. The great states of Europe, he claimed,

> will be weakened and undermined by the unsatisfied democratic strivings of a large part of their meanest citizens, their proletarians and beggars. But in Russia this cannot possibly happen. Our common people is satisfied, and the further we look into the future, the more satisfied it will be. . . . For this reason there will be left a single colossus on the continent of Europe—Russia. This will perhaps happen much sooner than people think. The future of Europe belongs to Russia.[10]

It is amusing to find Dostoyevsky here (without collusion) agreeing with Marx's contention, since belied by events, that a revolution described as proletarian would strike the advanced industrial countries of the world first.

Dostoyevsky admitted that West European countries had gone much farther than Russia in the development of science. But that would not save them. 'The passive Russians, while people over there [in Europe] were inventing science, were developing a not less astounding activity: they were creating the Tsarist system.' Dostoyevsky had shown himself less sanguine about Russia's prospects of becoming the colossus of Europe in 1873, the year in which the *Diary* first began to appear. Here, in what is perhaps the most remarkably prophetic passage in the entire *Diary*, he foresaw something in the nature of nuclear weapons. 'In about fifteen years perhaps people will no longer be firing guns, but some sort of lightning, some kind of all-consuming electrical stream out of a machine.'[11] From this Dostoyevsky deduced that Russia should spend at least as much on education as on her army in order to be able to compete scientifically with the West.

Later on he was more inclined to discount Russia's technical inferiority as he became increasingly impressed by her spiritual superiority to the West. The West was doomed in the last resort because it was eaten out by the corrupt materialism associated with the stereotype of the 'bourgeois', and because of its lack of serious spiritual resources. Above all Europe lacked genuine religious faith, whether one looked at the Catholic Church, which, according to Dostoyevsky, had compromised itself by seeking temporal power, or at Protestantism, which was entirely dependent on Catholicism since it consisted purely of a negation of Catholicism. Dostoyevsky believed that the time had now come when the Catholic Church would become demagogic and join forces with Socialism. He tended, no doubt to the astonishment of any Socialists and Catholics who may have read the *Diary*, to treat the words 'Socialism' and 'Catholicism' almost as synonyms. Dostoyevsky's mind had by now become a confused battleground in which various negative stimuli (not greatly distinguished one from the other) such as Atheists, Catholics, Socialists, Communists, Jesuits, Jews and stockbrokers were locked in conflict with other, positive stimuli, such as the Orthodox, the Russian, the Slav and the *narod*. The outcome in this unequal battle was inevitable: the enemy would collapse because of his corruption and ineffectualness, leaving the field to Russia and the Russian Idea. The 'Pan-European conspiracy' of Jews, Catholics and stockbrokers might be active at the time when Dostoyevsky was writing, but would disappear as soon as—an event repeatedly prophesied in the *Diary*—Russia decided to 'say a New Word'. The New Word, one of the more comic concepts of the *Diary*, occupies a somewhat shifting position, since it is sometimes described as being just about to be pronounced, and sometimes as already having been pronounced, while the identity of those who pronounce it vacillates between 'Russia' and the Slavs as a whole.

Though the approved concept of 'Russia' is everywhere opposed to the non-approved concept of 'Europe', Dostoyevsky's attitude to his mother-country was no more free from his usual ambivalence than any of his other attitudes. The most that may be said is that love seems to predominate over hate in his contradictory approach. Love is especially to the fore at times when Dostoyevsky considers Russia's relations with other countries. Here he constantly stresses the purity of Russian motives, which, because of their very selflessness, are misunderstood by European brains unequipped to recognize a truly disinterested action. Dostoyevsky even blames Russians for the excess of their kindness, contrasting the Russian 'army of gentlemen' with the atrocious Turks against whom they were fighting in 1877–8. This is the kind of war propaganda in which it is axiomatic that all atrocities are committed by the other side. Dostoyevsky speaks with particular indignation of the behaviour of various 'humane' Russian ladies towards Turkish prisoners of war (it should be remembered that 'humane' belongs to the Dostoyevskian vocabulary of abuse). These ladies annoyed Dostoyevsky by offering sweets and bouquets to Turkish prisoners on a railway station. What would they do if they were to meet a certain 'bashi-bazouk', whose habit had been to tear babies in two and cut strips out of their mothers' backs?

> I think these ladies would have met him with a screech of ecstasy, and would have been willing to offer him, not only sweetmeats, but something a bit better than that, and would then perhaps have begun a discussion in their ladies' committee about founding a scholarship in his honour in the local high school.[12]

It is difficult to complete the catalogue of the virtues attributed to Russia in the *Diary*. These include 'eternal service to common human ideals', a lack of territorial designs on any other country, a more democratic structure of society than that of any other country, and a superior tolerance of other people's faith.

So much for the idyllic picture of Russia when confronted with other countries. But when Dostoyevsky considers Russia in relation to himself, the picture becomes less idyllic, since there is scarcely a section of Russian society which escapes condemnation. This falls with particular severity on the privileged classes whose main defect in Dostoyevsky's eyes was that they had allowed themselves to become cut off from the common people (*narod*). He kept a close watch on this rift, and there were times when he seemed to see it narrowing. One of these had been the period of the Emancipation of the Serfs in 1861. Now the anti-Turkish feeling, which led to Russian volunteers going to fight against the Turks in 1876 and to actual war between the two countries in the following year, inclined Dostoyevsky to believe that the rift between the privileged classes and the *narod* was once more on the point of disappearing. But this was not his dominant impression.

Dostoyevsky's contempt for the powerful and privileged classes of Russia stopped short of the Tsar, of whom, as a fervent supporter of autocracy, he always spoke in reverential tones. With this exception the influential sections of Russian society aroused only his contempt—an indication has already been given of the scorn with which, in his fiction, he treated those high officials termed in Russia 'generals'. The same attitude is revealed in the passage of the *Diary* to which reference was made above, where he derides Russian society ladies who made Turkish prisoners of war the object of their charity on railway stations.

The contempt which Dostoyevsky felt for Russians at home was more than equalled by his contempt for Russians abroad, of whom he had given so unforgettable a picture in *The Gambler*. This was a time when former serf-owners, taking advantage of the relative freedom with which foreign passports were issued under Alexander II, had formed the habit of proceeding through the watering-places and fashionable centres of Europe surrounded with attendant governesses and French maids, and arousing envy for Russian wealth among European observers. What the observers did not know, according to Dostoyevsky, was that these Russian landowners were often using up the last of their capital on such ostentation.

These sybarites who lounge around the German spas and the shores of Swiss lakes, these Luculli consuming their substance in Parisian restaurants—they themselves know and, even with some degree of pain, foresee that in the end they will run through their entire funds and that their children, these same little cherubs in English costumes, will perhaps have to beg alms throughout Europe... or turn into French or German labourers. ....[13]

The ultimate crime of these 'Russian foreigners', in Dostoyevsky's view, was to teach their children to speak French. 'Oh, Mummy doesn't know with what venom she is poisoning her little child as early as the age of two, when she invites a French *bonne* to look after him.'

The main target for Dostoyevsky's ridicule, in the *Diary* as elsewhere, is not, despite the examples given above, the privileged categories of landowners and high officials, but a class which only overlapped with these categories to a limited degree, the Russian intelligentsia. The word 'intelligentsia', together with 'intellectual' (*intelligent*), 'enlightened', 'educated' and similar terms, belongs, as has already been indicated, to the vocabulary of Dostoyevskian abuse. It was a constant fear of Dostoyevsky's that he might be drawn into conversation with Russian intellectuals.

> The journey from St. Petersburg to Berlin is a long one, lasting almost forty-eight hours. So I took with me two pamphlets and several newspapers just in case. I say 'just in case' because I always fear being stranded in a crowd of unknown Russians of our intellectual class— anywhere, in a train carriage, on a ship or at some public meeting.[14]

The intelligentsia, in Dostoyevsky's view, carried the double taint of contamination with 'Europeanism' and of exalting itself over the common people.

It is the common people (*narod*) which Dostoyevsky uses as the main bludgeon with which to attack the Russian privileged classes and intelligentsia, 'our class'. 'Our class' might like to think itself superior to the common people, but this is the reverse of the truth. The common people is more educated than 'we'. It is 'we' who must learn from them, not they from us.

The picture of the common people is, however, no unrelieved idyll. They are described as 'dirty, ignorant and barbarous'. Reference is made to their penchant for 'debauchery' and to their 'stinking habits', including drunkenness, the peasant's practice (hallowed by years of tradition) of beating his wife, the ill-treatment of

G

children and ignorance of the prayers of the Orthodox Church. However, none of this mattered very much compared with the nugget of pure goodness which (as Dostoyevsky firmly believed) lay somewhere concealed in the *narod* if only one could grub around long enough in the dirt to find it.

> He who is a true friend of humanity, he whose heart has once beaten in sympathy with the people's suffering—such a man will understand and excuse all the impenetrable, piled-up muck in which our *narod* is immersed, and will be capable of finding diamonds in this muck.[15]

The superiority of the *narod*, in Dostoyevsky's view, rested on the proposition that the Russian common man, unlike the common man of other nationalities, did not commit evil without being aware that what he was doing was wrong. 'I am somehow blindly convinced' (the adverb is significant) 'that there is no one so scoundrelly and blackguardedly among the Russian *narod* as to fail to realize that he is base and disgusting, while others do evil deeds and go on to praise themselves for this, erecting their vileness into a principle.'[16] This underlines a basic tenet illustrated again and again in Dostoyevsky's fiction: it is better to commit murder or some other major crime, provided that you are instinctively convinced of the truth of Dostoyevskyism, than to abstain entirely from crime while remaining indifferent to Dostoyevskyism.

It is a characteristic Dostoyevskian paradox that the shafts of bitter sarcasm and hatred directed at so many sections of the human race in the *Diary* are fired by a man who placed love of his brother-man in a central position in his creed. Surveying the attacks on all foreigners, from the unspeakable Turks down to Western Europeans and the Slavs themselves (among whom the Poles come off particularly badly), one is at first inclined to discern a contrast in Dostoyevsky's mind between evil foreigners and virtuous Russians. It is only when one begins to dissect his attitude to various sections of Russian society that one begins to wonder whether Russians really come off much better than anyone else.

Reviewing in turn all the objects of Dostoyevsky's hatred, one begins to have the impression that one is peeling an onion. What will be left at the centre? The prophet himself, alone in his glory? Or nothing at all? It is true that the *narod*, despite various strictures made against it, remains relatively unscathed. But it is not easy to know exactly what Dostoyevsky meant when he spoke of the

Russian common people—at all events it seems to have little to do with any actual common persons. There is continual reference to the common people responding 'as one man' to various external crises, and the suspicion begins to arise that perhaps the *narod* in Dostoyevsky's mind really was one man—himself. Often on his pages *narod* seems to be used as a loose synonym for 'I'. Already in Dostoyevsky's time the word *narod* had become the supreme Russian nonsense-indicator, particularly when turned into an adjective and combined with another Russian nonsense-word, *pravda* (truth, justice). Thus the phrase *narodnaya pravda*, 'the People's Truth', comes as near to achieving an absolute vacuum as is possible in the sphere of semantics. This phrase, too, is lavishly used by Dostoyevsky in the *Diary*.

Dostoyevsky's prose style, at its best a very subtle instrument, is not seen to advantage in the *Diary*, which is so often hysterical and incoherent, despite patches of superb rhetoric. In general the style is one of the points which, taken together with certain features of Dostoyevskian teaching, make it possible to draw a parallel by no means far-fetched between the *Diary* and Hitler's *Mein Kampf*. Among the parallels of thought Dostoyevsky's attitude to Jews is particularly striking. Like Hitler, Dostoyevsky felt that he discerned an 'international Jewish conspiracy', but claimed 'All the Jews in Europe together shall not conquer us.' At home the Jews were accused of 'humiliating and debauching the *narod* . . . drinking their fill of its sweat and blood'. When Jewish readers of the *Diary* wrote to protest against its anti-Semitism, Dostoyevsky replied in an indignant harangue that he was not anti-Semitic at all. Could he help it if Jews happened to be objectionable? The offensiveness of his comments on the Jews is increased by his preference for the insulting term *zhid* ('Yid') to the neutral *yevrey*.

Amongst other features in which Dostoyevskian doctrine provides a foretaste of Hitlerism are his reflections on the destiny of a great nation:

> Every great nation believes and must believe, if it wishes to remain alive for long, that in it and in it solely consists the salvation of the world, and that it lives in order to stand at the head of the peoples, to join them all to itself in unity and to lead them in a harmonious chorus to the final goal.[17]

In keeping with the spirit of this passage, Dostoyevsky advocated an expansionist foreign policy, in which the main goal was to be the conquest of Constantinople by force of Russian arms.

Dostoyevsky did not neglect that essential piece of equipment in the armament of the aggressive-minded, a profession of peaceful intentions. Our people he says:

> do not want war at all . . . but by Jingo [this here seems an exact translation of the Russian particle *uzh*] if it should be necessary, if the great word of the Tsar should sound abroad, it [the people] will march in its entirety, in its whole mass of a hundred millions and will do everything which such a hundred-million-strong mass can do when inspired by a single impulse and in harmony as one man.[18]

Elsewhere Dostoyevsky puts forward the view that war is to be welcomed for its therapeutic effect on society. 'We need this war [against the Turks] ourselves; not only for our brother-Slavs, tortured by the Turks, do we arise, but for our own salvation. War will clear the air which we breathe and in which we have been suffocating, sitting in the sickness of corruption and in spiritual narrowness.'[19] This preoccupation with the desirability of war is also reflected in Dostoyevsky's correspondence, for example, in a letter of 1870 in which he says: 'Without war man congeals in comfort and riches, and completely loses the capacity for generous thoughts and feelings, becoming imperceptibly embittered and falling into barbarism.'[20]

Despite parallels in the exaltation of war, in the doctrine of the People's destiny and in anti-Semitism, Dostoyevskyism cannot be regarded in any important sense as being a forerunner of twentieth-century Fascism or of any other less short-lived totalitarian creed. The main point of difference is that Dostoyevsky did not seek to give to his views any organizational basis which would enable him to impose them on others. Nothing was further from his mind than the idea of founding a Movement. In his more sanguine moments he may have imagined the face of Russia being changed by the influence of his *Diary* and of the ideas from it which he embodied in his fiction. But such a change, in his view, must take place on an individual level, as the result of the conversion of large numbers of individual human beings. For it was a central item of his creed that society could only be transformed by the moral and religious changing of individuals, never by institutionalized pressures.

Here we meet yet another paradox in the complex of Dostoyev-skyism, where extreme intolerance went hand in hand with extreme claims for human freedom. Freedom was a central concept in his conception of the Christianity of the Orthodox Church. Again and again he emphasizes the fact that Christ cherishes the disciple who comes to Him of his own free will, and claims that the basic idea of Christianity is the recognition of the value of human personality and of freedom. The importance attached by Dostoyevsky to free-dom helps to explain the indignation which he repeatedly expresses, in the *Diary* and elsewhere, against the new and fashionable theory that crime was to be regarded as the result of environment. Dostoy-evsky interpreted this theory as an insult to humanity, since it denied human beings the responsibility which he regarded as an essential corollary of their freedom.

This reminds one of another important topic in the *Diary*, the proceedings of Russian criminal courts, in which Dostoyevsky took great interest. Owing to the reform of the Russian penal system in the early eighteen-sixties, these were often referred to as 'our new courts', and Dostoyevsky was anxious to observe the workings of that new institution, trial by jury. His general conclusion was that too many guilty people were acquitted, a tendency which he found less unfair to society than to the criminal himself, denied by his acquittal the opportunity of suffering.

Closely linked with the topic of the law courts is another staple theme of the *Diary*, the welfare of young children, and in particular the protection of children against cruelty. The obsession with cruelty to children as the ultimate manifestation of human evil runs through the *Diary* as it does through so much of the fiction.

The *Diary* is a fascinating and discursive work, liable at any moment to desert themes of more permanent interest to Dostoyev-sky for a discussion of such topics as birth-control and the impact of the Peabody rifle (capable of firing ten to twelve rounds a minute) on infantry tactics. But the book derives its main interest from what it tells the reader about a novelist of genius practising a craft—the dispensing of political-social homilies—in which he was far from a genius. He might well have applied to himself the criticisms of two predecessors among Russian writers, which he makes on the pages of his *Diary*. Gogol, he says, 'in those parts of *Dead Souls* where he ceases to be an artist and begins to discuss things directly on his own account, is simply weak and even lacking in character'. And

Griboyedov 'as soon as he deserts the role of the artist and begins disquisitions on his own behalf, originating in his own personal brain . . . at once descends to a most unenviable level'.[21]

Another idea put forward in the *Diary*, which again seems to apply with peculiar appositeness to Dostoyevsky himself, is his discussion of the Russian when he becomes seized of an 'idea'. 'The idea suddenly falls on a man like an enormous stone and half squashes him—and there he is writhing underneath it and unable to extricate himself.'[22]

•

One of the most notable passages in the *Diary of a Writer* is the text of the so-called 'Pushkin speech', originally delivered by Dostoyevsky on 8th June, 1880, during elaborate celebrations then held in Moscow to commemorate the unveiling of a monument to Russia's national poet.

Dostoyevsky had been invited to speak about two months previously by the President of the Society of Lovers of Russian Literature. He accepted with hesitation because, if rumour was to be believed, the occasion might well turn into a kind of pitched battle between the two main opposing politico-literary camps—the conservatives (to whom Dostoyevsky himself belonged) and the opposing camp of liberal 'Westernizers', of which the most prominent member was Turgenev. Before leaving for Moscow, Dostoyevsky had already heard rumours that a certain clique was 'raging' there with the aim of keeping the celebrations free from 'retrograde' speeches—the term 'retrograde' being the label attached to persons of Dostoyevsky's own school of thought by their liberal opponents. From what he could make out, Turgenev, the head of the opposing camp, was already turning himself 'into a sort of personal enemy of mine'.[23]

It is fascinating to read descriptions of the preliminaries to the celebrations contained in letters written by Dostoyevsky from Moscow. In reading them one seems to be carried back in spirit to the portentous and sinister 'build-up' passages which precede the explosion of his grandiose fictional Scandals, and the impression begins to be created that the Pushkin celebrations are about to go the way of the ill-starred Fête in *The Devils*. Among the portents of doom recorded in these letters are the mounting hysteria of the public, with as much as fifty roubles (a considerable sum at the time) being paid for the rental of windows overlooking the square on which the unveiling was to take place.

Everyone who bought a ticket to the public speeches wanted to know if Dostoyevsky himself was to speak. Meanwhile he was involved in an atmosphere of feverish intrigue and increasing tension as the inflammatory news filtered through that 'the party of our enemies wants to play down Pushkin's significance as a spokesman of the Russian national spirit'.[24] On the eve of his speech he was invited to a 'dinner for five hundred people with speeches and perhaps with a fight'[25]—which, however, seems to have passed off peaceably. Having retired from this to write a letter to his wife, he found himself in a condition which reminds one of Prince Myshkin on the night before the Chinese Vase Incident. 'Tomorrow's my big début. I'm afraid I won't sleep properly. I'm afraid of having a fit.'[26]

Dostoyevsky's speech did not after all turn into an occasion on which fact imitated fiction. Far from erupting into a Scandal it became the greatest triumph of his career. The atmosphere cannot be better conveyed than by quoting his own words, written to his wife on the evening after his triumph.

> The hall was packed. No, Anya, you'll never be able to picture to yourself and imagine the effect which it [the speech] created! . . . When I appeared, thunderous clapping burst out in the hall, and for a long, long time they wouldn't let me speak. I kept bowing and making signs asking them to let me speak—but it was no use. There was ecstasy and enthusiasm (all due to the Karamazovs). I spoke loudly and with passion. . . . (It's a terrific triumph of our ideas over a quarter of a century of errors!) But when at the end I held forth about the *world-wide unity* of people, the hall seemed to be having hysterics. When I'd finished—I can't convey to you the howl, the shriek of ecstasy. Strangers among the audience were crying, sobbing, embracing each other *and swearing to each other to be better, not to hate each other in future, but to love.* The meeting broke up and everyone rushed towards me on the platform.[27]

Thus the scene proceeded, amid tears, kisses and handkerchief waving. Shouts from the crowd acclaimed Dostoyevsky as a prophet. Two old men who had been enemies for the previous twenty years embraced each other and made up their quarrel on the spot. Dostoyevsky received a tearful embrace from Turgenev, while another of his former enemies, the memoirist Annenkov, rushed to shake his hand and kiss his shoulder. 'You are a genius, you are more than a genius', they told him. A new era of human brotherhood seemed to have been ushered in—an illusory impression, as was emphasized not long afterwards by the squabbles which broke out in print over Dostoyevsky's speech.

The scene of Dostoyevsky's triumph is of sociological interest to connoisseurs of Russian behaviour patterns, and of biographical importance in marking the most triumphant moment of his life. However, to the student of Dostoyevsky the artist, the Pushkin speech is of only limited interest, its chief importance being that it contains perhaps the most concentrated and typical expression of Dostoyevskyism to be found anywhere in *The Diary of a Writer*. To the study of Pushkin (Dostoyevsky's ostensible subject) the speech contributes little but confusion, although it is important as the crowning episode in a cult of Pushkin which Dostoyevsky had faithfully followed since he was a boy. Many of the ideas on Pushkin contained in the speech had been outlined previously in Dostoyevsky's journalism, beginning with articles in *Vremya* written in 1861.

One of the main contentions in the speech is the significance attached to two specific heroes of Pushkin: Aleko from the poem *The Gypsies* and Onegin, the hero of the verse novel *Yevgeny Onegin*. These two figures are put forward as specimens of a type which Dostoyevsky terms 'the Russian wanderer'. The two heroes are regarded as examples of the Russian intellectual wandering frustratedly over the face of the earth because he has become cut off from the common people and lost his roots with the soil. The Alekos of Pushkin's day had now, so Dostoyevsky maintained, turned to Socialism.

The messages read by Dostoyevsky into *The Gypsies* and *Yevgeny Onegin* were scarcely, if at all, present in Pushkin's mind when he wrote these two works. But even if this fact had been brought to the attention of Dostoyevsky's hearers, it is doubtful whether they would have been greatly concerned. It is true that Dostoyevsky was not much interested in Pushkin except as a source of texts on which to base sermons embodying his own social, religious and political ideas. But by treating Pushkin in this way he was only conforming with a dominant tradition in Russian literary criticism, which has so often sought less to illuminate the works of Russian writers than to use them as a pretext for agitational harangues embodying the views of the critic.

As harangues go, this was a good one, and whatever one may think of it more than eighty years later, it was an inspiration to Dostoyevsky's audience. It proceeds in an emotional crescendo as Dostoyevsky leaves the discussion of individual Pushkinian heroes and works up to a general assessment of the poet's importance. This, according to Dostoyevsky, rests on Pushkin's pre-eminence as the writer who most fully embodies Russian national feeling. 'Everywhere in Pushkin can be sensed a faith in the Russian character, a faith in its spiritual power.' 'Never yet has any single Russian writer either before him or after him been so sincerely and intimately united with his people (*narod*) as Pushkin.'

The feature which, in Dostoyevsky's view, most contributed to making Pushkin a great Russian national poet, was a 'capacity for universal responsiveness' which he shared with the Russian *narod*. This involved a capacity for understanding and 'getting inside the skin' of foreigners—a special Russian talent, according to Dostoyevsky, which was denied to the representatives of other nationalities. Hence it would be impossible to tell that the author of Pushkin's dramatic poem *The Stone Guest* (set in Spain) was not a Spaniard were it not for Pushkin's signature. By contrast with this Shakespeare's numerous Italians are almost all Englishmen in disguise. Thus Pushkin was, in Dostoyevsky's view, the supreme repository of the 'universality' (*vsemirnost*) and 'omnihumanity' (*vsechelovechnost*) regarded by him as the distinguishing feature of the Russian common people. To be a true Russian meant being a brother to all men.

This appalling but somehow inspired rubbish is one of the most remarkable examples on record of *vranyo*, a notoriously untranslatable word, which has been discussed above, and combines the concepts of lying, romancing, boastfulness and 'shooting a line', the nearest single equivalent being 'blarney'. But *vranyo* is altogether too subtle and Russian a concept to be effectively conveyed at all by the vocabulary of any other language. Those who wish to steep themselves in it should read the Pushkin speech.

*

It was Dostoyevsky's occasional practice to include short works of fiction in his *Diary of a Writer*. The most important of these is the story *A Gentle Girl* (*Krotkaya*), which appeared in November, 1876. The immediate inspiration for the story, as often happened

G*

with Dostoyevsky's fiction, was a newspaper report—on this occasion
of the suicide in Moscow of a young woman called Borisova, who
had thrown herself out of a window clutching an ikon. This last
detail particularly fascinated Dostoyevsky, who was in any case
much concerned with the prevalence of suicide among young people
in Russia at the time, a theme which occurs several times in *The
Diary*. Dostoyevsky's imagination linked Borisova's recent suicide
with two themes which he had noted down seven years previously as
suitable for development in fiction, the idea of discord between an
incompatible married couple and the idea of an ex-officer who had
come down in the world and become a pawnbroker.[28]

In this successful short story Dostoyevsky employs a device which
was for him a technical innovation, but one which, in his short
preface to the story, he claims had been used before by other
writers, notably by Victor Hugo in his *Last Day of a Condemned Man*.
The innovation consisted in writing down the thoughts of the
Narrator as if they had been taken straight down in shorthand. The
story thus consists of the disjointed reminiscences of a husband
shortly after his young wife has committed suicide in the manner
of Borisova by throwing herself out of a window. The entire story
is therefore a flash-back from its main crisis.

Despite the element of innovation and its superior technical
accomplishment, *A Gentle Girl* in many ways looks back to the period
before *Crime and Punishment*. In particular, the hero represents yet
another figure in the long line of 'St. Petersburg dreamers', his
closest affinity being with the Underground Man of *Notes from
Underground*. The connection with these predecessors is made quite
specific, the term 'dreamer' being actually employed in the text of
A Gentle Girl, and reference also being made to the 'corner' in which
the hero of the story has, like so many previous Dostoyevskian
underdogs, shut himself away from the human race. He runs true
to form by having been unpopular at school and in the army regiment in which he had served for a time, but from which he had to
resign owing to his unwillingness to take part in a duel. At the time
when the action begins he has, as it were, contracted out of the
human race, shutting himself up in his small pawnbroker's business
from which he eventually hopes by practising extreme self-denial
to make a small fortune of 30,000 roubles, a plan which recalls the
'idea' of Arkady Dolgoruky in *A Raw Youth*.

As a man of forty-one, the Narrator is ripe for a love affair with an innocent young Dostoyevskian girl, the 'gentle girl' of the title, who, at the age of sixteen, is ill-treated and beaten by the aunts who have brought her up since she was orphaned. The Narrator offers her marriage, thus providing her with an escape from her intolerable existence, and with the marriage one of the most notable duels on Dostoyevsky's pages begins. Crushed and humiliated by the circumstances of his previous biography, the Narrator views his marriage as an opportunity to pay back some of the humiliation which he has himself received. He regards his wife as an object for the exercise of power rather than of love. In this way he gradually kills the love which she feels, or might have felt, for him. By the time he has conquered his obsession with power and come to love his young wife she is no longer able to love him, and suicide is her reply to this unacceptable situation. Some of the details of the love-power duel in *A Gentle Girl*—notably the scene where the husband overhears the overtures made to his wife by the would-be seducer—seem too melodramatic, but this is redeemed by the skill with which Dostoyevsky deploys his favourite device of suspense. The nearest parallel in his earlier work to the duel between husband and wife in *A Gentle Girl* is the clash between the Underground Man and the prostitute in *Notes from Underground*.

*

The other pieces of fiction included in the *Diary* are shorter and less important than *A Gentle Girl*, but do include two intriguing excursions into fantasy. One of these, *Bobok*, describes a conversation between newly buried corpses in a cemetery. Another, *The Dream of a Ridiculous Man*, revives a theme of permanent fascination to Dostoyevsky—the idea of a utopistic human society such as he had previously associated with the symbol of the Crystal Palace. On Dostoyevsky's pages such utopias exist only to be destroyed, and here it is his own 'Ridiculous Man' who himself corrupts the paradise which occurs to him in a dream. Another well-known passage from the *Diary* is *The Peasant Marey*, which it is also tempting to call a piece of fiction, although it does in fact represent a reminiscence of Dostoyevsky's own childhood. He tells how, as a little boy, he had once been frightened by a wolf, but had been comforted by an old serf who took pity on him. With the passage of time this episode had become so overlaid in Dostoyevsky's mind with sentimentality about the Russian *narod* that one might be inclined to doubt whether it ever occurred at all. For some reason the excerpt has acquired anthological status in Russia, being automatically included in children's readers and collections of prose, but it would be difficult to select a passage which conveys a more misleading or deplorable impression of Dostoyevsky.

*

Though the *Diary* began to be published in 1873, the body of doctrine which it embodies had (as has been shown in Chapter Four above) taken shape nearly ten years previously. The crystallization of this doctrine in Dostoyevsky's mind coincided closely in time with his attainment of maturity as a writer. The question therefore arises whether this was perhaps a little more than a coincidence and whether the acceptance of this rigid framework of belief may not in some way have liberated creative powers which had hitherto not had full play.

It is impossible to be certain on such a point, but it would surely be wrong to claim that the formation of Dostoyevskyism was entirely without value in helping its creator to rise to his true stature as an artist. It seems likely that Dostoyevsky found himself in some way creatively liberated by a tension between his consciously held beliefs and the only partially conscious doubts which troubled him beneath the surface. This tension could only operate effectively when the conscious beliefs had hardened into a rigid doctrine against which it was possible for his creative self to kick. If this theory does not seem too fanciful, it may be helpful to change the image, and to think of the nonsensical doctrine of Dostoyevskyism as the surface crust of scum under which a rich jam was boiling in the hidden depths below.

The views presented in the *Diary* accordingly present the student with yet another Dostoyevskian paradox. On the one hand, it is impossible to understand Dostoyevsky without taking into account the *Diary*. On the other hand, it is also impossible to understand him without realizing that the views expressed in the *Diary* are in many ways irrelevant to his imaginative work, except in so far as they may have made possible a liberating psychological adjustment.

CHAPTER TEN

'THE BROTHERS KARAMAZOV'

The Brothers Karamazov, Dostoyevsky's last and longest novel, was published in *Russky Vestnik* in 1879–80. It has powerful claims to be regarded as his most important work, and is the novel best known to readers and most discussed by critics. But is it in fact the greatest of all his novels? Or should that title go, as has been claimed above, to *The Devils*? Or else, as some would maintain, to *The Idiot* or *Crime and Punishment*? There will never be general agreement on the answers to these questions, but that is no reason for not suggesting a ranking order of Dostoyevsky's last five novels, a harmless exercise which has been conducted many times in criticism with stimulating effect.

That *The Devils* is the best and *A Raw Youth* the weakest novel in the quintet has already been claimed. Of the three remaining novels *The Idiot* ranks lowest, leaving the difficult task of choosing the runner-up between *Crime and Punishment* and *The Brothers Karamazov*. These two novels are both built on a strong central situation. But whereas *Crime and Punishment* is everywhere taut and concentrated, *The Brothers Karamazov* produces a relatively sprawling effect, being more uneven and less unrelentingly concentrated everywhere on a single clear-cut target. On the other hand, the best passages of *The Brothers Karamazov* leave even the best of *Crime and Punishment* far behind. Furthermore the characters of *The Brothers Karamazov* represent an even more dazzling explosion of creative talent than those of *Crime and Punishment*.

The final ranking list, from the point of view taken in the present study, is therefore:

> *The Devils*
> *The Brothers Karamazov*
> *Crime and Punishment*
> *The Idiot*
> *A Raw Youth*

This ranking list differs from Dostoyevsky's own assessment.

He seems to have had a particularly soft spot for *The Idiot*. In 1877 he told a correspondent that many readers had spoken of this as his best work and that all such readers 'have something special in their cast of mind which always made a great impression on me and pleased me'.[1] It is to be noted that this comment was made before *The Brothers Karamazov* was written—it eventually superseded *The Idiot* as Dostoyevsky's own favourite work. Among recent assessments which go at least as far as the present study in dissenting from Dostoyevsky's own predilections, is that of Richard Curle, who is inclined to rate *The Brothers Karamazov* not only below *The Devils* but also below *Crime and Punishment* and *The Idiot*.[2]

Whatever one may feel about such differing judgements, there is at least one from which few readers and critics will dissent: *The Brothers Karamazov* is a work of genius and one of the world's greatest novels.

Of all Dostoyevsky's novels it carries the greatest load of philosophy. His major works since *Notes from Underground* had all been saturated with ideas, but it is only in *The Brothers Karamazov* (if one excepts the moralizing passages put into the mouth of Makar Dolgoruky in *A Raw Youth*) that Dostoyevsky himself seems to step forward in the mantle of the sage, particularly in the passages put into the mouth of Father Zosima. And though Dostoyevsky is renowned as a religious novelist, it is only in this last novel that religion is discussed so fully. Even Prince Myshkin in *The Idiot*, a character partly modelled on Jesus Christ, had spoken little of God and had not done much preaching. But on the pages of *The Brothers Karamazov* God appears repeatedly, in the mouths of many characters from the saintly Zosima to the atheistic Ivan Karamazov. There is also an occasional flirtation with mystical language from which Dostoyevsky's other fiction is almost free.

Not merely do ideas play a greater part in *The Brothers Karamazov* than in any of Dostoyevsky's other fictional works. They also figure in passages of theoretical discussion to an extent which finds no parallel in his fiction except in the much shorter *Notes from Underground*. This is particularly true of Book Five ('Pro and Contra') and Book Six ('The Russian Monk'). These passages, comprising about one-sixth of the total length, could be excised without loss to the novel as a story. This point is not made in order to put forward the absurd suggestion that they should have been excised, but in order to stress the contrast with the other novels, none of which contains theoretically excisable passages on this scale.

If the handling of the thought in *The Brothers Karamazov* represents an artistic defect, this must be due to the didactic spirit in which some of it is managed. Never before, except in non-fiction (notably the *Diary of a Writer*), had Dostoyevsky's readers been 'got at' to such an extent. This is the only fictional work in which he seems to seize the reader's ear, insistently whispering revealed truths. 'Whispering' seems to be the appropriate word because Dostoyevsky now tends to adopt a quieter manner, perhaps more eloquent of genuine conviction on his part than the frenzied tone often found in earlier writings.

A bland and silky note has crept into his Russian, which now lacks the taut vitality of earlier works, making one conscious of waning power and of the onset of old age. Even the skilful Scandal in the monastery, which occupies Book Two, pales before the riotous Scandals of *The Idiot* and *The Devils*. Dostoyevskian bile is here somewhat watered down. The texture of his prose has become laxer and less urgent, contributing to the general lowering of vitality which is to be found when *The Brothers Karamazov* is compared with its great predecessors. But Dostoyevsky seems destined to defy generalizations and constantly to surprise. Whatever may be said about the general level of vitality, he did create in Fyodor Pavlovich Karamazov a character of such blazing vigour as even he had never conceived before, and also constructed narrative sequences of frenzied suspense, humour and terror which rival anything in his work.

It is with diffidence that one puts forward the handling of the theoretical matter as a blemish in *The Brothers Karamazov*. If it indeed is a blemish, the brilliance of 'Pro and Contra' and of 'The Grand Inquisitor' do much to compensate for the slackening of tension which they involve. In condemning other sections of the novel one feels on firmer ground. These include Ivan Karamazov's well-known conversation with the Devil, which seems one of the occasions where Dostoyevsky's ranging imagination threw out something approaching nonsense. Less incomprehensible, but scarcely less tiresome, are some of the tirades in the lengthy trial scene, which, despite some spectacular writing and superb Dostoyevskian climaxes, gives the novel an ending below its general level. This section suffers from repetitiousness, some of the circumstantial evidence against Dmitry Karamazov being mulled over to a point where it becomes fatiguing. Dostoyevsky has also included too much Dostoyevskyism in the speeches at the trial. These speeches are of interest to the student of his thought, but do not compare in quality with 'The Grand Inquisitor'. Such defects have received gentle treatment in criticism of Dostoyevsky, possibly because the impact of Dostoyevsky at his best bludgeons the reader into a state where he cannot distinguish the relatively weak aspects of his work.

*

The Brothers Karamazov possesses a strong backbone in a central intrigue which runs through the book in a clear, broad line and thus calls to mind *Crime and Punishment*. In *The Brothers Karamazov* a murder is once more the theme, but in choosing this time the murder of a father rather than of an old pawnbroker, Dostoyevsky greatly increases his impact, whether or not one accepts entirely the comments of Freud:

> *The Brothers Karamazov* is the most magnificent novel ever written. . . .
> It can scarcely be mere coincidence that three of the masterpieces of the literature of all time, the *Oedipus Rex* of Sophocles, Shakespeare's *Hamlet* and Dostoyevsky's *The Brothers Karamazov*, should all deal with the same subject, a father's murder. In all three, too, the motive for the deed, sexual rivalry for the woman, is laid bare.[3]

The central plot is so simple that it can be summarized in a few words. Fyodor Pavlovich Karamazov, the evil-living, drunken and swindling father of four sons, is killed under circumstances which point to his eldest son, Dmitry, as the murderer. Though innocent of the crime, Dmitry is tried and convicted. This situation provides Dostoyevsky with three main suspense-hooks, of which he makes full use, surrounding them with the usual apparatus of foreboding and dark hints. These are: when will Fyodor Pavlovich be murdered? (He seems on the brink of it for several hundred pages.) Who did it? Will Dmitry be convicted? The first of these mysteries is resolved at the time of Dmitry's arrest, and the second when the lackey Smerdyakov, Fyodor Pavlovich's illegitimate son, confesses to Ivan Karamazov that it was he who smashed in the old man's skull with a paperweight. The last is resolved at the end of the book when Dmitry is sentenced to twenty years' hard labour in Siberia.

Strong and simple in its essentials, the central plot possesses a wealth of embroidery in its details, which, in accordance with

Dostoyevsky's long-established practice, revolve around inter-twined intrigues concerning love and money. It is love and money which cause Dmitry Karamazov to quarrel with his father Fyodor Pavlovich. Dmitry considers that he has been swindled out of part of his inheritance by his father, while he and his father have both fallen in love with the same girl, Grushenka. Since the impression exists that Grushenka is a loose woman, Fyodor Pavlovich has pre-pared an envelope containing three thousand roubles as a fee for the services which he hopes that she will render if she comes to collect.

Having baited his trap, the lustful old reprobate lurks in his house, alone except for his second son Ivan, the rats whose company he prizes in the evening and the black-beetles which he is in the habit of squashing with his slipper at night. Dmitry, more violent than his father and no less lustful, is driven to frenzy by this situation. Not only is the old man attempting to gain the love of the woman whom Dmitry himself desires, but he is using for this purpose money which Dmitry, considering that his father has cheated him over his inheritance, regards as his own. In a drunken rage in the local tavern he has already threatened to murder his father, a murder for which lust and money combine to give him a powerful motive.

These details comprehend only a tiny fraction of Dmitry's financial and amatory involvements. Before meeting Grushenka, he had been engaged to be married to the second most important female character in the novel, Katerina Ivanovna, with whom his relationship is particularly complicated. Katerina Ivanovna is bound to Dmitry by that violent wish to dominate and be dominated which is the hallmark of a Dostoyevskian love affair. When Dmitry deserts her for Grushenka, she makes the most of the situation's now increased inflammatory possibilities by clinging to him with a love charged with *nadryv* (psychological rupture or strain). She repeatedly says that she wants to save him, an emotion which alter-nates with a desire to ruin him. These two tendencies reach their most explosive expression during the trial, when she executes a violent change of course and clinches Dmitry's conviction by pro-ducing a telling piece of evidence of which the prosecution had not yet heard, a letter written to her in which he had actually announced his intention of killing the old man.

Meanwhile Dmitry's brother Ivan has fallen in love with Katerina Ivanovna. She returns his love (by love one must understand the

oscillatory love-hatred relationship found in almost all Dostoyevskian love affairs), but has nursed the grievance caused to her by
Dmitry into such a substantial emotional pustule that in her perversity she is unwilling to let it subside. To the earlier oscillatory
love patterns of *The Idiot*, *The Devils* and *A Raw Youth* must therefore be added the weird quadrille danced by Grushenka, Dmitry,
Katerina Ivanovna and Ivan, with Fyodor Pavlovich standing to
one side as a monstrously impressive embodiment of single-minded
lust who remains free from oscillation. Similar patterns are also to
be traced on the relationship between Alyosha Karamazov and the
fourteen-year-old Liza Khokhlakova, the most perverse of all
Dostoyevsky's heroines.

It is difficult to give an unequivocal verdict on the handling of the
love intrigues in *The Brothers Karamazov*. It is true that this world
of perverse oscillation in love was Dostoyevsky's own peculiar
terrain, and the patterns traced in *The Brothers Karamazov* show
him cultivating it as skilfully as anywhere in his previous fiction.
On the other hand, as already suggested, Dostoyevsky was a little
too prone to concentrate on oscillation in love.

Certainly the more oscillatory episodes are not among the most
effective of the novel's love-scenes. But the duel of lust between
Dmitry and his father, ending with the love which grows up between
Dmitry and Grushenka, provides the only passionate and full-
blooded love-intrigue in Dostoyevsky's work. Here too oscillation
is present but not so obtrusively as to swamp everything else. The
love affair between Grushenka and Dmitry, so superbly handled,
proves how unwise Dostoyevsky had been in the past to concentrate
too exclusively on oscillatory perversities in portraying love. His
achievements as a novelist would have been even greater if he had
earlier tested his strength in the direction taken by Dmitry and
Grushenka.

Dmitry Karamazov is the central figure in the plot. But his
younger brothers Ivan and Alyosha are no less important, their
involvement being more in the realm of ideas than of action. All
four Karamazov sons are represented as implicated in the murder.
Apart from Alyosha, Smerdyakov was the least guilty. He merely
committed it. Dmitry desired it (a worse offence, since to Dostoyevsky thoughts are more culpable than deeds) and came near to committing it. However, it is Ivan who bears the main burden of the
guilt.

It was Ivan who expressed his hope of Dmitry and his father that 'one reptile would devour another'. But his participation went further than wishes. It was he who made it possible for Smerdyakov to commit the murder by leaving unexpectedly for Moscow, thus withdrawing the protection of his presence from his father, left alone in his house on the fateful night. Moreover, Ivan's departure is represented as something more sinister than a sudden whim, following as it does his oblique hinting conversation with Smerdyakov, who urges him to leave in language so loaded with ambiguities that he can plausibly interpret Ivan's actual departure, when it occurs, as a tacit indication to go ahead with the murder.

Though the inner meaning of this arrangement is not shown as having penetrated Ivan's conscious mind, there are few things more subtle in Dostoyevsky than the way in which he is revealed to have approved the plan subconsciously. Dostoyevsky had already experimented in murder by proxy in similar fashion when, in *The Devils*, he made Stavrogin, without openly committing himself in any way and on a similarly subconscious level, consent to the slaughter of his imbecile wife. Since Smerdyakov was a creature of Ivan's, seduced by the heresies of atheism and intellectual self-sufficiency, Dostoyevsky found no difficulty in regarding Ivan as the principal in the crime and Smerdyakov as an assistant. Ivan was an intelligent man who chose not to believe in Dostoyevskyism. Smerdyakov merely banged an old man on the head.

Ivan's guilt is thus in keeping with his position in the ideological structure of the novel as the embodiment of Dostoyevsky's conception of Evil. But even the youngest son, Alyosha, who embodies Dostoyevskian Good, is represented as not entirely guiltless, for he knew that events were approaching a crisis, but had been so preoccupied by his personal reaction to the death of Father Zosima, that he forgot at the crucial moment to seek out Dmitry as he had intended—a course of action which, it is suggested, might have led to the prevention of the murder. By any commonsense scale of values Alyosha cannot be considered guilty at all, but such a scale of values operates only sporadically in Dostoyevsky's work. One must also remember the importance which he attaches to the concept of guilt. The thesis that 'all men are guilty before all men for everything' is an important part of the message which he set himself to convey. This being so even the pious Alyosha could not hope to escape. Nor, as a good Dostoyevskian, would he have wished to do so.

The above interpretation of the four sons' guilt for the murder of their father seems to flow naturally from a study of the novel and of Dostoyevsky's ideas in general. But it can only be accepted tentatively because of a letter written by Dostoyevsky in 1879, while *The Brothers Karamazov* was in the middle of being serialized, to a correspondent who must have questioned him on this point.

> Old Karamazov was killed by the servant Smerdyakov. . . . Ivan . . . took part in the murder only indirectly and distantly, solely by refraining (deliberately) from making Smerdyakov see reason when talking to him before his departure to Moscow . . . and thus *so to speak granted permission* to Smerdyakov to commit this evil deed. . . . Dmitry . . . is quite innocent of his father's murder.[4]

This commonsense version of the responsibility for Fyodor Pavlovich's murder must of course be taken fully into account, but it does not square very well with the handling of the guilt-theme in the novel, of which the interpretation suggested above seems to give a more accurate picture. On the other hand, one is reluctant to put forward an interpretation which conflicts so directly with a statement made by the author himself.

*

The Brothers Karamazov shares with *A Raw Youth* a preoccupation with family life such as appears nowhere else in Dostoyevsky's writings. In choosing the family as the theme of his last two novels Dostoyevsky challenges comparison with the supreme Russian novelist of the family, Tolstoy. There is evidence that this comparison was deliberately challenged by Dostoyevsky, who sought to undercut Tolstoy by showing his families in a spectacularly different light.[5] Tolstoy's families are often united, while Dostoyevsky's are disunited. Tolstoy's seem to live in a happy, patriarchal world of love and sunlight, and have solid ground beneath their feet. Even when they are not illegitimate, the children in Dostoyevsky's families tend not to have been brought up by their parents. They tread in darkness among quicksands. Tolstoy's sons love their fathers. Dostoyevsky's murder theirs.

One can scarcely imagine a family less Tolstoyan than that of the Karamazovs. Dmitry's mother had run away from his father when the boy was three years old. His father pretended not to know that he had a son at all, and Dmitry was looked after by the servant

Grigory for a time, after which he was taken over by his great-uncle, Miusov, who in turn handed him over to one of his great-aunts, from whom he gravitated to one of her married daughters. Alyosha and Ivan were also lucky enough to be brought up outside their father's orbit. Fyodor Pavlovich's first wife (Dmitry's mother) had actually beaten her husband. His second wife, the mother of Ivan and Alyosha, had been a gentle, shy creature, who had once tried to hang herself and was subject to hysterical fits. When Alyosha returned to his father's house, Fyodor Pavlovich was unable even to show him where his mother's grave was situated.

No more a respecter of God than of his own family, Fyodor Pavlovich bears the load of the blasphemy theme in *The Brothers Karamazov*. His blasphemous impudence plays an important part in the main Scandal in the novel, which occurs in Book Two and takes place in the local monastery. There is a relative lack of energy in the style which detracts slightly from this scene, but it is one of the best passages in the book. It gives Dostoyevsky an opportunity to indulge in his special brand of humour which is in general more in the background in *The Brothers Karamazov* than it had been in *The Idiot* and *The Devils*.

Like its predecessors, the Scandal in the monastery is carefully 'loaded' in advance. Fyodor and Dmitry have agreed to meet there in the hope that this setting will enable them to discuss their differences calmly, since even they can scarcely quarrel in front of Father Zosima and various attendant monks. The usual notes of impending catastrophe are heard, among which Fyodor Pavlovich's remark ('we have all promised to behave ourselves') is, in the light of what is known of his character, particularly pregnant with foreboding.

Fyodor Pavlovich is an example of a Dostoyevskian type more common among relatively minor characters, the clown or buffoon. Catching sight of the pictures of saints above the gates of the hermitage inside the monastery, he immediately lives up to his reputation by crossing himself several times with unnecessary verve. He has not been talking long to Father Zosima before he suddenly falls on his knees and says, 'Master, what must I do to inherit eternal life?' Of this Dostoyevsky makes the characteristic non-committal comment that it was difficult to tell whether he was joking or not. But as the scene proceeds this question becomes less difficult to answer.

Fyodor Pavlovich is soon aping and exaggerating the biblical Russian in which the monks address each other. Additional scope for buffoonery is provided by the presence of Miusov, a relative by marriage and an anti-clerical 'liberal of the forties' (like Stepan Trofimovich Verkhovensky in *The Devils*), whom he chooses to accuse of having undermined his faith. After he has exhausted the variations of mock piety, the time has come for the predictable *volte face*. Fyodor Pavlovich rounds abruptly on the monks, whom he accuses of insincerity, lying and hypocrisy and of attempting to 'save their souls by living on cabbage'. He goes on to tell a story, the height of impropriety in a holy place, of a man who was murdered in a brothel and whose corpse was nailed up in a box while prostitutes danced and sang round it. And he concludes by issuing a preposterous order to his son Alyosha, who is living in the monastery as a novice, to take up his pillow and mattress and leave.

The prospect of a settlement with Dmitry, for which the meeting in the monastery was originally conceived, has already disappeared after an exchange in which Fyodor Pavlovich says that if Dmitry was not his son he would challenge him to a duel with pistols at three paces. Of these doings Dostoyevsky comments, 'he wished to avenge himself on everyone for his own vileness', and, elsewhere:

> Old liars, who have spent their whole life acting, have moments when they put on such a performance that they genuinely shake and weep with emotion, despite the fact that at the same moment or only a second afterwards they might be able to whisper to themselves 'you're lying, you shameless old man'.

The shameless old man is conceived as a monster of animal vitality who dominates the scenes, all in the early part of the novel, in which he takes part. Though Dostoyevsky generally pays less attention than other novelists to details of physical appearance, he gives a vivid description of Fyodor Pavlovich with fleshy bags below his impudent eyes, the large number of wrinkles on his small fat face, his large, fleshy adam's apple, black rotting teeth and habit of spluttering when he begins to speak. He is a liar and a cheat, as well as a buffoon. His most notable characteristic is lust and he is commonly referred to as 'the old sensualist'. He says that he wants to live as long as possible and is making financial provision for his old age so as to procure for himself the women who will then no longer come to him voluntarily, for 'I wish to live in my vileness to the end of my days'. It is in keeping with Dostoyevsky's taste for the dramatic that the old man is murdered at a time when he is in the grip of his ruling passion, shortly after Dmitry, by tapping the prearranged code signal on his window, has indicated to him what is in fact not the case—that Grushenka has arrived to claim the three thousand roubles.

Though Fyodor Pavlovich is one of the most evil figures on Dostoyevsky's pages, he retains some hold on the reader's sympathies because of his animal vigour or because of something which Dostoyevsky cannot consciously have intended to gain him sympathy, his explosive incursion into the world of unctuous monkishness surrounding Father Zosima. It would be going too far to call Fyodor Pavlovich a likeable rogue, but he falls short of the ultimate odiousness of his bastard son Smerdyakov. Nor does he rate so very low on the Dostoyevskian scale of values, for at any rate Dostoyevsky left him untainted with that intellectual evil which was to him the supreme crime and of which he made Ivan the embodiment. Fyodor Pavlovich is merely an extreme example of one of Dostoyevsky's sinners, of his evil-doers, for whom, as opposed to his evil-thinkers, there is always hope.

The other important evil-doers in the novel actually show signs of realizing Dostoyevsky's hopes and of undergoing character changes in the desired direction. The central figure in this respect is Dmitry, subject to the opposing pulls of the wicked Ivan and the good Alyosha. These three brothers accordingly stand in a triangular relationship similar to that found in *Crime and Punishment* and elsewhere.

Each brother has his satellites. The salvation-prone Dmitry is to be associated with two other salvation-prone sinners, Grushenka and Kolya Krasotkin. The intellectual heretic Ivan has a larger group of hangers-on, including Smerdyakov, the atheist theologian Rakitin and the old-type liberal Miusov, to whom may be added those children of Ivan's own imagination, the Grand Inquisitor and the Devil. On the side of virtue Alyosha is powerfully supported by Father Zosima, a figure too important to be rated as a mere satellite, and by the brotherhood of the monastery from Father Paisy downwards. Characters which do not fall into this pattern include Fyodor Pavlovich, the perverse Katerina Ivanovna and the ultra-perverse Liza Khokhlakova, Fyodor Pavlovich's servant Grigory and Grigory's wife Marfa, together with a few pure figures of fun such as Liza's mother, the maniac monk Father Ferapont and Grushenka's contemptible Polish lover.

The schematic structure of the characterization gives the fabric of *The Brothers Karamazov* a latent toughness which is further strengthened by underlying allegorical tendencies. Not only is Fyodor Pavlovich Karamazov easily remembered as an embodiment of lust, but his three sons Dmitry, Ivan and Alyosha can also be equated (provided that one does not push the equation too far or allow it to obscure the fact that each of them is an individual) with Body, Mind and Soul respectively.

As these equations indicate, the three brothers are strongly differentiated, but there is also continued insistence in the novel on their family resemblance to each other and to their debauched and cynical father. The key concept in this respect is 'Karamazovian impetuosity', a potentiality for plunging into extremes, whether of sinfulness or saintliness. Dostoyevsky thought that this potentiality was a special attribute of the Russian people, so that he uses his adjective 'Karamazovian' as a sort of symbolical equivalent for 'Russian', this equation being another of the struts in the concealed structure of the novel and a further source of its strength.

●

As the loose equation of Dmitry with the concept of 'Body' indicates, it is in him that the strongest resemblance is to be found to old Karamazov. In his initial relations with Grushenka, Dmitry reveals a savage lustfulness which matches his father's. As befits his comparative youth—he is described as twenty-eight years of age—he is more violent than Fyodor Pavlovich, being inclined to use his fists where his father would employ low cunning. Like so many other Dostoyevskian heroes, Dmitry is depicted as a retired army officer. Like Stavrogin, he had been reduced to the ranks for duelling, before recovering his commission again. His early manhood has been spent in a whirl of debauchery, drinking and debts. He is described as of medium height, but powerful and muscular, and there is much insistence on a physical trait such as Dostoyevsky commonly neglected, his long, determined strides. Despite his physical strength, there is something unhealthy about his appearance with his sunken cheeks and yellow complexion.

Dmitry is impulsively violent. He is given to shouting out indiscretions when drunk in the local tavern, where he has been known to boast of his intention of murdering his father. His style of speaking is highly individual, being comically poetical in its extravagance as where he says he 'thirsted and hungered [for Grushenka] with every crook of his soul and even with his ribs'. A sullen, thoughtful expression on his face is always liable to give way to a sudden violent laugh.

His violent actions include a tragi-comic assault on the miserable Captain Snegiryov, whom he on one occasion pulls out of the local tavern by his sparse, ginger-coloured beard. Another and more powerful scene occurs when Dmitry bursts into his father's house under the impression that Grushenka has gained entry. After striking the old servant Grigory, he seizes his father by the hair, hurls him to the ground and several times kicks him in the face with his heel. A further savage assault on Grigory occurs when Dmitry, shortly before the murder, breaks into his father's garden.

Such is Dmitry the sinner—drunken, lustful, violent and something near to a thief in his appropriation of three thousand roubles entrusted to him by Katerina Ivanovna. But in Dostoyevsky's conception the hot-blooded sinner is only one step removed from salvation, whereas a cold and reasoning man like Ivan, who rejects God, is damned however well or badly he may behave. Dmitry's evil actions are in any case balanced by his generosity and warm human sympathies, but what particularly redeems him in Dostoyevsky's eyes is his pervading sense of guilt. No other character in Dostoyevsky's work indulges in such orgies of self-condemnation. Dmitry is constantly referring to himself as a 'reptile', a 'worm', an 'insect'. He speaks of himself as a man who 'loved debauchery', who 'loved also the shame of debauchery . . . loved cruelty'. After his arrest he tells his interrogator that he had been tormented all his life by a thirst for virtue, while continuing to commit vile deeds. Dmitry occasionally pauses in heaping reproaches on himself in order to stress the guilt of others, embracing even the seemingly pure Alyosha in his definition of 'all us Karamazovs' as insects, in whose blood lustfulness raises tempests.

Dostoyevsky takes pains to show Dmitry as a sincerely religious man. During the Scandal in the monastery his behaviour, at any rate at the beginning, is sincerely reverent. The name of God comes easily to his lips. When, after his arrest, he learns that the old servant Grigory (whom he had assaulted) still lives, his first thought is to thank God for a great miracle.

It is typical of Dostoyevsky's methods of characterization in their rich complexity that Dmitry, a figure of immense seriousness with elemental allegorical and symbolical implications, is also treated as a figure of fun, being incidentally the only one of the Karamazov brothers to be tinged with a comic streak. This is most evident in Book Eight, which challenges comparison with the Fête scene in *The Devils* as Dostoyevsky's finest piece of sustained writing. The first three chapters are devoted to Dmitry's frenzied attempts to possess himself of three thousand roubles, so that he can discharge the debt to Katerina Ivanovna which weighs so heavily on his conscience, and also—though the reader does not know this at the time —make use of the fifteen hundred roubles which he secretly carries round his neck and which he knows he will need if Grushenka accepts him as her lover. Though these three chapters are amusing, one has once more the sensation that Dostoyevsky is tormenting the victim of his humour, in the manner familiar ever since the days of Golyadkin in *The Double*.

In the first chapter Dmitry applies to the bad-tempered, ill and despotic old merchant, Samsonov (Grushenka's 'protector'), who, he hopes, will have sufficient interest in her welfare to further Dmitry's suit, if only in order to save her from falling into Fyodor Pavlovich's squalid clutches. Dmitry's fatuous offer to make over all his remaining claims against Fyodor Pavlovich, in return for the sum of money which he requires, is not advanced by his tactless reference to the fact that Samsonov, by virtue of his age and illness, has 'long been out of the running' as Grushenka's lover.

The drama and humour of this scene and those which follow derive from the fact that Dmitry is approaching breaking-point. Scarcely less amusing is his time-consuming expedition into the country, made on Samsonov's malicious advice, in order to get money from a peasant timber-dealer who turns out to be a hopeless drunkard. His final and even more desperate appeal to the ridiculous Madame Khokhlakova, a triumph of mutual misunderstanding, is funnier still. She immediately promises him an infinitely larger sum than the three thousand roubles for which he asks. It is some time before Dmitry realizes that she does not in fact intend to give him any money at all, but is merely expressing her instinctive conviction that he is destined to make his fortune if only he will follow her advice and become a gold prospector. When this fact finally settles in Dmitry's confused brain, he adds to his other misdemeanours by spitting at his would-be benefactress.

These three comic scenes proceed in an atmosphere of mounting tension. When they are over the mood changes to terror and violence in a scene of even greater tension—the chapter 'In the Darkness'. Here Dmitry, now suddenly struck by the fact that, while he has been wasting time, Grushenka may have gone to his father, breaks into the old man's garden in order to discover whether or not she is in the house. Assuring himself that Grushenka is in fact not there, Dmitry fights back his impulse to murder his father. After assaulting Grigory he rushes to Grushenka's lodgings, where he discovers that she has gone to the nearby village of Mokroye in order to be united with her original seducer, the Pole.

With that feeling for convincing inconsistency which Dostoyevsky often uses so artistically, he endows Dmitry in his attitude to this unexpected turn of events, not with jealousy of the Pole such as he had felt for his own father, but with a wish to step on one side in a grand act of renunciation. He now proposes to turn up at Mokroye with a lot of food and drink. His plan is that Grushenka and her Pole should join him in a wild orgy, after which, when dawn breaks, he will shoot himself with one of his duelling pistols. It is in the preparation for the ride to Mokroye and in the ride itself that Dostoyevsky reaches the high-water mark in this astounding sequence. Brandishing a sheaf of rainbow-coloured hundred-rouble notes which he holds ostentatiously in front of him in hands still stained with the blood of old Grigory, Dmitry appears, his face and coat also covered in blood, as a titanic figure of criminal violence. And as he orders large quantities of champagne, caviar, fruit and chocolate from the astonished shop assistants who had fitted out his previous expedition to Mokroye, one has the feeling that his 'broad Russian nature' and 'Karamazovian impetuosity' have been distended to exploding point. Always deft in details of this sort, Dostoyevsky skilfully provides Dmitry with a foil in a young man called Perkhotin, a model of ordinary common sense who tries to curb his extravagance and save him from being cheated by the shop assistants.

Various conflicting pressures add more tension to the scene. Grushenka's maid arrives before his carriage leaves and implores him not to destroy her mistress, for Dmitry's pistols suggest that, even though he may not have killed his father, he has murder on his mind. The incoherent and delirious speech of a person in the grip of drunkenness, hysteria, rage or jealousy is a device often used by Dostoyevsky, and he uses it with great effect in the disjointed language which he puts into Dmitry's mouth in this scene. As he drives off with the coachman and an advance portion of food and drink, while the rest is packed in readiness to follow later, an additional 'Russian' note is struck because of the emotional significance possessed for Russians in the age of coaches by swift dangerous driving and the tinkling of bells with which it is accompanied.

During this ride Dostoyevsky's pace is terrific. Dmitry babbles to the coachman about the need, which any coachman will appreciate, of 'giving way' to others at the right time, while the kindly coachman compares Dmitry (as Dostoyevsky's characters are so often compared) to a little child and says that 'God will forgive him for his simplicity of heart'. Dmitry utters a frenzied prayer that God should receive him in all his lawlessness and not judge him, for he has already condemned himself. 'I am vile, but I love Thee. If Thou sendest me to Hell, even there will I love and from there will shout that I love Thee for ever.'

When Dmitry reaches Mokroye and intrudes upon Grushenka and her Pole, a quieter tone at first reigns and Dostoyevsky reverts to the broad comedy which he had relinquished at the moment when Dmitry spat at Madame Khokhlakova. Grushenka's Pole, a pompous little man with a pipe, turns out, as any student of Dostoyevskian Poles could have predicted, no serious partner in life for a thorough-paced 'Russian woman' such as Grushenka. It transpires that he has a companion as preposterous as himself, another Pole. Polish nationalism and preoccupation with frontier lines receive a typical Dostoyevskian buffet when a toast is drunk to Poland by the ill-assorted company, the Poles refusing to raise their glasses to Russia except with the reservation, 'in its boundaries before 1772'. Even the bemused Dmitry at last realizes that he has nothing to fear in Grushenka's Pole, and after the two Poles have finally been discredited as a pair of card-sharps, they are removed to another room. The wheel of Dmitry's fortune is seen to have spun right round when Grushenka at last makes it clear to him that it is after all he whom she loves.

In Dostoyevsky's work, as in his life, one sudden spin of fortune's wheel is always likely to be followed by a spin in the opposite direction. So Dostoyevsky, who in *The Devils* had caused Shatov to be murdered at the moment of his greatest happiness, strikes a similar dramatic blow at Dmitry at the moment when his obsessive and devouring love for Grushenka is to be gratified. The blow is one which the reader has long been subconsciously awaiting and which lands with superb artistic inevitability as the authorities arrive and arrest Dmitry on the charge of murdering his father.

It is a feature of *The Brothers Karamazov* that Dmitry and the two relatively minor characters who play an ideological role similar to his—Grushenka and Kolya Krasotkin—show development of character during the course of the novel. One is again reminded of the contrast between Dostoyevsky, in whose works the development of character over a period of time occupies the smallest possible role, and Tolstoy, who was particularly interested in studying such development. For example, readers of *Crime and Punishment* and *A Raw Youth* are informed that Raskolnikov and Arkady Dolgoruky underwent conversions, but are given little opportunity to study the effects of these conversions.

Because of their oscillatory tendencies, Dostoyevsky's characters cannot be called stable or static. But their oscillatory behaviour patterns, however violent, usually undergo no significant change during the course of the novels. The oscillators, or at any rate those of them who escape suicide, murder or lunacy, are still oscillating away just as hard and in just the same way at the end as at the beginning. To this generalization Dmitry, Grushenka and Kolya Krasotkin are exceptions. Here again the bulk of Dostoyevsky's attention is devoted to the period before the change which takes place in each character, but at least some attention (such as was not devoted to Raskolnikov and Arkady Dolgoruky) is paid to the period after the change.

The sense of development in Dmitry's character begins when the reader realizes that his love for Grushenka is something nobler than the violent lust in which it had originated. But the real turning-point comes with an event which by any commonsense scale of values could only be regarded as a calamity, his arrest for a crime which he had not committed. A similar stroke of good fortune disguised as calamity had overtaken Dostoyevsky himself more than thirty years before *The Brothers Karamazov* was written when he was arrested for complicity in the Petrashevsky conspiracy.

The desire to be punished for which Dostoyevsky had found relief in the Petropavlovsk Fortress and later in the Omsk Prison, was made to bring similar relief to Dmitry. Before his suffering began Dmitry had been conscious of his own sinfulness and anxious to undergo regeneration, but in attempting to accomplish this had only floundered more hopelessly in crime and violence. After his arrest things became easier. 'I accept the torment of the accusation and of my public shame [he says]. I want to suffer and shall be purified by suffering. . . . I accept punishment not because I killed him, but because I wished to kill him and might actually have killed him.'

While in prison awaiting trial, Dmitry shows that he has absorbed the great Dostoyevskian truth that all are guilty for all. He will go to Siberia (he assumes that he will be convicted) as a scapegoat for all men. In a lyrical speech to Alyosha he imagines himself as one of hundreds of subterranean men in the Siberian mines with hammers in their hands. 'Oh yes, we shall be in chains and there will be no freedom, but then in our great grief we shall be resurrected anew.' Dmitry is not afraid of twenty years in the mines. All he is afraid of is losing the sensation of having become a new man. Dmitry is thus the embodiment of one central message of the novel, that man should cultivate and distend to its ultimate limit the feeling of guilt inside him and find relief and purification in suffering. As Dostoyevsky himself knew, this doctrine runs contrary to common sense. The logic on which it is based is 'not of this world'. It operates, as interpreters have explained, on a 'heavenly' or 'metaphysical' level and is not susceptible of discussion in everyday terms.

Was Dostoyevsky an enunciator of genuine profundities about the laws of God and of the human spirit? Or was he merely a man who attempted to erect a personal neurotic aberration into a universal law? Or was he perhaps some sort of mixture of the two? Readers of his work who disagree on these important points need not necessarily disagree about his greatness as a novelist. It is possible to be a sincere admirer of Dostoyevsky's art without being at all a disciple of Dostoyevskyism. To enjoy *The Brothers Karamazov* one does not have to be obsessed with a desire to purify oneself by suffering. One does not even need to feel that this is a serious concept.

It is in his original and brilliant handling of the novelist's technique and in his portrayal of human behaviour, especially of human behaviour under pressure, that Dostoyevsky's greatness lies, more than in the general laws which he deduced from that behaviour. To this must be added an acute artistic sensibility and discipline which sometimes deserted him, but enabled him by strokes of telling convincingness to keep his feet firmly on the ground even in his most far-fetched scenes.

Dostoyevsky is always carrying things to absurd extremes, but

instances have already been considered where he draws back on the
brink of some ultimate absurdity or horror. These include the seduction under blackmail of Dunya by Svidrigaylov in *Crime and
Punishment*, which does not take place, and the hundred thousand
roubles which Nastasya Filippovna throws into the fire in order to
torment Ganya in *The Idiot*, and which are not allowed to be burnt.
This practice of drawing back, of suggesting in the middle of his
most extravagant scenes some ultimate extravagancy which might
have taken place, but did not, acts regularly as ballast which saves
Dostoyevsky from flying off into clouds of fantasy. If the word
'realism' had not long ago been thoroughly discredited in criticism
of Russian authors, it would be possible to describe this as a realist
device in an author who does not generally lend himself to description as a realist.

Dmitry's fate at the time of his trial also illustrates the artistic
instinct whereby Dostoyevsky ingeniously extricates himself from
the impasse into which his moralizing fervour had shown signs of
leading him. However much he might play with metaphysical profundities and paradoxes 'not of this world', he knew very well that
it would have been ridiculous to lead Dmitry Karamazov off in
fetters to Siberia, singing hymns of praise to God for allowing him
to be sentenced for a crime which he had not committed. So he skilfully draws back. He allows Dmitry's associates to arrange his
escape to America. Dmitry resists this plan at first, regarding it as
running away from his own crucifixion. Later he is inclined to
accept it, comforting himself with the casuistry that, since America
cannot fail to be hateful to any full-blooded Russian, his life there
will be at least a sort of hard labour affording him sufferings
comparable to those which he might have undergone in Siberia.
Thus, in a sense, Dostoyevsky satisfies both the demands of
'this world' and of 'the other world'. Dmitry gets the suffering
which he needs, but without outrage to that everyday common
sense which Dostoyevsky respected more than is sometimes
appreciated.

Dmitry's reflections on America allow the reader to part company
with him on a note of ecstatic tribute to his native land. He hates
the idea of America. What hell it will be for a woman like Grushenka
who is Russian to her bones! 'I love Russia', Dmitry tells Alyosha.
'I love the Russian God. I shall die there!' (in America). He plans
to return one day to Russia in disguise, even if it means getting a

doctor to give him synthetic warts, or putting out an eye and growing a long beard which homesickness can be guaranteed to turn grey.

●

Grushenka's spiritual path repeats the pattern of Dmitry's. At the same time she is the most memorable portrayal of a young woman by an author whose female figures yield greatly in interest to the male, and whose most successful female studies had previously been confined to older women such as Yepanchina in *The Idiot* and Stavrogina in *The Devils*. Tall, beautiful and well-built with a figure said to resemble that of an exaggerated Venus de Milo, Grushenka is the only woman on Dostoyevsky's pages, apart from Dunya in *Crime and Punishment*, who radiates sensual attraction.

At the beginning of the novel the reader sees this seductress in an unsympathetic light during her odd interview with Katerina Ivanovna, her rival for Dmitry's love. Speaking in an unpleasant, drawling 'sugary' voice she promises to relinquish Dmitry and is getting on just a little too well with Katerina Ivanovna when she executes a characteristic Dostoyevskian *volte face* and viciously insults her. As the former mistress of her impossible Pole and of the old merchant Samsonov, Grushenka is deliberately surrounded by Dostoyevsky with potentialities of unchastity and it is only fairly well on in the book that it becomes clear, perhaps disappointingly, that she is in fact no 'loose woman' at all, and has never really been one.

In keeping with her tarnished reputation, Grushenka has plotted at one stage the seduction of the virtuous Alyosha, of whom she threatens that she will 'have his novice's cassock off him'. But though Dostoyevsky's pages contain many instances of seductions recorded as having taken place in the past, it is a curious law of his fiction that none of his many foreshadowed seductions ever takes place. When Alyosha is eventually lured to Grushenka's dwelling by the unscrupulous Rakitin, he finds in her the affection of a sister. Bold, impudent, acquisitive, proud and mean with money, Grushenka also has other sins which make her ripe for salvation, since she has become enamoured of the injury done to her by the original seducing Pole. By setting herself as if in revenge on the male sex to torment both Fyodor Pavlovich and Dmitry, she bears her share of responsibility for the murder of the one and the wrongful arrest of the other.

After Dmitry's arrest, though still liable to the riotous gusts of emotion expected from a Russian woman, she takes on a more serious colouring. The seductive adventuress has given way to a woman transformed by her love for Dmitry.

The third figure in whom the workings of Dostoyevskian grace are shown is a thirteen-year-old boy, Kolya Krasotkin, the most important among Dostoyevsky's many portraits of children. Children had played no part in his major fiction since Kolya Ivolgin in *The Idiot*. In *The Brothers Karamazov* this lapse is fully remedied since Dostoyevsky here studies a whole circle of young boys, the most important after Kolya being Ilyusha Snegiryov, whose tragic funeral concludes the Epilogue. The adventures of these boys provide an opportunity for Alyosha Karamazov, the embodiment of Dostoyevskian Good, to bring to bear his beneficent influence, thus reinforcing the general message of the novel. The importance here attached to the threshold of life, serving as a balance to the aged Father Zosima and to Fyodor Pavlovich (who both die during the course of the novel in such strikingly different ways), gives a fullness of horizon to *The Brothers Karamazov*, which thus serves as a study of sin and salvation in humanity of all ages.

Before his regeneration under Alyosha's influence, Kolya stamps himself on the reader's mind as an outstanding representative of that class of Dostoyevskian characters which sets itself to acquire ascendancy over others. He is preoccupied with his own prestige, showing an underdog feature in his obsession with his short stature. To compensate for this he indulges in wild escapades, one of them an outstanding example of a Dostoyevskian 'dare'; he had lain between railway lines and allowed a train to pass over him.

Kolya tyrannizes his devoted widowed mother and also the younger boys with whom he is friendly and with whom he enjoys playing, though he considers it beneath his dignity to admit this. He is particularly comic in his affectation of pompous adult speech and soon makes it clear that, despite his youth, he has picked up all the ideological heresies which Dostoyevsky most violently rejected. He says that he is a Socialist. Among the subjects which he studies he respects only mathematics and the natural sciences. He regards God as a hypothesis and though he is 'not against Christ' insists that He would have been a revolutionary if He had lived in later times. He tells Alyosha that he knows him to be a mystic, but adds reassuringly 'contact with reality will cure you'.

H

This precocious young nihilist, though described affectionately and amusingly, is by Dostoyevskian standards a hard case of heresy. Consistently with this, he allows himself unintentionally to behave with cruelty to the nine-year-old Ilyusha, after the latter, instructed appropriately enough by Smerdyakov, had thrown a piece of bread containing a pin to a stray dog which had rushed off howling. Now dying of consumption, little Ilyusha cannot forget the dog, imagining that he has caused it to die an agonized death. Frantic attempts have been made by Ilyusha's father and his small friends to find the dog, in the hope that it might still be unharmed, so that the remorse of the dying boy might be alleviated.

Meanwhile Kolya has found the dog, which is indeed unharmed. But he is heartless enough to conceal his discovery, setting himself to teach the dog various tricks so that he may eventually produce it under the most dramatic possible circumstances. Despite Ilyusha's relief the emotional shock of the dog's reappearance affects him badly, and the shock to Kolya himself is equally strong as he fights back his tears in this overwrought atmosphere. When he appears at Ilyusha's funeral there is no more talk of socialism and allied heresies. Now he wants to die for humanity and sacrifice himself for Truth, and he receives the final Dostoyevskian accolade when Alyosha predicts that his life will be an unhappy one. Like Dmitry and Grushenka, Kolya has stepped from the ranks of Dostoyevskian heretics to the ranks of potential Dostoyevskian saints. The atmosphere surrounding Ilyusha's death is tragic, but there is a playful tone in the account of Kolya's spiritual journey which makes it a more palatable lesson than the monkish homilies of Father Zosima.

*

Alyosha represents Dostoyevsky's most impressive attempt to put flesh on what, in the conscious levels of his complex mind, he fervently accepted as his ideal of Truth, Beauty and Goodness. Now a weary and battle-scarred warrior in the struggle to portray his ideal, Dostoyevsky approached this task in *The Brothers Karamazov* with more sophistication and ingenuity than hitherto.

Here again Dostoyevsky the moralist and Dostoyevsky the artist have worked out an impressive compromise. Dostoyevsky the moralist wanted to portray a prophet proclaiming sweeping verities on things human and divine. Dostoyevsky the artist knew that sweeping verities must not be overdone. So in *The Brothers Kara-*

mazov he splits the Good into two. Father Zosima carries the burden of the preaching and moralizing, leaving Alyosha free to act and react. Moreover, Zosima is not quite allowed to have things his own way as was Makar Dolgoruky in the lengthy tirades which proceeded from his death-bed in *A Raw Youth*. Ivan Karamazov puts out a flood of eloquent anti-Zosima argument in 'Pro and Contra'. And various dissociative devices are also brought to bear, softening the impact of Zosima's exhortations. At the elbow of Dostoyevsky the devout there usually stood Dostoyevsky the irreverent joker with his water-pistol, sneezing powder and stink bomb.

In an early scene the quiet and dignified world of the monastery had been defiled by Fyodor Pavlovich. An even greater Scandal takes place after Father Zosima's death when the faithful, instead of witnessing the miracles for which they had hoped, are assailed by the powerful smell of his prematurely corrupted corpse. They are further scandalized by the savage irruption into the vigil over the dead Elder's body of the grotesque Father Ferapont, an irruption preceded by a formula on the model hallowed in Dostoyevskian Scandal scenes: 'the door opened wide and on the threshold appeared . . .' A heroic mortifier of the flesh, Father Ferapont proceeds to exorcize the devils which (he claims) have been breeding like spiders in Father Zosima's cell, and denounces the dead man for not keeping his fasts and for being seduced by gifts of sweetmeats and tea. Such are the devices whereby Dostoyevsky the artist jerks the soapbox from under Dostoyevsky the moralist.

No such dissociative devices were necessary in the case of Alyosha, the least intolerable of the ideal personages put forward in Dostoyevsky's novels. Alyosha abstains from edifying tirades, and is free from the eccentricity attributed to previous representatives of goodness. He slaps no faces and breaks no Chinese vases.

Alyosha shares with his precursors one basic ingredient of Dostoyevskian goodness in remaining serenely untouched, either as victim or inflicter, by the world of humiliations, insults and injuries in which Dostoyevsky's sinners and heretics are caught up. 'He was convinced', the reader is told, 'that no one in the whole world would ever wish to offend him, and not only that no one would wish to, but that no one would be able to.' Incapable of taking offence, he is equally incapable of giving it. His father's heart was touched by the fact that Alyosha was able to live in his house, a witness to his evil way of life, without condemning him and by the fact that

Alyosha was attached to him by sincere and straightforward affection.

Dostoyevsky's Narrator is made to apologize for introducing his hero in a novice's cassock, and emphasizes that this is no sickly, pale fanatic or mystic, but a healthy and handsome specimen of young manhood. Calm and even-tempered, he loves people and is in turn loved by them. His love is always active, and this love in action is most effectively illustrated in his relations with the school-boy circle of Kolya Krasotkin and Ilyusha Snegiryov. Alyosha easily attracts children by his matter-of-fact approach and habit of treating them as his equals.

What makes Alyosha reasonably acceptable as a character is not so much his armour of virtue as the chinks in it. This paragon of faith is capable of admitting on occasion that perhaps he does not really believe in God. And the point is repeatedly made that Alyosha too is a true Karamazov, not only in his love of life but in the specific characteristic of lust, which in his case is potential rather than actual. In speaking of Alyosha as his 'main hero' (which in the novel as it stands he certainly is not) Dostoyevsky's Narrator is made to refer to a sequel which was planned but not written. In this Alyosha would have been the principal character and his involvement with sin would have gone further than the embryonic stage attained in *The Brothers Karamazov*.

Among the chinks in Alyosha's armour is his bitter reaction to the odour of corruption from the corpse of Father Zosima. His basic faith is recorded as unshaken by this severe emotional shock, but the incident causes him to stage a 'rebellion'. He bursts out of the monastery without accepting a blessing from Zosima's associate, Father Paisy, and so far abandons the mood of decorous grief which would have been appropriate to the death of his beloved teacher as to accept from the atheist Rakitin an offer of sausage and vodka and to allow himself to be lured to the apartment of the seductress Grushenka. It is on this occasion that Alyosha, by neglecting what he knows is his duty—to seek out his brother Dmitry in the atmosphere of mounting crisis which precedes Fyodor Pavlovich's murder—involves himself however remotely in the guilt of that murder, which falls upon all Fyodor Pavlovich's sons.

Alyosha's mentor Zosima moves in a similar aura of calm, confident and serene joy. But whereas these qualities had been Alyosha's birthright, Zosima had won them as a young army officer in a world of self-centredness and aggressiveness similar to that of Dmitry. After savagely ill-treating his soldier servant just before engaging in a duel, he had seen the light suddenly and had resigned his commission in order to become a monk.

Zosima's acceptability as a character must vary with the individual reader's tolerance of edifying abstract nouns, long moralizing passages couched mainly in the imperative mood and lyrical exhortations to look around at God's gifts—the clear sky, the pure air, the tender grass, the little birds. The keynotes of Zosima's teaching are—firstly an emphasis on the joy of life, to which his more sombre monastery colleagues take exception, and secondly the thesis 'all men are guilty before all and for all', which (as already mentioned) runs through the whole novel. Finally, he bears the burden of Dostoyevskian polemics against the point of view chiefly represented by Ivan Karamazov and especially by that creature of Ivan's brain, the Grand Inquisitor, that man can 'arrange his affairs justly by his mind alone, without Christ'. Such people, he says, 'have already proclaimed that there is no longer any crime, no longer any sin'.

Zosima is thus made to express Dostoyevsky's conviction, so often illustrated in his novels, that exclusive reliance on the human intellect leads logically to violence. And what leads to murder and suicide on an individual plane will lead to massacre and general bloodshed on a political plane. 'Having rejected Christ,' Zosima says, 'they will end by bathing the world in blood.' To the secular evil of materialism and the mistaken path of those who see freedom as the multiplication and quick satisfaction of their needs, Zosima contrasts the monk's way of cutting off superfluous and unnecessary needs. Salvation will come from the 'God-fearing' ordinary Russian people, 'great in its humility' which, despite the grave faults of drunkenness and cruelty, never forgets that it does wrong in sinning and that sin is cursed by God.

Such is the central message of The Brothers Karamazov. It was his interest in this message which helped to inspire Dostoyevsky, and the novel is unthinkable without it. Alyosha and even Zosima are memorable literary creations, but they look anaemic when set beside Fyodor Pavlovich, Ivan, Dmitry and Smerdyakov. Dostoyevsky remains stronger in attack than defence, a more potent purveyor of vitriol than of milk. As a literary symbol Zosima's little birds are of less significance than Smerdyakov's mucus-stained handkerchief.

The artistic impact of Alyosha and the monastery is a relatively modest one, but its importance should not be underrated. A necessary counterweight to the violence, absurdity and complexity of the main intrigue is provided by the untroubled serenity of these representatives of Goodness. Because of this counterweight Dostoyevsky was able to push his nightmare fantasies to an extreme which would otherwise have thrown him off-balance. In essence Alyosha and Zosima are one more example of the Dostoyevskian 'softener'. Artistically their role is a secondary one.

*

It is a typical Dostoyevskian feature that Ivan Karamazov, the evil genius of the novel, is a more potently realized character and also makes a bigger impact in the sphere of ideas than the Alyosha-Zosima combination. As befits the allegorical representative of Mind in the fraternal triptych, he is a highly educated person. Moody, sullen and shut up within himself, but 'far from timid', he had begun to make a name by publishing articles in the press. One of these, purporting to be a defence of the Orthodox Church, had, like Samuel Butler's *Fair Haven*, led churchmen to think quite mistakenly that Ivan was on their side, while only a few enlightened spirits recognized it for what it was, a satirical burlesque. When taxed with this by Father Zosima, Ivan produces a vague answer reminiscent of Stavrogin's replies when questioned about the biting of the Governor's ear, and one richly typical of Dostoyevsky: 'All the same I wasn't entirely joking.' Ivan claims that there is no sanction which can make men love each other except belief in God and immortality. Destroy these beliefs and 'everything is permitted' (a formula many times repeated in the novel's theoretical passages), even cannibalism. Thus atheism leads logically to murder and every other kind of violence.

Since Ivan (despite one qualified denial of this, highly in accordance with Dostoyevskian 'wrap-up' technique) himself is an atheist, he must logically end, even on his own premises, as a murderer. And in fact, as already mentioned, he does bear the chief load of guilt for his father's murder. It was because of the ideological contamination irradiating from Ivan and his central formula 'everything is permitted' that Smerdyakov, his chief ideological dupe, felt moved to do the actual killing. Lest the point should be missed, Dostoyevsky causes Smerdyakov to throw this explosive formula ('You said everything was permitted') back at Ivan when, in the third of the three barbed duologues with Ivan preceding Dmitry's trial, Smerdyakov finally confesses to the murder.

Earlier in the book Dmitry too is shown under the influence of this contamination. On hearing of Ivan's ideas he asks if it is true that criminal acts are to be regarded as the inevitable conclusion of atheism, and upon receiving confirmation of this makes the curt comment, sinister in the context of his quarrel with his father and threats of violence, 'I shan't forget it.' Since it was Ivan's own dupe Smerdyakov who taught Ilyusha Snegiryov to throw pieces of bread containing concealed pins to stray dogs, Ivan also bears responsibility for Ilyusha's estrangement from his school-friends and for the deterioration of his health. All are indeed 'responsible for all'.

It is Alyosha whom Ivan in the chapter 'Pro and Contra' makes the target for the most sustained campaign of ideological seduction in Dostoyevsky's work. Ivan steers the argument off the question of God's existence, which he is willing to concede, for he himself has long given up the problem of whether God created man, or man God. What Ivan cannot accept is God's world because of the suffering of the innocent and particularly of children. The instances of this which he quotes range from the tossing of babies on bayonets by Turks to savage beatings and other refinements of vile cruelty to children.

After describing how a Russian General had once set a pack of hounds on an eight-year-old boy before the eyes of his mother, Ivan finally forces Alyosha to admit that the General deserved shooting, an admission which, in Ivan's view, amounts to the renunciation of Zosima-inspired ideology. 'Bravo', says Ivan. 'What price our hermit! So that's the kind of devil that lurks in your heart!' And he adds later, 'I won't yield you to your Zosima.' Ivan cannot accept 'higher harmony' at the price of the tears of a tortured child. He hastens therefore to 'return his entrance ticket' to God's world. Alyosha is forced to agree that he too would not consent to be the architect of world harmony at the price of a tortured child, but points out that one man, Jesus Christ, has the right to forgive such horrors. This provides Ivan with the cue to relate his Legend of the Grand Inquisitor.

The Legend is regarded by some as Dostoyevsky's supreme achievement, and perhaps nowhere else is the roving of his fantastic imagination more brightly illustrated, which tends to make readers

lose sight of the Legend's bearing on the novel. But this connection
can easily be defined. Where Ivan is the Dostoyevskian heretic
operating on the level of the family and of private life, the Grand
Inquisitor is the Dostoyevskian heretic operating on the level of
world-wide statecraft. Part of the difficulty of the Legend lies in the
fact that what Ivan intended as a refutation of Christ was intended
by Dostoyevsky to impress his readers as a vindication. The reader
of the Legend, who does not get very much help from Dostoyevsky
in this respect, must therefore bear firmly in mind throughout,
firstly that Ivan is to be identified with his Grand Inquisitor and
secondly that, in recounting the Legend, Ivan is supposed to be
discrediting both himself and the Grand Inquisitor while attempting
to do the opposite. One reason why this is made less obvious by
Dostoyevsky than it might have been is probably his own latent
sympathy with the cause which he was hoping to overthrow.

The scene is set in sixteenth-century Seville at the height of the
Inquisition. Christ appears and, after being quickly recognized by
the throng and performing some miracles, is put in prison on the
orders of the Grand Inquisitor, a ninety-year-old man, tall and erect
with a dried-up face and sunken, glittering eyes. At night the
Inquisitor comes alone to the prisoner's cell and begins to reproach
Him in a lengthy monologue to which Christ makes no reply at all,
except in one possible variant of the ending discussed by Ivan, to
kiss the old man, when he has finished speaking, on his bloodless
lips, the only answer which Dostoyevskian love can make to the
wicked machinations of Dostoyevskian reason. The Grand Inquisitor begins, 'Why hast Thou come to hinder us? Tomorrow I will
burn Thee at the stake as the most vicious of heretics.' He promises
that the same people who so recently were kissing Christ's feet will
rush to heap coals on His pyre.

Soon he is operating on a more theoretical level. The essence of
his principles emerges—the organization of the world on a rational
basis 'by the mind alone', and without Christ. Christ came to give
men freedom. But for fifteen centuries this freedom has caused man
nothing but torment. Accordingly the Grand Inquisitor and his
associates have now at last done away with it, moved by motives of
philanthropy. The freedom of choice which Christ gave to man
turns out to have been a burden and not a blessing because man,
with the exception of a few chosen spirits, is essentially a feeble
creature. Jesus had been wrong in rejecting the three Temptations

in the Wilderness. In refusing to turn stones into bread, to make Himself master of the world and to cast Himself down unharmed from the pinnacle of the Temple, He had neglected the opportunity of conquering and capturing man's faith in the only possible way, by miracle, mystery and authority. Though man does have rebellious tendencies, he is a feeble rebel whose main need is to find someone before whom he can bow down and to whom he can present this terrible gift of freedom which had been Christ's mistaken legacy to him. Hence the need to 'correct' Christ's teaching, by substituting miracle, mystery and authority for freedom and hence the need, now that Christ has appeared in sixteenth-century Seville, to burn Him at the stake before He can do any more harm.

What was Dostoyevsky trying to convey in the Legend? On the more trivial level he used it as a means of continuing his polemic against the Roman Catholic Church with its authoritarian trends and claim to infallibility. And lest anyone should be led into error by the implied attack on the Church, Alyosha is made in the discussion which follows to point out that this criticism falls only on Rome and has nothing to do with Orthodoxy.

Secondly, and not for the first time in Dostoyevsky's polemics, the Socialist movement is closely associated with Catholicism as an ideological heresy. Since Dostoyevsky could not make a sixteenth-century prelate refer to Socialism by name, these passages are likely to remain obscure to those unversed in Dostoyevskian lore. Instead of Socialists the Grand Inquisitor refers to certain people whose activities he foresees in the future and who will one day proclaim that there is no such thing as crime and therefore no such thing as sin—there are only hungry people.

Here Dostoyevsky is once again working off his long-established irritation against the contemporary 'progressive' tendency to regard crime as exclusively the result of environment. The Grand Inquisitor goes on to speak of a 'horrible Tower of Babel' (Socialism) which will arise in place of Christ's Temple. 'They [the Socialists] will not complete it; we [the Roman Church] shall. Having begun to build their Tower of Babel without us, they will end in cannibalism. The "unrestricted mind" will lead men to destroy each other, and the survivors will crawl to us like a herd in order to submit once and for all. . . . We will give them the quiet humble happiness of feeble creatures such as they were created. At last the countless millions of mankind will know happiness. Only a few hundreds of thousands

H*

of organizers, who preserve the secret, will be unhappy. This section of the Legend embodies what is perhaps the most eccentric idea in the whole corpus of Dostoyevskyism, the claim that the Roman Catholic Church would become demagogic and 'capture' the proletarian revolution which Dostoyevsky believed imminent in Western Europe.

The sweep of the Legend, accordingly, takes in much more than the parochial territory of Dostoyevsky's polemic with contemporary Catholicism and Socialism, because it is an attack in the name of the individual and of Christ on all forms of organization of Man for his own good. It contains and greatly deepens the lesson implied in Shigalyov's teachings in *The Devils*, where a society had been foreseen in which a cynical élite would organize the human insect on a similar ant-heap basis. The tendencies here attacked by Dostoyevsky were in relatively embryonic form during the nineteenth century and have grown so vastly in the twentieth that it is difficult entirely to deny him the status of 'prophet'. The Legend of the Grand Inquisitor strikes wide and deep and its blows fall in many places. To refer to only one of these, anyone who has ever visited a Soviet 'Palace of Culture' cannot fail to read with renewed interest the simple but telling words of the Grand Inquisitor when he says of the human race: 'We will make them work, but organize their leisure like children's games with singing and dancing.'

Clear though the central intention of the Legend may be as a hymn to individual freedom, it is difficult in the case of Dostoyevsky to accept entirely at its face value an interpretation so undilutedly edifying. It is not the main purpose of this study to examine Dostoyevsky as a personality, but reference may again be made to a feature of his character which has already been noted, his addiction to strong mental sensations, which he tended to use as a drug or stimulant. He seems to have used his religious strivings, based on the freedom of conscience championed in the Legend of the Grand Inquisitor, in the same way as he had once used his gambling, financial scrapes and love affairs, as a means of keeping himself in the condition of agonized suspense which he found so gratifying. In his oscillations between belief and unbelief he was perhaps subconsciously powered less by a concern with religious truth than by a need to keep in a state of perpetual vibration a mental mechanism which could never be contentedly still.

The Grand Inquisitor is only one of Ivan Karamazov's numerous ideological satellites. Others include the Devil, who appears in a hallucination as a shabby gentleman in order to torment Ivan with a hotchpotch of his own most trite and vulgar thoughts. The absurd liberal of the forties, Miusov, whom Fyodor Pavlovich mocks during the scandalous scene in the monastery, and the vicious atheist student of theology Rakitin are variants respectively of the 'father' and 'son' types described more fully in *The Devils*. Rakitin is the nihilist without whom no Dostoyevskian novel had been complete for over a decade.

Of all Ivan's satellites the most fascinating is the reptilian Smerdyakov whom Ivan's philosophy brought to murder and suicide, and who seems to leave a trail of slime on every page on which he appears. This pomaded figure with his dandified dress, known for his habit of hanging cats and teaching small boys to torture dogs, also carries more serious stigmata of Dostoyevsky's loathing in his contempt for the Russian peasant, hatred of Russia and idealization of the French. But Dostoyevsky gave him one of his own characteristics when he made him an epileptic, whether or not the attribution of Dostoyevsky's own disease to the actual slayer of Fyodor Pavlovich is, as Freud maintains, an echo of his feeling of guilt for the murder of his own father. Dostoyevsky who spent so much time constructing Bogeymen, never conceived a Bogeyman more horrible than Smerdyakov.

•

A dubious position is occupied in *The Brothers Karamazov* by the pathetic Captain Snegiryov and his consumptive son Ilyusha whose funeral takes place in the Epilogue. Snegiryov and his family represent an ingredient common in Dostoyevsky's earlier work, but one which had been relatively neglected since *Crime and Punishment*, his 'Poor Folk'. It is interesting that he chose to conclude his last novel on a note similar to that which he had struck when, in his first work of fiction, he had described Makar Devushkin and his circle.

The poverty-stricken Snegiryov, with the sparse ginger-coloured beard by which Dmitry Karamazov had once hauled him out of a tavern, is yet another Dostoyevskian underdog on the Devushkin model. Not quite so downtrodden as Devushkin, he retains a greater ability to protest. 'He looked like a man who would terribly like to hit you, but who was terribly afraid that you would hit him.' He also differs from Devushkin in having a family, which, however, merely serves to strengthen the 'Poor Folk' aura around him, since it consists, besides the dying Ilyusha, of a mad crippled wife and a hunchback crippled daughter.

The description of this milieu, while reproducing to a notable extent the atmosphere of *Poor Folk* itself, is naturally on a higher artistic level. But it raises a problem which arose in less acute form with reference to *Poor Folk*, an artistic failure in its sentimentality and pursuit of the pathetic to the point of absurdity. Is one to feel moved to tears or embarrassment when Snegiryov tells funny stories and does animal imitations, annoying to Ilyusha who prizes his father's dignity, over the sickbed and then runs off to cry quietly so that Ilyusha should not hear him? Or when Ilyusha tells his father to find a good little boy when he himself is dead and call him Ilyusha and love him instead, to which Snegiryov replies in a wild whisper, grinding his teeth, 'I don't want a good little boy.' Similarly confusing are the Captain's piteous antics over Ilyusha's grave when he runs after the coffin (just as thirty years previously old Pokrovsky had been made to run after his son's coffin in *Poor Folk*), drops a flower and insists on picking it up, will not allow the lid of the coffin to be closed and finally goes home to weep over the dead boy's little boots.

Dostoyevsky has pitched these happenings somewhere between tragedy and sentimentality in an area where it seems heartless to treat them flippantly, yet difficult to surrender to the emotion for which he too strongly plays. The literary artistry with which the 'Poor Folk' of *The Brothers Karamazov* are handled is formidable, but the rampant emotionalism of these scenes must be rated as an artistic blemish. It was only when he kept off the 'Poor Folk' theme that he reached his greatest creative heights.

CONCLUSION

I SHOULD like to end this book on a more personal note than has been aimed at in the previous chapters. There it seemed appropriate not to use the first person singular and also to avoid conjuring up that mysterious community called 'we' which some critics like to invoke but to which, when reading works of criticism, I have not usually felt myself to belong.

'I' and 'we' have been avoided, but the view of Dostoyevsky presented here is of course highly personal. Though phrases like 'I think that' or 'my own impression is' have not been used, such reservations should be everywhere understood where literary judgements are made.

By this I do not mean to suggest that something approaching absolute validity is a theoretical impossibility in assessing literature. For instance, to say that *The Brothers Karamazov* is a better novel than *Poor Folk* is surely to make a valid judgement. However, it is precisely such incontrovertible judgements which are least worth making when discussing literature. The valuable literary judgement is always the disputable one. Such is the nature of literary study. Critics who do not think so might be happier writing books on chemistry, but they would not necessarily be better employed, for a reader may be just as stimulated by a critic who believes or implies that he is in touch with absolute truth as by someone who does not.

It seems important to make this point, if only because the presentation of Dostoyevsky attempted here differs so greatly from previous interpretations, and is (so far as I am aware) unique in print, although it is shared to some degree by a number of fellow-students of the subject. In fact, as indicated in the Foreword, my disagreement with existing presentations of Dostoyevsky has been one of the main reasons impelling me to make my own attempt.

I have accordingly tried to disentangle Dostoyevsky from what I regard as misinterpretations by defining what it is that he has not done as well as attempting a picture of his positive achievement. In discussing the latter I have relied more on illustration than analysis, because it seems to me that criticism is almost helpless when it tries to define the nature of an author's positive achievement—as, indeed, is the author himself. Here one is reminded of the story of Tolstoy, who once wrote that if anyone asked him what he had been trying to express in *Anna Karenina*, he could only reply by writing the novel out again.[1] However, I should not like to leave Dostoyevsky without making a brief attempt to sum up his positive achievement, which inevitably involves touching once more on some points already made.

One of his achievements is that of all great novelists, and lies in having created a world of his own, a world which did not exist before he created it, and which never would have existed if he had not written. This involved the creation of some of the most fantastic characters ever to have been conceived by a human brain and of some of the most breathtaking narrative sequences ever written.

Even more important is the fact that, having entered Dostoyevsky's world, one can never again look upon the real world with quite the same eyes. His reader has acquired a new insight and new terms of reference with which to interpret his own world. It may seem that I am coming nearer here to accepting the view of Dostoyevsky as a 'great teacher' or 'great thinker' than earlier pages would suggest. However, such an impression would be misleading. The point here is that Dostoyevsky's views when formulated theoretically by himself or others are of importance chiefly for understanding him, and scarcely at all for understanding the world outside his novels. His views on politics could no longer be held by anyone outside a lunatic asylum, and his views on religion (where he still has a few converts) will never command wide adherence. It is the images which he created, not his theoretical views, which cause his readers to look on the world with new eyes.

Most human beings do not closely resemble Dostoyevskian characters, but after reading his work it is astonishing how many one meets who seem to. In any case, there are few human beings who do not exhibit in less extreme form some of those characteristics which Dostoyevsky picked out and exaggerated to the ultimate limit of their potentialities with his own special technique of inspired literary distortion. Nor can one by any means discount all his theorizing. In particular it is impossible to read his interpretation of human freedom, as embodied in *The Brothers Karamazov* and elsewhere, without being provoked to thought.

REFERENCES

The full titles of works to which reference is made will be found in the Bibliography under authors' or editors' names.

The following abbreviations are used in the list of references for certain works given under 'Dostoyevsky, F. M.' in the Bibliography.

Diary   *Dnevnik pisatelya* (*The Diary of a Writer*), Vols. XI and XII in the *Polnoye sobraniye*, etc., of 1926–30.
L.   *Pisma* (*Letters*).
Works *Sobraniye sochineniy* (*Collected Works*) of 1956–8.

CHAPTER ONE

1. Cheshikhin-Vetrinsky, I, p. 37.
2. *Diary*, Jan. 1877.
3. Ibid.
4. Belkin, p. 16.
5. See the article on Dostoyevsky in the *Bolshaya sovetskaya entsiklopediya*, Moscow, 1950–8.
6. Belkin, pp. 310, 332.
7. L. I, p. 100.
8. Belkin, p. 13.
9. Ibid., p. 27.
10. Carr, *Dostoevsky*, p. 43.
11. Belkin, p. 32.
12. *Diary*, Nov. 1877.
13. L. I, p. 80.
14. Cheshikhin-Vetrinsky, I, p. 35.
15. Ibid., p. 43.
16. Ibid., pp. 28–9.
17. Ibid., p. 43.
18. L. I, p. 84.
19. L. I, p. 127.
20. L. I, p. 129.
21. L. I, p. 130.
22. L. III, p. 23.

CHAPTER TWO

1. *Works*, II, p. 657.
2. L. III, p. 85.
3. L. I, p. 246.
4. L. III, p. 86.
5. Mochulsky, pp. 141–2.

6. L. I, p. 246.
7. Italics not original.
8. Mochulsky, p. 145.
9. Dostoyevsky, A. M., *Vospominaniya*, pp. 78–79.
10. Chulkov, p. 16.
11. Grigorovich, p. 55.
12. L. I, p. 47.
13. L. I, p. 57.
14. L. I, pp. 138–9.
15. *Diary*, Nov. 1877.
16. L. I, p. 167.
17. See Michael H. Futrell, 'Dostoyevsky and Dickens'.

CHAPTER THREE

1. L. I, p. 293.
2. L. I, p. 260.
3. L. I, p. 286.
4. *Works*, III p. 707.
5. L. I, p. 169.
6. L. I, pp. 175–6.
7. L. I, p. 189.
8. L. I, p 206.
9. L. I, p. 213.
10. L. II, p. 605.
11. L. I, pp. 135–6. Italics not original.
12. L. I, p. 139.
13. L. I, p. 135.

CHAPTER FOUR

1. L. I, p. 310.
2. Virginia Woolf, p. 177.
3. Carr, *Dostoevsky*, p. 84.
4. Bem, Vol. II, pp. 31–50.
5. See p. 139.
6. L. IV, p. 109.
7. L. I, p. 85.
8. L. I, p. 54.
9. L. I, p. 353.
10. L. I, p. 324.

CHAPTER FIVE

1. See L. I, p. 435.
2. Glivenko, p. 173.

CHAPTER SIX

1. L. II, p. 13.
2. L. II, p. 257.
3. L. II, p. 283.
4. L. II, p. 141.
5. L. II, p. 161.
6. L. II, p. 261.
7. L. II, p. 71.
8. Made to me by Dr. George Katkov.

9. Sakulin, p. 130.
10. Other autobiographical traits attributed to Myshkin are discussed in Grossman, *Seminary po Dostoyevskomu.*
11. Carr, *Dostoevsky*, p. 217.
12. Ronald Hingley, 'Leonid Leonov', *Soviet Survey*, July–Sept. 1958, p. 72.
13. Mochulsky, p. 316.
14. L. II, p. 239.

CHAPTER SEVEN

1. Carr, *The Romantic Exiles*, p. 337.
2. L. II, p. 288.
3. Konshina, p. 61.
4. L. III, p. 21.
5. Mochulsky, p. 376.
6. See Futrell, 'Dostoyevsky and Dickens'.
7. Konshina, pp. 251 and 271.
8. For more detailed reviews of the evidence, see Slonim, pp. 167–73, and Carr, *Dostoevsky*, pp. 113–14.

CHAPTER EIGHT

1. L. III, p. 40.
2. L. III, p. 240.

CHAPTER NINE

1. *Diary*, Dec. 1877.
2. *Diary*, Dec. 1876.
3. L. III, p. 206.
4. *Diary*, July–Aug. 1877.
5. *Diary*, Nov. 1877.
6. *Diary*, Sept. 1876.
7. *Diary*, Sept. 1877.
8. *Diary*, Sept. 1873.
9. *Diary*, July–Aug. 1877.
10. *Diary*, Apr. 1876.
11. *Diary*, Nov. 1873.
12. *Diary*, Nov. 1877.
13. *Diary*, May–June, 1877.
14. *Diary*, July–Aug. 1876.
15. *Diary*, Feb. 1876.
16. Ibid.
17. *Diary*, Jan. 1877.
18. Ibid.
19. *Diary*, Apr. 1877.
20. L. II, p. 284.
21. *Diary*, Apr. 1876.
22. *Diary*, May, 1876.
23. L. IV, p. 144.
24. L. IV, p. 157.
25. L. IV, p. 168.
26. L. IV, p. 170.
27. L. IV, p. 171.
28. *Works*, X, p. 519.

CHAPTER TEN

1. L. III, p. 256.
2. Curle, p. 176.
3. Freud, 'Dostoyevsky and Parricide', pp. 18 and 28.
4. L. IV, p. 117.
5. Mochulsky, pp. 407–9.

CONCLUSION

1. Letter to N. N. Strakhov of April, 1876.

BIBLIOGRAPHY

Abraham, Gerald. *Dostoevsky*. London, 1936.

Bakhtin, M. M. *Problema tvorchestva Dostoyevskogo*. Leningrad, 1929.

Belkin, A. A. (editor) *F. M. Dostoyevsky v russkoy kritike*. Moscow, 1956.

Bem, A. L. (editor) *O Dostoyevskom. Sbornik statey*. Prague, 1929–36. 3 vols.

Berdyayev, N. A. *Dostoievsky. An Interpretation*. London, 1934.

Carr, E. H. *Dostoevsky*. London, 1931.

The Romantic Exiles. London, 1949.

Cheshikhin-Vetrinsky, V. E. (editor) *F. M. Dostoyevsky v vospominaniyakh sovremennikov i yego pismakh*. Moscow, 1923. 2 vols.

Chulkov, Georgy. *Kak rabotal Dostoyevsky*. Moscow, 1939.

Curle, Richard. *Characters of Dostoyevsky*. London, 1950.

Dolinin, A. S. 'Ispoved Stavrogina', *Literaturnaya mysl*, Vol. I, 1922, pp. 139–62.

V tvorcheskoy laboratorii Dostoyevskogo. Istoriya sozdaniya romana 'Podrostok'. Moscow, 1947.

(editor) *Dostoyevsky, statyi i materialy*. Moscow-Leningrad, 1922–4. 2 vols.

(editor) *F. M. Dostoyevsky, materialy i issledovaniya*, Leningrad, 1935.

Dostoyevskaya, A. G. *Dnevnik, 1867 g*. Moscow, 1923.

Vospominaniya. Moscow, 1925.

Dostoyevsky, A. M. *Vospominaniya Andreya Mikhaylovicha Dostoyevskogo*. Leningrad, 1930.

Dostoyevsky, F. M. *Die Urgestalt der Brüder Karamasoff erläutert von W. Komarowitsch*. München, 1928.

Pisma. Moscow-Leningrad, 1928–34, 1959. 4 vols. (See review of vol. 4 by Goldstein, below.)

Polnoye sobraniye khudozhestvennykh proizvedeniy, Vols. I–XIII. Moscow-Leningrad, 1926–30.

Sobraniye sochineniy, Vols. I–X. Moscow, 1956–8.

Freud, Siegmund. 'Dostoyevsky and Parricide', *The Realist*, Vol. I, No. 4, London, 1929, pp. 18–33.

Futrell, Michael H. 'Dostoyevsky and Dickens', *English Miscellany*, 7, Rome, 1956.

Gide, André. *Dostoevsky*. London, 1925.

Glivenko, I. I. (editor) *Iz arkhiva F. M. Dostoyevskogo. Prestupleniye i nakazaniye.* Moscow-Leningrad, 1931.

Goldstein, David I. 'Rewriting Dostoyevsky's Letters', *American Slavic and East European Review*, Vol. XX, No. 2 (April, 1961), pp. 279–88.

Grigorovich, D. V. *Literaturnyye vospominaniya.* Leningrad, 1928.

Grossman, Leonid. *Poetika Dostoyevskogo.* Moscow, 1925.

Put Dostoyevskogo, Vols. I–II. Leningrad, 1924.

Seminary po Dostoyevskomu. Moscow, 1923.

(editor) *Tvorchestvo Dostoyevskogo.* Odessa, 1921.

Zhizn i trudy F. M. Dostoyevskogo : biografiya v datakh i dokumentakh. Moscow-Leningrad, 1935.

Kirpotin, V. Ya. *F. M. Dostoyevsky.* Moscow, 1947.

Molodoy Dostoyevsky. Moscow, 1947.

F. M. Dostoyevsky : tvorchesky put, 1821–1859. Moscow, 1960.

Komarovich, V. L. 'Neizdannaya glava romana "Besy" (Ispoved Stavrogina)', *Byloye*, 18, 1922, pp. 219–52.

Konshina, E. N. (editor) *Zapisnyye tetradi F. M. Dostoyevskogo.* Moscow-Leningrad, 1935.

Lavrin, Janko. *Dostoevsky. A Study.* London, 1943.

Lloyd, J. A. T. *Fyodor Dostoevsky.* London, 1947.

Merezhkovsky, D. S. *L. Tolstoy i Dostoyevsky.* 2 vols. St. Petersburg, 1901–2 (translated into English as *Tolstoy as Man and Artist with an Essay on Dostoyevsky.* New York, 1902).

Mikhaylovsky, N. K. 'Zhestoky talant' in his *Sochineniya*, Vol. 5, St. Petersburg, 1897, pp. 1–78.

Mochulsky, K. Dostoyevsky. *Zhizn i tvorchestvo.* Paris, 1947.

Murry, J. M. *Fyodor Dostoevsky, A Critical Study.* London, 1916.

Panayeva, A. Ya. *Vospominaniya.* Moscow, 1956.

Pereverzev, V. F. *F. M. Dostoyevsky*, 3rd edition. Moscow-Leningrad, 1928.

Rozanov, V. V. *Legenda o velikom inkvizitore.* 3rd edition. St. Petersburg, 1906.

Sakulin, P. N. and Belchikov, N. F. (editors) *Iz arkhiva F. M. Dostoyevskogo. Idiot.* Moscow-Leningrad, 1931.

Seduro, Vladimir. *Dostoyevski in Russian Literary Criticism.* New York, 1957.

Shestov, L. I. *Dostoyevsky i Nietzsche.* St. Petersburg, 1903.

French translation. *La philosophie de la tragédie. Dostoïewsky et Nietzsche.* Paris, 1926.

Simmons, Ernest J. *Dostoevsky. The Making of a Novelist.* London, 1950.

Slonim, Marc. *Les trois amours de Dostoievsky.* Paris, 1955.

Steiner, George. *Tolstoy or Dostoyevsky.* London, 1959.

Suslova, A. P. *Gody blizosti s Dostoyevskim.* Moscow, 1928.

Troyat, Henri. *Firebrand. The Life of Dostoevsky*. London, 1947.
Volynsky, A. L. *Kniga velikogo gneva*. 2nd edition. St. Petersburg, 1906.
Woolf, Virginia. 'The Russian Point of View' in her *The Common Reader*
    [First series], London, 1938, pp. 172–81.
Yarmolinsky, Avrahm. *Dostoevsky. His Life and Art*. London, 1957.

Note on bibliographies of Dostoyevsky. A comprehensive bibliography
in Russian for the period 1924–9 (together with a list of earlier bibliographies) will be found in Vol. XIII of the *Polnoye sobraniye*, etc., of
1926–30, listed above under 'Dostoyevsky, F. M.' Bibliographies in
English will be found in the works of Ernest J. Simmons and Vladimir
Seduro listed above.

Index